✯ And ✯ Brave Men, Too

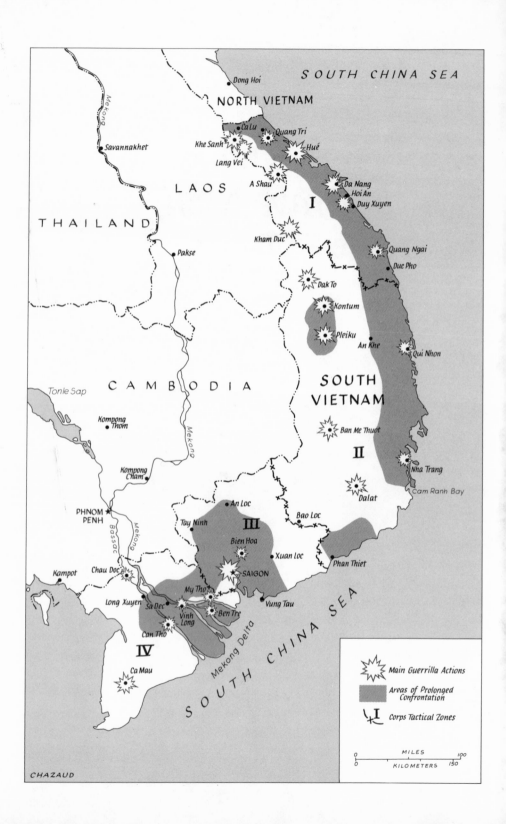

SOUTH CHINA SEA

Dong Hoi

NORTH VIETNAM

Savannakhet

Ca Lu
Quang Tri
Khe Sanh
Hué
Lang Vei
A Shau
Da Nang
Hoi An
Duy Xuyen

LAOS

I

THAILAND

Kham Duc

Quang Ngai
Duc Pho

Pakse

Dak To

Kontum

Pleiku

An Khe
Qui Nhon

SOUTH
VIETNAM

Tonle Sap

CAMBODIA

Kompong
Thom

Ban Me Thuot

II

Nha Trang

Kompong
Cham

Dalat

Cam Ranh Bay

PHNOM
PENH

An Loc

Tay Ninh

III

Bao Loc

Bien Hoa

Xuan Loc

Kampot

Chau Doc

SAIGON

Phan Thiet

Long Xuyen

My Tho

Sa Dec

Ben Tre

Vung Tau

Vinh
Long

Can Tho

IV

Ca Mau

Mekong Delta

SOUTH CHINA SEA

CHAZAUD

Main Guerrilla Actions

Areas of Prolonged
Confrontation

Corps Tactical Zones

MILES
0   100
0   150
KILOMETERS

TIMOTHY S. LOWRY

⋆ And ⋆
Brave Men,
Too

CROWN PUBLISHERS, INC.
NEW YORK

Grateful acknowledgement is made for the following:

Excerpt from *Soldier: The Memoirs of Matthew B. Ridgway.* Copyright © 1956 by Matthew B. Ridgway and Harold H. Martin. Copyright © 1956 by The Curtis Publishing Company. Reprinted by permission of Harper and Row Publishers, Inc., New York.

Selection from "Flanders Field" by John MacCrae taken from *The Family Book of Verse,* selected and edited by Lewis Gannett, published in 1961 by Harper and Brothers, New York.

Selection from "I Dig Rock'n Roll Music" by Paul Stookey, James Mason, and Dave Dixon, copyright © 1965 by Pepamar Music Corporation.

Material has been quoted and adapted from the following:

"Hell in a very small place" by Don Tate, from *Pacific Stars and Stripes,* February 19, 1984. Used by permission.

U.S. Marine Corps Official Operational History of Vietnam, *U.S. Marines in Vietnam,* History and Museums Division, Headquarters, U.S. Marine Corps, Washington, D.C., specifically from the following volumes:

U.S. Marines in Vietnam: An Expanding War 1966 by Jack Shulimson, 1982; *U.S. Marines in Vietnam:* The Landing and the Buildup 1965 by Jack Shulimson and Major Charles M. Johnson, USMC, 1978; and *Small Unit Action in Vietnam Summer* 1966 by Captain Francis J. West, Jr., USMCR, 1967, 1977.

Medal of Honor Recipients 1863–1978, 96th Congress Senate Committee Print Number 3, U.S. Senate Committee on Veterans Affairs, February 14, 1979.

Published by Crown Publishers, Inc., One Park Avenue, New York, New York 10016 and simultaneously in Canada by General Publishing Company Limited
Manufactured in the United States of America
CROWN is a trademark of Crown Publishers, Inc.
Library of Congress Cataloging in Publication Data
Lowry, Timothy S.
  And brave men, too.
  1. Medal of Honor. 2. United States—Armed Forces—Biography. 3. Vietnamese Conflict, 1961–1975—United States. I. Title.
UB433.L69 1985   959.704'38   84-28521
ISBN 0-517-55707-X
Design by Lauren Dong
10 9 8 7 6 5 4 3 2 1
First Edition

959.7
Lo

★ Contents ★

14.95

10/27/86

√168072

★ | Acknowledgments | ★

This project began over twenty-one years ago when as a 17-year-old kid, I joined the Marine Corps and sailed to Vietnam. When I returned, America was in the midst of great changes, and there didn't seem to be time to break out the welcome home banners and the marching bands. One evening, though, Don Leckenby, Bob Good, and I were at a tavern when Don said something about Vietnam. A stranger named Inger Christiansen asked if we had been to Vietnam and when I nodded, she smiled broadly.

"Well, let me buy you guys a beer and say welcome home," she said. "It's good to have you back." I will never forget that beer or that smile.

Not knowing what else to do after my discharge, I enrolled at the University of Northern Colorado on the G.I. Bill where a couple of professors, Dr. William Hartman and Dr. Walter Stewart, patiently guided me through to graduation. The students at UNC lost an irreplaceable source of information with Dr. Stewart's retirement, and a pal when Dr. Hartman retired.

Dr. James Bowen, then a dean of students, was there too. Jim not only gave me encouragement but stood by me and the other veterans when it wasn't popular.

I have always been proud of being a Vietnam veteran, but reluctant to try and express it. While many shook their heads and said nobody wanted to read about Vietnam, a young woman named Linda Eddington Stevenson encouraged me to write about some of the brave men I knew. Linda read and critiqued the manuscript first. Without her I couldn't have done it, because in addition to her enthusiastic support, she chased away the shadowy nightmares.

In Palm Springs, literary agents Jim and Polly Fox helped me get started, and then worried about me once I did. My brother Mike—a fellow Vietnam veteran—Jimmie Sommers, and Jan Hurley Ruetmann helped me in California. When I got lost in Maryland and in the District of Columbia, John and Jean Smith were able to find me.

John Mofield's support and help in New York City was invaluable. When it was all done, senior editor Jim Wade and Jane von Mehren at Crown took a jumbled pile of pages and molded them with care. Because he has a teenaged son in the Marines, Jim understands.

At a bistro in Greeley, a Green Bay Packer fan named Robbie Johnson served an occasional beer, and Paul ("Big Daddy") Greene provided the Thanksgiving turkey. Robbie has been there from the beginning, and his friendship has meant more to me than I can express. Mike Wilson, a buddy from high school and Vietnam, was there at the beginning, too.

And there were the brave men who not only shared their experiences, but also their homes. I was always amazed that they treated me, a stranger, so well and were so kind. If this book has any merit it is because of them; if not, it's because of me.

Preface

The Vietnam War was not only this nation's most divisive conflict since the Civil War, but also its most complex. In fact, the war in Southeast Asia consisted of two separate and distinct wars: the one going in and the one coming out. The "going in" war began, for the most part, with the passage of the Tonkin Gulf Resolution in 1964 and lasted until the Tet Offensive of 1968.

During this period, the American commitment to South Vietnam grew from approximately twenty thousand U.S. troops to over half a million. This changing troop level was accompanied by changing objectives. The mission of the first Marines to land in the early months of 1965 was to defend the Da Nang airfield from air raids by North Vietnamese aircraft and from ground attacks by small Vietcong guerrilla forces. By the end of 1967, the mission was sweeping and clearing large sections of the country of regular units of the North Vietnamese army.

These different missions resulted in veterans with different experiences. Some sat in foxholes at night waiting for the Vietcong to slip in and slit open their throats; others awaited the suicidal charges of North Vietnamese regiments. Yet each of these veterans had something in common—they were fighting their way in.

The Tet Offensive changed that.

After the January 1968 country-wide attack by North Vietnamese and Vietcong forces, the war changed from one of escalation to one of extrication. No longer were Americans dying to get in; we were dying to get out. As a result the morale of the troops sank.

After January 1968 there were new agonies that the pre-Tet vets, for the most part, did not suffer. Drug usage, racial friction, increased desertions, and refusals to obey orders began to occur in some units. The goal became one of enduring that year or those hundred missions, and returning home.

As with previous conflicts, the veterans of Vietnam were honorable, patriotic, and brave men, too. This is the story of some of these brave men who fought in that first war, a new type of war with new rules, regulations, and restrictions. It is also the story of a rapidly changing nation and how it sometimes overlooked and misunderstood these men.

As the sixties began, revolutionary concepts and events were occurring that would alter the course of American history, changing forever how the world viewed America, how America viewed the world, and, most important, how America viewed itself. Everything seemed to be happening at the same time—civil-rights workers were being murdered in the South while topless dancing was being introduced on the West Coast; former head Mousketeer Jimmie Dodd died while drugs were beginning their assault on middle-class youth; and while Congress was passing the Tonkin Gulf Resolution that would give President Lyndon B. Johnson unprecedented war powers, University of California students at Berkeley were sowing the first seeds of campus unrest.

At the same time, traditional American values and institutions were increasingly being subjected to unprecedented attacks by the nation's youth. These assaults would intensify in the early seventies before finally subsiding. To many of the sixties generation, anything old was bad and should be discarded, while virtually anything new was good and should be retained. Included in the young people's attacks were parents, marriage and the family, schools, religion, the police, big business, the government, and the military.

In their fight against the "Establishment," the young seemed to be enjoying the shock effect of this iconoclasm on their parents as much as the new freedoms—free love, long hair, mod dress, etc. However, the most distancing aspect of the new generation's battle with the old was the Vietnam War. This war about a "nonwar" raged from 1964 until the last American troops returned home in 1975. Caught in the middle of this bitter quarrel between the generations were the veterans who served in Vietnam— vilified by the young for representing the old, and distrusted by the old for being young. In the end, the antiwar protesters won; the veterans returned home, but not to parades and appreciation. It wasn't that America was unappreciative of the horrible ordeal that its young men and women had suffered in Vietnam; rather, the country seemed emotionally exhausted by everything that had happened during this period.

While Americans were fighting and dying in rice paddies around nameless *villes* and on the slopes of numbered hills, stories were being reported about American atrocities, increased desertion rates, and drug abuse in Vietnam. Meanwhile, back in the United States, reports of assassinations, mass murders, racial strife, and terrorist activities were all screaming for America's immediate attention. (There were so many bombings in Boulder, Colorado, in 1969 that one disgruntled citizen exploded a bomb on Flagstaff Mountain west of town to protest the other bombings.)

When Saigon fell to the North Vietnamese and Vietcong in 1975, the polarization that the war had helped create began to subside as the U.S. tried to forget the unpleasant memories of Vietnam. However, one highly decorated veteran remarked, "What they don't realize is that there are thousands of us who cannot." One man wrote: "Thousands of our men will be returning to you. They will have been gone a long time and done and felt things you cannot know.

They will be changed. They will have to learn to adjust themselves to peace." The writer was Ernie Pyle. The men he wrote about were the veterans of World War II.

During the summer of 1981, several Vietnam veterans staged a hunger strike in Los Angeles to protest what they claimed was unresponsive treatment from the Veterans Administration. When the VA failed to answer their demands for better treatment, the veterans moved their protest to Washington.

During the summer of 1932, an "army" of twenty-eight thousand protesting World War I veterans descended on the nation's capital demanding payment of government-promised war bonuses. President Herbert Hoover responded to the protest by ordering the Army to disperse the veterans. Under the command of Army Chief of Staff Douglas MacArthur and his aide, Dwight D. Eisenhower, the regular soldiers routed the veterans, some of whom had served with MacArthur during the Great War. Six veterans died in the protest.

While the Los Angeles veterans from Vietnam's "non-war" were staging their hunger strike, a young Vietnam veteran died in a one-car accident in the mountains west of Denver. It had been ten years since his return from the war, but he was still haunted by the memories of the 114 enemy soldiers he had killed and of the friend who had bled to death in his arms. Late in July of 1981 he began taking tranquilizers and smoking pot in an attempt to forget those memories. His stomach was filled with downers and his mind occluded by marijuana when he climbed into his van and drove off one day. His experience in Vietnam had taught him to fear tunnels. The police estimated that his van was doing eighty miles an hour when it emerged from the Eisenhower Tunnel near Loveland Pass and struck a concrete retaining wall. He was alive when he was pulled from the crumpled van, but as motorists and highway patrolmen administered first aid trying frantically to save him, he merely watched and said nothing. Before the ambulance arrived, this troubled veteran of Vietnam finally succeeded in not remembering. He was not the first to suffer from "postwar stress."

The battle for Iwo Jima during World War II was the bloodiest in the history of the Marine Corps, resulting in almost twenty-four thousand casualties. Associated Press photographer Joe Rosenthal's dramatic picture of the American flag raising on Mount Suribachi was used as the model for the Marine Memorial at the Arlington National Cemetery—"Uncommon Valor Was a Common Virtue." Because of his participation in the flag raising, Ira Hayes returned home a hero. Later, he would say, "I couldn't take it . . . thinking of all those other guys who were better men than me not coming back at all." After his discharge, Hayes began a ten-year odyssey of aimless wandering and habitual drinking. He was arrested fifty-one times for drunkenness, sometimes barefoot and usually incoherent. Finally, in 1955, this native American drank too much cheap wine and died on the freezing sands of an Arizona Indian reservation.

"I heard of a high British officer," Ernie Pyle wrote during World War II, "who went over the battlefield just after the action was over. American boys were still lying dead in their foxholes, their rifles still grasped in their dead hands. The veteran English soldier remarked time and again, in a sort of hushed eulogy spoken only to himself, 'Brave Men. Brave men.' " Vietnam had its brave men too, but this fact seems to have been eclipsed by other events and tragedies of the time. During World War II, 469 Congressional Medals of Honor were awarded for valor. In Vietnam, there were 238. Per capita, there were more awarded to Vietnam's two million-plus veterans than to World War II's twelve million.

One reason that many people are unaware of this fact is that the newspaper and television coverage from Vietnam had to compete for space with coverage of sensational events at home. Therefore, film and photographs of an American torching a Vietnamese hootch, or the execution of a Vietcong prisoner, or a child victim of an American napalm attack were more competitive than a dozen bland

Congressional Medal award ceremonies. Americans had a unique opportunity to *see* the nation and world around them; but television could also provide an escape from this often dreadful reality. While America was chuckling over the antics of Gomer Pyle, ten thousand miles away a young Marine, on his nineteenth birthday, died after diving on an enemy hand grenade in order to save his buddies. While "Hogan's Heroes" were amused by the bumbling antics of Sergeant Schultz, an American airman died after fourteen hours of beatings in a North Vietnamese POW camp. While the Hillbillies were romping through Beverly Hills, an American fire team leader, blind in one eye, charged into the midst of a battalion-size enemy attack after hearing his buddies cry for help.

Because the actual coverage from Vietnam was often brutal and gruesome, people back home were not only becoming increasingly ignorant about Medal of Honor recipients but, in an attempt to minimize their own agony over the war, they began blocking it out entirely. When the television screen revealed wounded and dying Americans far from home, it was less painful to change the channel or turn the set off. Soon, anything associated with Vietnam was being blocked out—the B-52 strikes, search-and-destroy missions, KIA, MIA, POW, napalm, booby traps, rice paddies, Medal of Honor winners, and, ultimately, Vietnam veterans. Despite the unacceptable images on the TV tubes, the killing, dying, and suffering went on and on, and when the "boys and girls" returned home from the war, it was difficult to look them in the eyes, let alone cheer them in a parade. As more years passed, some Americans became disturbed by their treatment of these veterans and tried to rationalize their guilt by pointing out the differences between them and previous war veterans. *They* lost the war, *they're* drug addicts, *they're* aloof and uncommunicative, *they're* cry babies, *they're* ungrateful. Eventually, some Americans began believing only what they wanted or needed to believe about the Vietnam veterans.

In the summer of 1982, ABC Television broadcast a

news special about Vietnam veterans and noted that 34 percent of the Americans who saw heavy combat in Vietnam were later arrested for civilian offenses after returning home. In an effort to explain why a small number had trouble adjusting to civilian life, a news crew visited several prisons and interviewed some convicts who were also Vietnam veterans. Later, a viewer, who was asked what he thought about the program, responded that it surprised him to learn that over 30 percent of the Vietnam veterans came home and were later sent to prison for drugs and violent crimes. That was not what the statistics indicated, nor what the prison interviews had revealed. It didn't make any difference. This viewer had been so conditioned to think the worst about Vietnam veterans, it was easy for him to reach this conclusion.

Recently, two Vietnam veterans were sitting in a neighborhood lounge watching an NFL football game on TV. At halftime, they began to quietly talk about their war; they did not want to disturb or annoy the other patrons. A woman at a nearby table started to say something to them, but then stopped. "What is it?" one of the vets asked. "What did you want to say?"

Shy, tentative, the woman paused and then said, "I just wanted to know if you are ashamed of being a Vietnam veteran."

Both of them were astonished. "Ashamed?!" exclaimed one. "I'm not ashamed. In fact, I'm quite proud of being a Vietnam veteran."

The woman smiled with apparent relief and said, "Thank you. I'm so glad to hear somebody say that."

The veteran couldn't explain exactly why he was proud, even to himself. Part of it was because he had done nothing to be ashamed of, part of it was because he had done what he thought was required of him, and part of it was because of other veterans he had come to know. But mostly, it was because he was proud of 238 men . . . brave men.

In the spring and summer of 1964 the civil-rights movement was slowly gaining momentum through Freedom Rides and voter registration drives across the South. The young people on the nation's campuses were beginning to assert themselves with demands for more freedom for themselves and more accountability from their elders. At the same time, the American commitment in Vietnam was growing slowly and with this escalation came agonizing questions. Did we belong there? What was our goal? When would we leave?

These three forces were converging and over the next ten years would develop a new national consciousness that would demand participation and action. "Compared to the Korean War generation," an Ivy League administrator said, "this one is more committed. They will get off the fence."

They got off the fence all right, but not all on the same side. There also seemed to be more than two sides to the fence. On any given subject, ten of these non–fence sitters could come up with twenty-five different opinions. If young people tended to pat themselves on the back for being committed, elders shook their heads and wondered, "To what?"

In March 1964, a young woman named Kitty Genovese was attacked while walking home from work one evening. "Oh! My God!" she screamed. "He stabbed me! Please help me!" The attacker fled, leaving Kitty lying in a pool of blood and crying for help. Thirty-eight of her neighbors heard Kitty's pleas, but not one would help. Recognizing one of her neighbors watching from a window, Kitty called him by name, but silence was his only response. The attacker returned and continued his deadly assault. The highly public murder of Kitty Genovese and the resulting furor seemed to serve as a cautionary tale; young people clamored to become involved in preventing other deaths. However, there was a darker side to involvement.

In June, three young civil-rights workers were attempting to help register black voters in Mississippi. The mother of one worker asked, "Ain't you afraid of this?"

"Naw, mama," her twenty-year-old son replied. "That's what's the matter now—everybody's scared."

Later, after the three young men had disappeared, the sheriff of the county where they had last been seen said, "They're just hiding out and trying to cause a lot of bad publicity for this part of the state."

"Well," another Mississippian said, "we would feel sorry that they were dead, and if we caught them, we might indict the men who killed them, but we would also feel that they were asking for trouble when they came down here trying to change the customs of other people."

There was only one "custom" the workers were trying to change. A Mississippi plantation owner put it succinctly: "If any of my niggers try to register [to vote], I'll shoot them down like rabbits."

In August the bodies of the three young men were found under a newly constructed earthen dam. The body of the black man, who had told his mama that he was not afraid, had been so badly mangled that it reminded a coroner of an airplane-crash victim. But the Ku Klux Klan joked that the FBI was able to find the bodies only because a postal letter carrier happened to be walking by the dam and the black man reached up to get his welfare check. And the sheriff who had dismissed the disappearance of the three workers was later indicted in their murders. He was acquitted, but he was later convicted of violating the three young men's civil rights.

In addition to the Freedom Rides and voter registration drives across the South, the 1964 Civil Rights Act in Congress raised the temperature further. After passage by the House of Representatives, the bill—which advocated voting rights for blacks as well as access to public restaurants, housing, transportation, education, and banning employer discrimination due to race—met bitter opposition in the Senate. "I can see no room for compromise," one southern opponent in the Senate said. "We are preparing for a battle to the last ditch—to the death."

A filibuster of the bill backed by a block of southern senators (eighteen Democrats and one Republican) began. Meanwhile, a black mother of ten was shot down in Florida while searching for her lost wallet along Highway 1. She died before reaching the hospital. Senator Sam Ervin—the Democrat from North Carolina who would chair the Watergate hearings a decade later—responded to one critic of the filibuster, saying, "I assure my good friend and the senator from Pennsylvania that we are not engaged in a filibuster. We are engaged in an educational debate." The laughter that followed was not included in the *Congressional Record*. The filibuster was broken, and in July the new bill became law.

That same month the slums of Harlem and Bedford-Stuyvesant in New York erupted in violence. A white building supervisor who was washing down the sidewalk in front of his building sprayed three passing black youths, and they chased him inside. A thirty-six-year-old white New York Police lieutenant emerged from a nearby store and confronted the youths. The confrontation resulted in the death by shooting of a fifteen-year-old black boy. The police officer claimed that he fired only in self-defense, but black witnesses said the boy had had no weapon. The grand jury ruled that the police officer was justified.

"This is worse than Mississippi," one black girl screamed.

The resulting riots spread to Rochester, and before they ended, 4 people had been killed, 350 injured, and 973 arrested. A white woman who could not understand the riots lamented, "Why are they doing this? Why don't they stop?"

While the National Association for the Advancement of Colored People, Congress of Racial Equality, and other black-oriented organizations advocated nonviolence, an angry black parent in Harlem exclaimed, "We can't sit back and wait on the so-called Negro leaders. These are our children and we've got to be the ones who act!"

In an attempt somehow to explain the acts of violence in New York and across the South, many whites adopted the theory that these disruptions were communist-inspired. "It's the rats, the roaches, the futility, the despair that comes from being kept down," an angry black retorted. "Damn Communism, damn Socialism. I'm talking about being free!"

The passage of the Civil Rights Act was the basis for another racial confrontation in September. The New York City Board of Education, in an attempt to equalize racial quotas in the classroom, inaugurated a new plan to move students by bus to racially imbalanced schools in the city. Over two hundred fifty thousand children were kept home from class by parents protesting the new plan designed to promote educational parity. Those children who did attend class met vicious verbal attacks. A white picketer protesting the busing plan snarled at a young white student who was attempting to go to school: "If you go to school today, you'll turn into a nigger!" The anger subsided and the schools began attracting more students, and the boycott began to peter out. However, the country had hardly seen the last of these problems.

"More and worse riots will erupt," black nationalist Malcolm X predicted in the *Saturday Evening Post*. "The black man has seen the white man's underbelly of guilty fear."

A Los Angeles teenager said that the underlying reasons for the rioting were obvious—". . . seeing the terrible condition Harlem is in, I think those riots are somewhat understandable. This can happen to any low-class people who have to live around dirt, filth and frustration. [We should] try to do something soon about the poverty of the Negro." But a black revolutionary offered *his* solution: "There is only one thing that can correct the situation and that's guerrilla warfare." It would come.

The racial disorders of the sixties were nothing new. There had been outbreaks off and on since before the Civil War. What made the current unrest different was the *coverage* it was being given in the nation's newspapers, magazines, and, most important, on television. This had an interesting side effect on the nation's young. In the classroom, students were being taught about equality, freedom, and happiness for all, yet on television they saw black people (both young and old) being beaten with clubs and attacked by police dogs, children being escorted to school by soldiers, and cities being patrolled with tanks. Churches and organized religion were another source of confusion for the young. As one youth put it, "You see a picture of a thousand corpses being bulldozed into a mass grave by the Nazis, and then you hear about this great Greco-Roman-Judeo-Christian tradition of the inviolability of the human person, and you begin to wonder if it isn't all a great deception."

Baby doctor Benjamin Spock noted this youthful cynicism when he said, "Adolescents speak with bitterness about the possibility of no future."

☆ ☆

An indication of what was coming occurred in the summer when youngsters around the country rioted for no apparent reason. On Labor Day thousands of youths in Seaside, Oregon, rebelled. For two nights they threw rocks and sand-filled beer cans at local police who were merely trying to restore order. Ninety-five young people were arrested.

At the same time in Hampton Beach, New Hampshire, seven thousand high school and college students charged into the center of town from the beach. In what was possibly a reaction to the rioting and racial confrontations they had seen on television earlier in the summer, the youngsters screamed at the officers trying to control the situation, "Kill the police! Kill the police!"

"It was one of the most appalling things I've ever seen," a local restaurant owner said. "Girls and boys alike, some as young as thirteen and fourteen, were chanting in a near frenzy." Twenty-two were injured in the rioting that followed and 139 arrested. New Hampshire Governor John King theorized that the incident at Hampton Beach "is a symptom of moral sickness in American youth which is potentially explosive and must be dealt with accordingly." But the explosive potential of the new generation became even more apparent that fall when students at the University of California at Berkeley rebelled against the school administration's ban against outside political activities, e.g., on-campus recruitment of civil-rights workers for voter registration drives in the South. The Free Speech Movement (FSM) was formed and student activists began to confront the school administration's policy.

The confrontation came to a head in December when the FSM seized the administration building, Sproul Hall, and demanded an end to the ban. At first tentative and unsure about how to handle the unruly demonstrators, officials finally decided to get tough and clear the building of protesters. Police stormed Sproul Hall, arresting over seven hundred students and supporters. Many students resented the strong-arm tactics utilized at Berkeley. *Life* magazine predicted, "The result at Berkeley could foreshadow the spread of civil disobedience to other campuses around the country."

In addition to questioning authority and the inflexibility of its rules, young people were beginning to discard the Victorian sexual taboos of their parents. In a 1916 survey of college seniors, 20 percent of the male respondents said that they had never even been kissed. By the fifties, 20 percent of the college women polled in a similar survey admitted to having premarital sex. Then, in the sixties, the advent and accessibility of the Pill greatly increased this number. This changing attitude also spawned a new "retailing" openness. In a California bar that summer, a young waitress began serving drinks in her new topless bathing suit and was arrested. Nineteen hundred and sixty-four became the Year the Bottom Fell Out of the Top.

"The coolest customers in the U.S. these days," noted *Time* magazine (October 9, 1964), "are the nation's teenagers, who number 22 million and are growing as a group three times faster than the total population."

Not only was this rapidly growing group of young people providing an economic boon for the nation, but it was also injecting a new vitality. "Americans are dancing again, staying up late to do so, as they have not for many years," one journalist observed. "Girls are showing their knees, as they did . . . in the Twenties. War and depression seem remote dangers, in spite of irritants like Vietnam."

Their music, their cars, their ideas, their dress—everything about the new generation seemed fresh and novel. But this new world also possessed new dangers. *Look* magazine (September 8, 1964): "We are living in a new world and are being tested everywhere—Vietnam, New York, Mississippi—in ways we have never been tested before."

By the summer of 1964, several thousand Americans were serving in Vietnam as advisers to the South Vietnamese army. Over a hundred Americans had been killed in action, and many questioned the reasons for these combat deaths of "advisers." Why were we there?

"To begin with," former Assistant Secretary of State for Far Eastern Affairs Roger Hilsman explained,

Southeast Asia is, of course, important strategically. But South Vietnam is also important as an example. Our missile and bomber programs have deterred nuclear war. The Communists . . . tried large-scale conventional war, in Korea. . . . Now the Chinese Communists think they have found a chink in our armor with a new tactic—internal war, a mixture of the political and military. If we don't meet it in Vietnam, we are going to see it in other parts of the world.

In an attempt to allay fears that his administration was planning to escalate the American role in Vietnam, President Johnson said, "The United States intends no rashness, and seeks no wider war. But the United States is determined to use its strength to help those who are defending themselves against terror and aggression."

A popular joke at the time had President Johnson saying, "We are assisting the South Vietnamese government strictly in an advisory capacity. Last week we dropped four thousand pounds of advice on a suspected Vietcong position."

In May of 1964, *Life* magazine published a series of letters from a U.S. Air Force pilot who was serving as an adviser to the South Vietnamese air force. In a letter to his pregnant wife, he wrote:

I'm over here to do the best job possible for my country —yet my country will do nothing for me or my buddies. Why? Because votes are more important than my life or the lives of my buddies. What gets me is that they won't tell you people what we do over here. I'll bet that anyone you talk to does not know that American pilots fight this war. We—me and my buddies—do everything. The Vietnamese STUDENTS we have on board are Airman basics. They don't even know their own serial numbers. The only reason they are on board is in case we crash there is one American "adviser" and one Vietnamese "student." They are sacrificial lambs. They are a menace to have on board.

Two days after sending his last letter home, this American "adviser" and his Vietnamese "student" were killed when their plane was shot down by Vietcong ground fire. If American pilots were increasingly fighting the air war, Americans were still serving the South Vietnamese army strictly in an advisory capacity. It could often be an incredibly frustrating role.

The Economist, June 27, 1964:

A French reporter was out in the field with [a South Vietnamese army] artillery battalion that was being advised by an American captain. The two stopped to have a drink, and when they came out of the hut, they were surprised to see the column about to make off in an unexpected direction.

"We have just heard there is a strong Viet Cong barrier on the road," the South Vietnamese commander explained, "so we shall take another route."

"But you can attack and break it with your guns," the astonished reporter said.

"If he"—designating the American with his head— "wants to go, he is free to do so, but this is not our war," replied the [Vietnamese] officer, climbing into his jeep and leading the convoy in the opposite direction from the enemy.

Likewise, it was becoming increasingly frustrating for the American diplomats. In September, Stuart Alsop wrote in a column for the *Saturday Evening Post:*

There are, in fact, sensible people at the second policy-making level who are convinced that the war has been lost already. "There's just no good way out of this anymore," said one younger official long involved in the struggle to keep Vietnam from Communist control. "Maybe we'll just have to accept defeat."

"Accept defeat?" said another. "We've been defeated already. We just don't know it yet."

This degree of gloom is not shared by the President's top-level advisors . . . [but] there is no real optimism left.

ROGER HUGH C. DONLON

Rank: Captain
Unit: Special Forces Detachment A-726
Birthplace: Saugerties, New York

Place: Nam Dong
Date: July 6, 1964

Birthdate: January 30, 1934

It happened thirty miles northwest of Da Nang, near Khe Sanh (names quite alien to America in 1964) on a small hill that was surrounded by larger hills. There were 311 militiamen in the force that defended the region—a couple of South Vietnamese regular soldiers, sixty Nung mercenaries, and the rest members of the Civilian Irregular Defense Group (CIDG). The regulars and the Nungs had proven to be dependable in a fight, but the CIDG were, well, irregulars, who often came into camp with their families, their animals—and sometimes even the Vietcong.

Advising this motley crew was United States Army Special Forces Detachment A-726, a twelve-man unit under the command of Capt. Roger Donlon. Together, they protected the peaceful valley below that was dotted with villages with a total population of about five thousand. In addition to advising the militiamen about counter-guerrilla-warfare tactics and how to defend themselves from the harassing tactics of the Vietcong, the team of Green Berets also provided the villagers with medical aid, helped build schools, and assisted the South Vietnamese in locating and digging water wells.

When the opportunities presented themselves, the thirty-year-old Donlon would pause and forget the war for a minute.

"I remember sometimes in the early dawn, that fog layer being there, and you could see the mountaintops . . . the sun would just be coming through dimly, then brighter. Things would still be damp, cool from the night, and we would watch the morning burn off little by little. . . . Sometimes it could be beautiful . . ."

Only for a minute could he pause, because the enemy—the Vietcong—was amid the beauty . . . waiting.

On the Fourth of July after several weeks of VC infiltration, there were indications that the enemy was getting ready to pounce. They were outside the camp; they were inside the camp; the captain could feel it. The villagers also felt it, and their anxiety increased after the Vietcong assassinated two village chiefs in the valley. The attack was coming, everybody could feel it, but when?

The answer came at 0225 on July 6.

"I was getting off watch and heading into the mess hootch to check the roster. As I grabbed the door, a white phosphorous round hit the place, blew me down. I don't know whether I picked myself up or not, but I did a fast, low-ass crawl away from there." Wearing a fatigue blouse and black pajama bottoms, Donlon lost one of his combat boots from the explosion.

An Australian member of the team—yes, the Aussies were there, too—who had more combat experience than the rest of the team combined, remarked, "Well, we're in for a bloody good one tonight." Immediately, he went down, an AK-47 round in the head.

"I have to say, after he got killed, I was fighting mad right from the start, I also felt fear from the start . . . fear anybody would feel."

Pitted against the defenders of Camp Nam Dong were about seven hundred enemy soldiers who were storming the outer defenses. From the inside, God and the Vietcong only knew how many guerrillas were fighting against the camp's defenders.

"The eerie thing was that our commo [communications] got knocked out right away. We got one message out. The CP [command post] got hit right at the beginning. It was no accident where the round landed. They had it paced off, had it measured. They would rehearse and rehearse before attacking."

The captain and the other members of his team immediately began removing ammunition from the CP. Then Donlon sprinted around the compound consolidating his defenses and checking his five mortar positions. Because key personnel had been posted in vital defensive positions, the camp defenders were able to ward off the enemy's initial surprise attack.

"We were able, within a minute, to illuminate, send up hand-held flares right off the bat, and take from the Vietcong one of their most powerful weapons. And that was the cloak of darkness, and the fear that goes with it. It took confidence away from the attackers and gave confidence to the defenders."

After this initial assault, Sgt. Marvin Woods began directing the fire from one of the camp's mortar positions, alternating high-explosive and illumination rounds. This helped keep the VC pinned down, and at the same time revealed where they were assembling for the next assault.

"They're over here!" one of the team sergeants shouted from the eastern side of the camp. Donlon dashed to that side of the camp and found the enemy coming:

". . . literally through and right over that wire, most of them barefoot and stripped down to loincloths, hundreds of them. Some had penetrated the interior perimeter; the outer perimeter was penetrated all over the place. The infiltrators inside the camp had stripped to the same-color loincloths, identifying themselves to the attackers. They were sturdy fighters. You had to respect them. They had grit."

The illumination was good at that point, and he saw a

Vietcong demolition team consisting of three sappers coming up the hill near the camp's main gate. As he raced to that location, he found that he had a slight problem.

"Ran out of ammo. But I yelled to one of our mortar pits for someone to throw me some. . . . Just about everybody was wounded or dead in there. . . . I heard something hit beside me, and what I grabbed made the pit of my stomach fall out.

"Just one clip of ammo in a cardboard box. One. Oh, hell."

The three Vietcong were unaware of the captain's presence: They had something else on their minds. The VC were loaded down with satchel charges slung all over themselves; they were bulging with explosives. Their job was to blow the main gate, and once that was accomplished, their comrades would swarm into the camp and overrun the defenders. But first, they had to blow that gate.

Twenty yards away Captain Donlon with one clip of ammunition was all that stood between the sappers and victory or defeat, depending on which side of the fence you were on.

"I'll just sit right here, I thought. Right out in the middle of bare-ass nothing. It went back to all the training I could remember. Coaching out on the firing line . . . 'Watch your breath . . . Get a good bead . . . If you are going to shoot, shoot low, get 'em on a ricochet . . .' What was my best firing position? Where did I get my Expert? I wasn't about to stand. I had a little common sense left. I went right into a kneeling position."

While he was loading his AR-15, a mortar shell exploded nearby and the captain received a severe stomach wound. He knew that he was bleeding, but he didn't know how bad the wound was. . . . He didn't want to know. He ripped off part of his T-shirt and stuffed it into the wound to slow the bleeding.

"I reached down and felt a lot of wet. Thought I was urinating on myself. Maybe I was. Everybody who's been in combat has done that once or twice."

He couldn't dwell on that, though. He still had the three sappers to deal with. He put the AR-15 on semiautomatic, don't jam now, and resumed his kneeling position.

"I took all single shots. Picked them off one by one. They never knew they were zapped. In that situation, every round was vital."

And that situation was getting worse. The outer defensive perimeter was coming under increased attack, and when he realized it could not be held any longer, Captain Donlon ordered the withdrawal of his forces to the interior defensive positions. There he found that most of the men in one of the mortar pits were critically wounded. He disregarded his own injuries and went to their aid.

"Down in the pit with the wounded, it got to the point where we were throwing the enemy's grenades back at them. Just picking 'em up and throwing those damned grenades back before they could blow. ChiCom [Chinese Communist] grenades. Thank goodness a lot of them were duds. Finally I yelled, 'That's enough of that! Let's get aft of this place!' Getting out. Going elsewhere. Had enough of that hole.

"My team sergeant was in real bad shape and I picked him up. Got him on my shoulder. Got him out as far as I could. Then another round hit. Big flash, big white flash, maybe inside my head. And there was this sensation of 'shuuuuu' falling. That's it, lights going out, meeting my Maker.... What seemed like a very long fall ... into eternity ... we were blown back into the mortar pit, all of four feet. I don't know ... maybe I was unconscious for a while."

When he regained his senses, his team sergeant was dead and he had taken a chunk of shrapnel in his left shoulder. The fight was still going on as he staggered back to the inner defense perimeter barefoot; his other boot had been blown off. Mortar shells were raining all around.

The inner perimeter with its thatched buildings—the living quarters, the CP, the supply room, the dispensary, the ammo bunkers—was a shambles. Everything was all shot up and the only thing standing was a jerry-rigged shower, a fifty-five-gallon drum on stilts with a thatched screen around it. Fires were burning everywhere.

Donlon kept fighting and moving from position to position, encouraging his men. His wounds were excruciating, yet he kept going. Adrenaline was surging through his veins and it was keeping him pumped up. It was keeping him going.

"This chunk of shrapnel had lodged in my shoulder. That smarted, that really smarted. I couldn't move my left arm really, but it worked out. I just stuck it down there holding the place in my belly, and that sort of semi-immobilized it. Yeah, just stuck it down in the old black pajamas. But pain, the sensation of pain, can be masked by other emotions in a situation like that."

The dead were sprawled everywhere while the living fought to remain so. Ten of Donlon's A-Team were dead or wounded . . . other emotions.

The captain continued to consolidate his positions. Ignoring his painful injuries—trying to—he carried an abandoned 60 mm mortar to a safer location where he administered first aid to three wounded militiamen. He returned time and again to the mortar position and began removing other weapons and ammunition, thus keeping the Vietcong from using them against the defenders.

"Send out the Americans," the VC began shouting through a bullhorn. "Throw down your arms! We only want the Americans!"

While helping direct the camp's returning mortar fire, Donlon put an end to that nonsense.

"Right in the middle of one of those sentences, we put an 81 mm mortar round down the guy's mouth."

Two hours after the attack began, a flare ship arrived from Da Nang. While there was no sign of an American air strike, the mere presence of the friendly aircraft helped boost the defenders' morale. Finally, at dawn, the Vietcong broke off their attack and slipped back into the jungle.

It was over. Camp Nam Dong had held. One last time,

Donlon staggered around the smoldering wreckage of the camp, surveying the damage. Finally, near the main gate, he came to the three sappers he had killed, cluttered with unused satchel charges.

"But I didn't look at them much, didn't much dwell on them. There were fifty-four enemy dead scattered around, another one hundred in a mass grave, the ones they left behind.

"But at that point I was looking at one of the camp's family women. She had her arm blown off. She had a child in her other arm. She was asking one of my medics to kill her."

The American medic tended her injuries instead.

When a relief column reached the camp later that day and while bleeding from his numerous wounds and while his left arm dangled uselessly by his side, Capt. Roger Hugh C. Donlon snapped to attention, saluted the senior American officer in the column, and requested permission to turn over his command. Then, tired, bloody, and drained, Captain Donlon sat down.

"No more adrenaline, I guess. I was empty."

He was awarded the Bronze Star by General Westmoreland and later put in for the Congressional Medal of Honor.

"Not win. Excuse me, not *win*.

"Every man I know who's *received* the medal has said, 'I did at the time what I felt was my duty.' Because you don't go out and win it. It's not the Super Bowl. I don't know any warrior who went to war for the sake of winning an award. It was a specific military task that he was doing. It was a mission.

"And not just to kill an enemy. When you think of that . . . in the middle of mortal combat, what rises above everything else is not necessarily the elimination of the enemy, but an action directed at saving, not destroying life.

"To be in the front lines is the greatest privilege a man

can have. . . . As you age, as you grow in rank and responsibility, your definition of the front line broadens. The diplomatic corps . . . terrorism . . . the Korean airliner shot down . . . that's front line.

"Maybe standing up to your boss in peacetime and saying, 'Sir, based on my experience and beliefs, this is what I know is right,' is front line.

"I know a very brave lady who served on the front line for years—my mom. Raising the ten of us, she knows what the heck a front line is.

"There's no smoke in those battles, but it takes courage.

"I found the press and the overwhelming attention a little hard to handle for a while. Things got a little wild for a while. But I never did anything to disgrace the uniform. I've always felt proud to be in the Army. I never lost that. If I had, I never would have stayed in.

"We couldn't have survived at Nam Dong without teamwork. It's okay to talk about individual heroes sometimes. Sometimes it's good to pause and recognize the contributions our service people have made. History is good to study and necessary to understand, but you don't want to get stuck in it.

"It's not something you plan. You're trained to perform. I was equipped for anything then. My physical equipment could maybe use some spare parts now, but mentally and morally, there's no question, I would be ready."*

In Washington, the administration was faced with a dilemma—how could the United States support the South Vietnamese government if some of the Vietnamese commanders, as indicated by the story in *The Economist*, were reluctant to fight the Vietcong? Compounding the problem was the fact that there were pockets like Nam Dong where

---

* Adapted from "Hell in a very small place" by Don Tate, *Pacific Stars and Stripes*, February 19, 1984.

the South Vietnamese villagers, with the help of some American advisers and Nung mercenaries, were able to drive off the numerically superior Vietcong.

Committing American ground forces to help the sometimes timid Army of the Republic of Vietnam (ARVN) repel the VC and their sponsors in North Vietnam, was not possible at that time. President Johnson would need congressional approval for such a move, and, since 1964 was an election year, it was highly doubtful—considering pressing issues at home—that Congress would agree to an increased American presence in South Vietnam without some sort of justification.

In August, North Vietnamese torpedo boats attacked two Navy vessels, the U.S.S. *Maddox* and the U.S.S. *Turner Joy*, patrolling in the Bay of Tonkin thirty miles off the North Vietnamese coast. At the same time, South Vietnamese forces were attacking North Vietnamese coastal installations in the vicinity. Subsequent data indicated that the North Vietnamese believed the American vessels were participating in the South Vietnamese raids.

Nevertheless, President Johnson ordered immediate retaliatory air strikes against the bases of the North Vietnamese torpedo boats. At the same time, LBJ asked Congress for a resolution authorizing him to respond to other belligerent acts in the region as he saw fit without additional congressional approval.

While hardly a Pearl Harbor, these two attacks helped dissolve much of the opposition to the administration's policies in Vietnam. One senator, Democrat Wayne Morse of Oregon, did express his doubts about the resolution and the course the nation was about to embark upon:

> The Pentagon almost goes into a paralytic stroke when someone suggests that we are involved in a civil war in South Vietnam. But so we are and have been from the beginning. . . . If we go into South Vietnam and North Vietnam, so far as the people are concerned, we cannot

tell the difference because they are all one nationality and race. But unfortunately the people in North Vietnam have been sucked in by Communism. The people in South Vietnam are being dominated by a military dictatorship. The people in North or South Vietnam do not know what freedom is . . . [and] would not recognize democracy if they met it on the streets of Saigon. . . . If the senators want my opinion, a snow job is being done on us by the Pentagon and the State Department in regard to the [Bay of Tonkin] incident . . . the resolution will pass and senators who vote for it will live to regret it—I am satisfied that history will render a final verdict in opposition to the resolution.

The Tonkin Gulf Resolution did pass, and of the over five hundred votes cast in Congress, only Morse and fellow Democrat Senator Ernst Gruening from Alaska voted against it.

Across the continent at La Jolla, California, a small ceremony was taking place that signaled the end of one era and the beginning of another. The Marine Corps rifle training facility at Camp Mathews was closing and being deeded to the University of California at San Diego.

During its half century of existence, Camp Mathews had trained over a million Marines, many of whom saw action in World War I, World War II, and Korea. The Pacific-based Marines would now receive their rifle training at the new facility located ten miles north on the sprawling base at Camp Pendleton just off Highway 101. In addition to the over three hundred million rifle slugs buried in the berms north of San Diego, the Marines were leaving something else behind at Camp Mathews that August morning.

After his landslide victory over Barry Goldwater in the November election, President Johnson moved a Marine missile battalion attached to Force Troops, Fleet Marine Force (Pacific), at Twenty-Nine Palms, California, westward. On November 18 at 0230 the battalion, equipped with HAWK antiaircraft missiles, sailed out of San Francisco Bay aboard two Navy ships, the A.K.A. *Union*, a World War II vintage assault ship, and the L.P.D. *Vancouver*, a brand-new troop ship.

The Marines were told that they would spearhead the landing of the Third Marine Division at Da Nang, South Vietnam, within three months. As they continued to sail west in the first week of December, a couple of Mathews-trained Marines on the *Union* listened to a radio broadcast, possibly from the Armed Forces radio station on Guam. Included in the newscast was a report about a student strike at the University of California at Berkeley protesting the court arraignments of those who had been arrested in the takeover of Sproul Hall. The newscaster also noted that President Johnson had just awarded the Medal of Honor to Army Special Forces Capt. Roger Donlon for his actions during the fight at Nam Dong.

After the newscast, Tony Bennett crooned, "I Left My Heart in San Francisco."

Just as the final straw didn't break the camel's back, the attack against the American installations at Pleiku didn't start the Vietnam War. Rather, it was merely another cause added to a list of causes that had begun years before.

As Leo Tolstoy explained in *War And Peace:*

> . . . What brought about this extraordinary event? What were the causes? The historians, with naive certainty, tell us that its causes were the wrongs inflicted on the Duke of Oldenburg, the nonobservance of the Continental system, the ambitions of Napoleon, the firmness of Aleksandr, the mistakes of the diplomats and so on.
>
> . . . Accordingly all of them—myriads of causes—coincided to bring about what occurred. And so there was no single cause for the war, but it happened simply because it had to happen. Millions of men, renouncing human feelings and reason, had to move from west to east to slay their fellows just as some centuries earlier hordes of men had moved from east to west slaying their fellows.
>
> . . . And by the law of coincidence, thousands of minute causes . . . the number depending on the multiplicity of points of view . . . fitted together and com-

bined to produce that movement and the war . . .
undertaken (as it seemed to Napoleon) for the sole purpose of obtaining an armed peace.

. . . In historic events the so-called great men are but
labels giving names to events, and like labels they have
only the slightest connection with the event itself.

Every act of theirs that seems to them an act of their
own free will is, in the historical sense, not free at all,
but is connected with the whole course of history and
determined from eternity.

Slowly, quietly, they inched their way forward through
the elephant grass around the United States military com-
pounds at Pleiku and nearby Camp Holloway in the Vietnamese Central Highlands. Once in position the Vietcong
waited silently; at midnight the Tet Lunar New Year cease-
fire would end, and their work could begin. Finally, in the
early morning hours of February 7, 1965, the guerrillas
noiselessly crossed the ground like shadows—shadows that
would haunt the nightmares of thousands of Americans in
the coming years—and launched their attack.

The combined ground assault and mortar attack was
brief, lasting only fifteen minutes, and costly—eight Americans were killed and one hundred twenty-six were
wounded. World War II cartoonist Bill Mauldin was there
and reported back, "Badly wounded men were sprawled
over every bit of floor. . . . Blood was pooled and splattered
everywhere and I kept slipping in it as I made my way
through barefooted."

When Gen. William Westmoreland, the new commander of the 23,500-man American force in South Vietnam, informed Washington of the attack, President
Johnson was incensed and convened the National Security
Council. "I've had enough of this," he angrily told the
council members. "I want three things: I want a joint attack; I want it to be prompt; I want it to be appropriate."

Four hours later, at 2 P.M. Saigon time, forty-nine carrier-based American jets attacked and destroyed a guerrilla training base at Dong Hai, forty miles north of the demilitarized zone separating North from South Vietnam. This event (Flaming Dart I) marked the beginning of the American air war against targets in North Vietnam.

"The people of South Vietnam have chosen to resist," President Johnson told the American people. "At their request, the United States has taken its place beside them in their struggle. We have no choice but to clear the decks . . . As the United States government has frequently stated, we seek no wider war. Whether or not this course can be maintained lies with the North Vietnamese aggressors."

In addition to the air strikes being flown against North Vietnamese targets, the President also ordered the Marine First Light Antiaircraft Missile Battalion from its temporary base at Camp Hague, Okinawa, to Da Nang. The battalion's mission was to protect the large American air base from possible reprisal attacks from the North Vietnamese air force. Also, the missilemen would provide cover from air attacks when the additional units from the Ninth Marine Expeditionary Brigade landed.

A month later, the Pentagon announced that two infantry battalions from the Ninth MEB (elements of the Third Marine Division) were being sent to South Vietnam. Their mission was to protect the Da Nang air base from possible Vietcong ground attacks similar to the ones launched against Pleiku and Camp Holloway. Secretary of State Dean Rusk told a national radio and television audience that the Marines would return enemy fire if fired upon, but their primary mission was to put a tight ring of security around the Da Nang air base, thus freeing South Vietnamese army units for combat against the Vietcong.

However, from Vietnam, Marine Corps Commandant Wallace Green said that he didn't want his men ". . . sitting around on their ditty boxes. The job I want them to do is to find the Vietcong and kill them. We got one today and we're going to get more. . . . We're fighting a war here now."

There were more sporadic attacks around South Vietnam, leaving some to feel that the Americans were no longer controlling events but that events were controlling them. The *Kansas City Star:* "Do we have a specific, unwavering policy or are we improvising from crisis to crisis?"

Newsweek (January 18, 1965): "The problems which the U.S. faces in its costly effort to stave off Communist domination of all Indo-China have lately grown so complex and threatening that no policy planner . . . can reasonably argue that the course which he favors offers more than an outside chance of success. Even the fundamental question of what U.S. goals in Vietnam should be is now without a clear answer."

In May, halfway around the world, President Johnson sent Army paratroopers and Marine infantrymen into the Dominican Republic after insurgent rebel forces there initiated guerrilla attacks against government forces, including several inside the capital of Santo Domingo. Over two thousand Americans were in the Dominican Republic at the time, and when President Johnson ordered in the American forces, he said, "Our people have to be protected, and we intend to protect them."

When the Marines stormed ashore at Da Nang in March, civil-rights demonstrators began a march in Alabama to petition the state government for increased voting rights for blacks. The march had been highly publicized, and while black leaders asserted that there would be no violence by the marchers, opponents made no such promises.

At Selma, Alabama, the state police and sheriffs' posses met the marchers in a violent confrontation. *Newsweek*'s Bill Cook reported,

The charge was swift and horrible. Impersonal behind their gas masks, the troopers clubbed their way through the screaming demonstrators. Blue-gray clouds of eye-stinging tear gas were released. Hurt and unconscious Negroes lay on the highway shoulder. A trooper walked by and dropped a tear gas grenade by each fallen Negro. Across the highway, hundreds of white spectators cheered.

Two days later, a white Unitarian minister who was supporting the Negro voter registration drive was beaten to death by white prosegregationists. A couple of weeks later a white mother of five who supported improved civil rights for blacks was shot to death by the same forces.

In an address before a joint session of Congress, President Johnson declared, "It is wrong—deadly wrong—to deny any of your fellow Americans the right to vote. . . . We have already waited one hundred years and more, and the time for waiting is gone. . . . We will not be intimidated by the terrorists of the Ku Klux Klan anymore than we will be intimidated by the terrorists in Vietnam."

This comparison between the terrorists in Vietnam and the KKK in Selma evoked emotional responses from some Negro servicemen. In a letter to *Newsweek*, a black Air Force sergeant from Selma named Edward A. Maull wrote,

> . . . I am sitting in Korea under the guns of 600 million Chinese, yet the government of the United States cannot stop a few sadistic racists from ambushing my people. It is a bitter pill to swallow . . . The conditions that the Negroes are living under in Selma . . . are no different from those oppressed peoples in North Korea, China, Russia, Poland, East Germany. You may print this letter. I am not afraid and, frankly, I just don't give a damn.

In July Watts, the black section of Los Angeles, California, erupted in violence after a white police officer pulled over a black motorist and tried to arrest him for driving under the influence of alcohol. Soon a crowd gathered, mostly youths, and surrounded the police car and began threatening the officer, who immediately called for help.

Dozens of police vehicles responded and the ensuing riot—called the Six Day War by some—quickly spread as fire-bomb-carrying youths stormed around their neighborhood, lashing out at the police, the firemen, and, ultimately, themselves. The National Guard was called in to help restore order and when the battle was over, 34 people had been killed and 1,032 had been injured.

As with Pleiku, the attempted arrest of the black motorist was but a cause on a list of causes, chief among them high unemployment, high crime, and inadequate education. Two thirds of the high-school students in Watts dropped out before graduating and joined the swelling ranks of the unemployed and/or the criminal elements. Another factor was a sense of powerlessness to determine their own future that many Watts residents felt: over 70 percent of those polled thought that they could do nothing to shape their own destiny.

In an attempt to escape this despair, many blacks were beginning to resort to drugs. This retreat into drugs had been a fact for years, but in the sixties it became almost a flood. As *Newsweek* reported at the beginning of 1965, drug addicts in America were no longer restricted "to the far away people, faceless in the most obscure and undesirable corners of society . . . The addict has lost his isolation. He is impinging on the middle-class world that has never felt him. Suddenly, he is contagious."

Rock-and-roll was another phenomenon that was sweeping the country. The kinetic tom-tom beat of this new wave of music was, to many critics and adults, too loud, too monotonous, and, in the vernacular of the time, just too much. Nevertheless, as one Princeton senior said, "It really turns everybody on." The new music created new dances as well. No longer did couples dance together as their parents had. Instead, each partner expressed him- or herself independently while shaking to the pulsating new music with dances like the monkey, the watusi, the hully-gully, the mashed potato, the swim, and countless other variations of Chubby Checker's twist.

Politically, the young people were equally as spontaneous and innovative. The Free Speech Movement at Berkeley had spawned other protests around the nation. Collectively known as the Movement, it grew to encompass Stalinists, Maoists, Communists, Trotskyites, Socialists, DuBois Clubs, Students for a Democratic Society (SDS) and the Student Nonviolent Coordinating Committee (SNCC), the latter two being core units for many future protests and antiestablishment crusades.

"We are trying to change society," a Movement member from Tufts University noted. "In the fifties, the Beat Generation ran away from it. My generation knows we have to strike at the system to make it respond."

The politics, music, dress, and attitudes of the young were something new that their elders were having trouble coping with. *Irresponsible, unmannered, undisciplined, disrespectful,* and *wild* were all adjectives used to describe the young. However, when a Tennessee farmer was asked what bothered him most about teenagers, he paused before lamenting, "The fact that I'm not a teenager myself."

Life magazine pointed out in its April 30 edition, "Grabbing the nation by the ear, protesting in loud and earnest demonstrations, American college students are telling the whole country where to get off. . . . Most realize that they are making a gesture. They hope that enough gestures will make something happen to their colleges and to the U.S."

As the war in Vietnam began to escalate and the civil unrest at home began to spread, the Movement seemed to be gathering momentum. Growing numbers of young people were becoming increasingly disenchanted with traditional American institutions and leaders. This seemed to be underscored when Yale students were surveyed about whom they admired most. The top answer: Nobody.

The pressures to succeed at the nation's colleges and

universities had increased over previous generations, because of the pressure put on the students themselves and the pressure put on them by their parents. "When I think about not making it at Yale," a freshman said, "I know I would be ashamed. I guess that's what makes me scared." A sophomore at Harvard noted, "Every time I succeed, my success is immediately taken over by my parents. The only thing I can do that will be peculiarly my own is to fail." However, failure had a new, dark implication for some of the students. A joke at the time on college campus was that the faculty had devised a new grading system: A for excellence, B for above average, C for fair, D for poor, and V for Vietnam.

The draft system had been criticized by many for allowing the upper and middle classes to send their sons to college, enabling them to avoid military duty, while the poor were being tossed into the eligibility pool for possible duty in Vietnam. A student could continue into graduate school and avoid military service altogether when he reached the upper limit of the draft age. This merely added another complex issue to the confusing nature of the escalating war.

In the spring of 1965 a government team went to a number of college campuses to try to explain the administration's policies. It was met with opposition. "Come on," a University of Wisconsin student said to government officials, "why not be honest with us? Like Johnson, you think we're a bunch of idiots." Another said, "Get this straight, sweetie. We're not going to fight your filthy, fascist war. Go fight it yourself."

This antiwar sentiment on the nation's campuses, at first almost insignificant in size, was growing. During the Easter break, while many students frolicked at Ft. Lauderdale and other resorts, fifteen thousand demonstrated at the White House against U.S. policies in Vietnam, three hundred Columbia University students sent a letter to North Vietnamese President Ho Chi Minh apologizing for the American bombing raids over his country, and University of Michigan students began collecting medical supplies to send to North Vietnam.

By the summer of 1965, the core units from the Army's 173rd Airborne Division, the 101st Airborne Division, the First Division (The Big Red One) and the newly formed First Air Cavalry Division had taken up positions in enclaves in the Central Highlands and the Mekong Delta region of South Vietnam. In I Corps to the north, the Marines from the First and Third divisions had taken up coastal positions from Chu Lai to the south of Da Nang and Phu Bai to the north. By June there were seventy-five thousand American troops in South Vietnam, and on June 9 the White House revealed that Gen. William Westmoreland had been given the authority to send American troops into combat ". . . when other effective reserves are not available and when in his judgment the military situation urgently requires it."

A couple of weeks later, Washington gave Westmoreland permission to commit U.S. ground forces into battle ". . . in any situation . . . when in [his] judgment, their use is necessary to strengthen the relative position of the GVN [Government Vietnam] forces."

"No more niceties about defensive posture and position," Westmoreland said later, ". . . we had to forget about enclaves and take the war to the enemy."

During the last week of June, Hanoi Hannah, the North Vietnamese radio propagandist, boasted that the Communist troops would be coming down to Da Nang and help the Americans celebrate the Fourth of July. On the first, Vietcong guerrillas supplemented by North Vietnamese regulars showed up and gave the Americans a pre-Fourth fireworks display.

The eighty-five-man Vietcong attack force consisted of a special operations and a mortar company, and was armed with four 81 mm mortars, a 57 mm recoilless rifle, automatic weapons, and demolitions. This force was joined by a thirteen-man North Vietnamese sapper team, and these units crossed the Cau Do River south of Da Nang where they established positions on the southeastern edge of the American Air Force Base.

At 0130 a Marine sentry heard a suspicious noise and threw an illumination grenade. When the grenade exploded, the enemy opened fire, and under the protection of concentrated covering fire and grenades, ten sappers dashed onto the airfield. As a result of their satchel charges, a Convair F-102 and two C-130s were destroyed and two other planes were damaged.

Although the attack on the airfield resulted in minimal damage and few casualties, its spectacular nature caused negative worldwide publicity and drew attention to the growing vulnerability of the American bases.

The commander of the Marine forces in the Pacific later recalled that this attack on the airfield caused the Americans to expand and extend their patrols. Lt. Gen. Victor Krulak said, "I landed at Da Nang at 0800 that day, and it was already acknowledged that we had better get moving off the airfield perimeter, or there would be more of the same kind of attack."

However, in order to accomplish this the Marines' Tactical Area of Responsibility (TAOR) would have to be expanded, and this would require the landing of additional American units. After a series of discussions with his field commanders, General Westmoreland stated that the South Vietnamese troops were proving unable to hold critical rural areas and were unable to meet the growing VC threat. Without further American and allied forces, he noted, "there was little chance of arresting the trend."

On July 30, General Westmoreland told Lt. Gen. Lewis Walt, the Corps' ranking officer in Vietnam, that he expected the Marines to undertake larger coordinated operations with the ARVN at greater distances from the base areas. Walt reminded Westmoreland that his forces were bound by previous orders that limited the Marines to reserve/reaction type missions in support of the South Vietnamese.

Westmoreland replied that these restraints were no

longer realistic. He invited General Walt to rewrite the instructions, working into them the authority he thought he needed, and Westmoreland promised his approval.

FRANK S. REASONER

Rank: First Lieutenant
Unit: Third Marine Division
Birthplace: Spokane, Washington

Place: Near Da Nang
Date: July 12, 1965

Birthdate: September 16, 1937

In an attempt to gather intelligence about Vietcong troop strength and movements south of Da Nang, the Americans began to increase the number of reconnaissance patrols. The attack on the Da Nang airfield showed how vulnerable the base was, and to minimize the danger of similar attacks in the future, the VC had to be located.

A patrol from Company A, Third Reconnaissance Battalion, Third Marine Division, had penetrated deep into enemy-held territory on July 12 when it came under intense machine-gun and automatic-weapons fire from between fifty and one hundred entrenched Vietcong. The patrol was being led by First Lt. Frank Reasoner, who was with the advance point when the enemy attack began.

The lieutenant deployed his men for an assault against the enemy positions and established a base of fire. He kept encouraging his men as he moved from position to position. Because of the ferocity of the machine-gun fire from the enemy, the Marines' main force could not move forward to assist the point Marines. Reasoner repeatedly exposed himself to the devastating fire while he skillfully provided covering fire for his men, killing at least two VC and silencing one machine-gun position while attempting to evacuate a wounded Marine.

The casualties began to mount. When the radio operator was wounded, the lieutenant moved to his side to tend him. After being given first aid by the lieutenant, the radioman was wounded a second time while attempting to reach a more protected position. During Lieutenant Reasoner's rush to again help the fallen radio operator he was mortally wounded.

Lt. Frank Reasoner was posthumously awarded the Congressional Medal of Honor for his actions.

On August 15 the location of the First VC was finally confirmed after a deserter from the enemy regiment surrendered to the South Vietnamese. He revealed that the regiment had established its base in a village twelve miles south of Chu Lai and was planning to attack the American enclave. The Marines had two options: to remain in their defensive positions and wait for the enemy, or to go out and get them. They chose the latter. Operation Starlite, originally code-named Satellite, but a typographical error had changed it, was conceived.

Operation Starlite

The first major battle between American and Vietcong forces began on August 18. The attack plan called for units from the Fourth Marine Regiment to be heli-lifted inland several thousand meters from the coastal village of Van Tuong, where it was believed the Vietcong were headquartered. Marines from the Third and Seventh regiments. would make an amphibious landing a couple of thousand meters south of the village, then converge on the VC in Van Tuong.

The major action occurred near LZ Blue, a patchwork area of rice paddies, hedgerows, and woods. Two small knolls, Hill 43 and Hill 30, dominated the flat terrain and the nearby villages of Nam Yen and An Cuong (2).* When Company H, Fourth Marines, landed at LZ Blue, it was

---

* Some *villes* shared a common name so the (1) or (2) after the name was used to identify and differentiate them.

38

almost directly on top of the Sixtieth VC Battalion. The first few helicopters met little interference, but as the others came in, the enemy opened up. The company quickly established a defensive perimeter around the landing zone.

Company H then attacked the entrenched Vietcong on Hill 43. The VC fought back tenaciously, but the Marines, who were being supported by close air strikes and tanks, were too strong. The company then moved from Hill 43 into the open rice paddies between the villages of Nam Yen (3) and An Cuong (2), because the company commander mistakenly believed that the hamlets had been cleared of enemy soldiers by the Marines who had made the amphibious landing.

Suddenly, as H Company moved into the open, the VC opened fire with small arms and machine guns, catching the rear guard in a murderous crossfire while enemy mortars began to fall on the lead elements. The Marines were taking fire from all directions and the Ontos and tanks were having trouble maneuvering in the muddy rice paddies. The company commander drew his armor into a tight circle and then deployed his infantry.

JOE C. PAUL

Rank: Lance Corporal
Unit: H Company, Second Battalion, Fourth Marine Regiment
Birthplace: Williamsburg, Kentucky

Place: Near Chu Lai
Date: August 18, 1965

Birthdate: April 23, 1946

During the first few minutes of the attack, Lance Cpl. Joe Paul's platoon sustained five casualties while pinned down by devastating mortar, machine-gun, recoilless rifle, and rifle fire from the enemy position in and around Nam Yen (3). The wounded Marines could not move from their

exposed forward position when they were suddenly subjected to a barrage of white phosphorous rifle grenades.

Lance Corporal Paul charged forward and placed himself between his wounded comrades and the enemy. Fully
realizing that this action would almost certainly result in
serious injury or death to himself, the lance corporal, nevertheless, remained and delivered effective suppressive fire
with his automatic weapon in order to divert the enemy
attack long enough to permit the casualties to be evacuated
to a more protected position.

Although critically wounded himself in the course of
the battle, Paul stayed in the exposed position and continued to fire into the enemy positions until he collapsed and
was evacuated. Lance Cpl. Joe Paul was awarded the
Congressional Medal of Honor posthumously for his actions during Operation Starlite.

Company H then withdrew to LZ Blue and fought a
delaying action. Upon reaching the LZ, it established a defensive perimeter and awaited reinforcements.

Meanwhile, a supply column had left the regimental
headquarters located a thousand meters from the beachhead and had gotten lost between Nam Yen (3) and An
Cuong (2). It was following a trail flanked by rice paddies
on one side, trees and hedgerows on the other when the
Vietcong opened up with recoilless-rifle and mortar fire.
The column vehicles backed off the trail and turned their
weapons on the enemy's positions. The Vietcong infantry
attempted to advance but were held off.

An excited radio operator with the supply column com-
municated back to regimental command headquarters
". . . that the column was surrounded by VC and was about
to be overrun."

A staff officer at the headquarters recalled, "The radio
operator kept the microphone button depressed the entire
time and pleaded for help. We were unable to quiet him
sufficiently to gain essential information as to their posi-

tion. This continued for an extended period, perhaps an hour."

A relief force moved out to rescue the column but it came under heavy fire which killed five Marines and wounded seventeen. The resulting American artillery fire and air support caused the enemy fire to diminish but not stop. The commander of the relief force said, "It was obvious that the VC were deeply dug in, and emerged above ground when we presented them with an opportunity and withdrew whenever we retaliated or threatened them."

The ambushed supply column was extracted and the next day much of the enemy resistance had disappeared. The terrain was difficult—compartmented rice paddies, dikes, and hedgerows—and this hindered control, observation, and maneuverability.

The Vietcong were still holed up in the bunkers, trenches, and caves scattered throughout the area. As Marines swept through an area, snipers would fire on them from the rear. In many instances, the Marines either dug the enemy out of their positions or blew up their tunnels with explosives.

By nightfall on August 19, organized resistance had ended in the Starlite operational region. The Marines had suffered 51 killed and 203 wounded, while the Vietcong suffered 614 killed and 9 that died of wounds. This was a confirmed body count, but because of the numerous tunnel complexes the estimates ran much higher. One source estimated that over 1,400 VC had died in the Starlite fighting.*

This was the first major action between the Vietcong and the Americans. However, two weeks earlier an incident occurred that would have a tremendous impact on the Americans back home. This incident had repercussions

---

* Pages 40–44 adapted from *U.S. Marines in Vietnam: The Landing and the Buildup*, 1965.

analogous to the infamous George Patton slapping incidents during World War II: trivial in military terms, yet considerable in civilian terms.

After the July 1 attack against the Da Nang airfield, the Marine Tactical Area of Responsibility (TAOR) was extended south of the Cau Do River to deny the Vietcong easy access to the air strip from the south again. First Battalion, Ninth Marines ("One/Nine" in Marine shorthand) was ordered to "search out and destroy the VC, their positions, and fortifications . . ." in the sector.

In briefing his platoons before going into the Cam Ne complex immediately south of Da Nang, the commander of D Company, Capt. Herman B. West, told his men that if they received incoming fire from ". . . a position, a hedgerow, trench line, bunker, spider trap, hut, or any other location they were to overcome and destroy."

On August 3, D Company moved into the Cam Ne complex two miles south of Hill 327. Upon disembarking from the APCs, they were greeted by small-arms fire that wounded one American. The enemy withdrew immediately.

The entire complex favored the hit-and-run tactics of the Vietcong. The innocent-looking hootches harbored punji pits, spider holes, interconnecting tunnels between huts, and a civilian populace that, if not actual Vietcong itself, was sympathetic to the guerrillas. The Marines uncovered 267 punji pits and traps, six Malayan whips, three grenade booby traps, six antipersonnel mines, and a multiple-booby-trapped hedgerow. When the Marines began to withdraw, snipers popped up and took shots at them.

During an ensuing firefight, four Marines were wounded by a force estimated to have been between thirty and one hundred VC. A ten-year-old Vietnamese boy and four villagers were wounded in the crossfire between Vietcong and American forces. This would not be the last time the VC would use the civilian population as a shield.

The brutality of the village war was brought home to millions of Americans on their television screens. Lt. Gen.

Lewis Walt, commander of the Marines in Vietnam, gave a CBS Television crew a ride into Cam Ne in his helicopter, and, while circling the complex, he okayed the burning of "those thatched houses, which hid or camouflaged pill boxes." Walt said that CBS newsman Morley Safer heard him give that permission.

Safer later reported that the Marines "had orders to burn the hamlet to the ground."

Safer arrived after the action between the Marines and the Vietcong, and he reported that the Americans proceeded "first with cigarette lighters, then with flame throwers, to burn down an estimated 150 dwellings. Old men and women pleading with the Marines to spare their houses were ignored. . . . The operation netted four prisoners—old men . . . If there were any Vietcong they were long gone."

Safer's report was accompanied with film graphically showing a Marine torching a hootch with his lighter, and this caused a furor at home: An American boy burning down old folks' homes. However, the Marines countered the furor created by the report saying that D Company had received small-arms and automatic-weapons fire from an estimated platoon of Vietcong when they attempted to enter the hamlets. It was a Vietcong village, the Marine Corps argued.

The editors of the *Marine Corps Gazette* said, "War is a stupid and brutalizing affair. This type of war, perhaps more so than others. But this does not mean that those who are fighting it are either stupid or brutal. It does mean that the whole story should be told. Not just a part of it." Media analyst Marshall McLuhan said, "A hot war like Vietnam over a cool medium like TV is doomed."

When a survey revealed that the vast majority of Americans received most of their news from television, CBS's Walter Cronkite responded that the majority "of the public is inadequately informed. . . . It is impossible by the spoken word to communicate all the information that the individual citizen needs. . . . We are charged with a responsibility which, in all honesty, we cannot discharge. We do such a slick job that we have deluded the public into thinking that they get all they need to know from us."

As the war continued to escalate, official spokesmen for the United States both at home and in Vietnam began to deal less openly with the press. "My directive," a U.S. spokesman in Saigon, Barry Zorthian, said, "says that our policy is one of minimum candor."

Battle of the Ia Drang Valley

In mid-October, the North Vietnamese began a major offensive in the Central Highlands with an attack against the American Special Forces camp twenty-five miles southwest of Pleiku. On October 27, in response to this attack, General Westmoreland ordered the First Cavalry Division (Airmobile) to seek out and destroy the enemy force. For the first time in the war, the Americans engaged the North Vietnamese army regulars in a major battle.

The First CAV troopers were opposed by the Thirty-second, Thirty-third, and Sixty-sixth North Vietnamese army regiments. The month-long fight was to become known as the Battle of the Ia Drang Valley.

"These aren't the pajama boys who run when they see you coming," an Army colonel commented. "These guys came to fight." The battle proved to be a series of ambushes and counterambushes as each side jockeyed for position. One of the bloodiest actions began on November 14, when a battalion of the First CAV landed in the valley. Initially, the troopers met no opposition, but as they began to deploy, the NVA struck in waves of suicidal attacks. After three days of bitter fighting, the American machine gunners had to crawl forward and clear the corpses that had stacked up in front of their positions before they could continue firing. After losing an estimated 890 dead, the remnants of this NVA regiment pulled back. "It wasn't a cheap victory," said an American battalion commander near tears. "I've got men in rubber bags tonight who had only two weeks to go in the Army, but they fought all the way and didn't give an inch."

In another action, one American battalion walked into an NVA ambush. The enemy soldiers were in trees and fortified positions. The Americans were hit with crisscrossing mortar, rocket, and automatic-weapons fire. "Suddenly everybody around me was getting hit and dying," said one sergeant afterward. Vicious hand-to-hand fighting ensued, and American aircraft swept in and raked the NVA with cannon fire, bombs, and napalm. Because of the close proximity to our own lines, some Americans were inevitably hit too. After sustaining terrible losses, the North Vietnamese again slipped back into the jungle. After viewing the bodies strewn over the battlefield, one American said, "They [the NVA] will be able to hold their regimental reunion in a phone booth."

Shortly after dawn, the First CAV troopers left their foxholes and moved out in skirmish lines looking for their dead and wounded buddies. "My God, my God," gasped an eighteen-year-old Pfc. as he looked at the shattered bodies. "All of my friends."

From nearby a sergeant shouted, "Bring some more litters. There's four here and a whole lot more out through there."

As the flies and ants began crawling over the dead, one soldier spat. "Now, tell me when we goin' to bomb Hanoi?!"

When the fighting ended, 247 Americans were dead and 570 were wounded. The North Vietnamese army left 1,500 dead soldiers on the battlefields before slipping back into Cambodia.

Back home the antiwar rallies and protests continued. While the First CAV was slugging it out with the NVA, a thirty-one-year-old Quaker named Norman Morrison burned himself to death in protest of the war. A week later a thirty-two-year-old seminary student died in a similar fashion.

On December 7, 1965, the Vietcong proposed a twelve-hour cease-fire throughout Vietnam for Christmas, but the response from the American forces was cool and suspicious. In Saigon one skeptical military spokesman responded to the proposal, "We get paid 365 days a year . . . I know of no reason to suggest that we won't be fighting on Christmas." The American military experts also knew that the VC and the North Vietnamese followed the strategem of seeking a cease-fire only when it could be used to their advantage. If the enemy wanted a cease-fire, they reasoned, you could bet they would use it for resupply and repositioning.

However, Pope Paul VI made an impassioned plea for a temporary halt to the fighting in Southeast Asia, and President Johnson acquiesced. He ordered General Westmoreland to join the ARVN commanders in declaring a thirty-hour suspension of hostilities from 6 P.M. Christmas Eve to midnight Christmas. The diplomats hoped that this gesture would help turn the rising tide of anti-American sentiment pertaining to the Vietnam War and, as a result, get the North Vietnamese and Vietcong to the negotiating table. Regardless, the politicians felt that a brief halt to the fighting couldn't do any harm.

Former Marine Cpl. Mike Wilson remembers the "Christmas cease-fire":

"We were out on a sweep the day after Christmas in the Marble Mountain area south of Da Nang, and we saw three gooks running across the ridge with weapons. It was obvious that they were going across to set up and start sniping at us. I was on the point and wanted to open up. The lieutenant said, 'No, we are not going to make contact until we are fired upon.'

"They moved to our flank where I guess a mortar was already set up and started shooting. We had a black kid on flank who was shot in the leg and was pinned down out in a paddy. I went out to drag him back to a dike and I got shot in the back. The lieutenant came with a radio, waving his pistol and flapping his arms, and took a hit in the stomach. I got him knocked down, got on the radio and called in mortars. The gooks had already started firing mortars. We nailed them with our mortars and small-arms fire.

"The lieutenant was flown back to the Philippines or somewhere, because he was really in bad shape. The black guy had a bad leg wound and I had a superficial back wound. I'm not sure if there was anybody else hit that day, but there at least were the three of us.

"When I saw three guys running across the ridge with weapons, I should have been able to defend myself; that was my concern. But that was just one of a whole series of things we couldn't do. For instance, we boxed up our flame throwers a month after we landed and were not allowed to use them. I think that it was the result of the [televised] burning of Cam Ne.

"If you are in a life-and-death situation, then you need to be able to defend yourself. We had no guarantee that the guy on the other side of the fence had the same information about the cease-fire, or that he was going to honor it.

[A Vietcong officer said after the war that he preferred attacking U.S. positions to ARVN positions because the Americans were better disciplined and would hold their fire when so ordered.]

"I don't know what they thought, extending the cease-fire. Maybe they thought they could keep it going forever. I thought it was a joke."

A Harris poll in January showed that 73 percent of the Americans polled favored the cease-fire as a means to get the North Vietnamese and the Vietcong to the negotiating table.

In addition to the cease-fire, LBJ—ever conscious of public opinion—also halted the bombing of North Vietnam. Pentagon officials warned that the enemy would take advantage of this halt to resupply its cadres in the South and rebuild the damaged facilities in the North. The military believed that the bitter fighting in Starlite and the Ia Drang Valley had knocked the wind out of the North Vietnamese and Vietcong. Nevertheless, the bombing of North Vietnam was stopped.

President Johnson wanted a negotiated settlement to the war; so did the American people, as the Harris poll indicated. It was during this period that a delicate peace feeler from Hanoi appeared. It was a vague indication that perhaps the North Vietnamese might be persuaded to possibly begin considering negotiations—it was very tenuous. LBJ felt that the bombing halt would be a good-faith gesture on his part, but secrecy was paramount.

A reporter from the *St. Louis Post-Dispatch* got a tip that Hanoi had indicated a desire to talk, but that the United States had rejected this peace feeler. The *Post-Dispatch* correspondent attributed this information to an unidentified "well-informed [source] who is anxious to see an end to the war in Vietnam."

After the story appeared, the administration publicly proved that it had been actively pursuing the peace feeler. However, once the story was published, contact with North Vietnam was broken and the Hanoi regime hardened its position.

The St. Louis reporter later admitted, "I knew only a relatively small part of the story. My story was incomplete."

In addition to the cease-fire and bombing halt, President Johnson sent emissaries globe-trotting in a concerted effort to get world leaders to help try to persuade North Vietnam to agree to talks. W. Averell Harriman, former ambassador to Moscow, went to Warsaw; McGeorge Bundy, LBJ's special adviser on the National Security Council, went to Ottawa; U.N. Ambassador Arthur Goldberg went to the Vatican; and Vice President Hubert Humphrey went to Tokyo.

At the same time, three private citizens traveled to Hanoi at the invitation of Ho Chi Minh. The three—an American Communist Party member, a left-wing professor at Yale, and Tom Hayden, a co-founder of the Students for a Democratic Society (SDS)—sought Ho's conditions for ending the war. Upon receiving them, the three Americans planned to return to the United States and present the conditions at town meetings around the country for "ratification," side-stepping the governmental process.

Also, it was believed that the three were seeking Ho's permission to allow American "volunteers" to go to North Vietnam and help rebuild the areas that had been destroyed by American bombers. Antiwar activists felt that these "volunteers" could be used as hostages to deter future bombing of the North.

Because of this trip to Hanoi, the three Americans faced fines up to five thousand dollars and imprisonment up to five years under a 1918 law which prohibited travel to un-authorized countries. They also faced prosecution under the Logan Act, passed a century and a half earlier, which forbade private citizens from negotiating with a foreign country on behalf of the United States.

No one had ever been prosecuted under either law, and the administration didn't feel it would be appropriate to go after these three. "There is nothing they would like better," one official said, "than to be made martyrs of and we are not going to oblige." This reluctance to prosecute Hayden and the others opened the door for additional private citizens—from former U.S. Attorney General Ramsey Clark to movie star Jane Fonda—to travel to North Vietnam and condemn America's involvement in the war.

While U.S. government-approved travel to North Vietnam was not possible, travel to South Vietnam was, and in January *U.S. News and World Report* surveyed several congressmen who had recently visited the war zone. L. Mendel Rivers, a Democrat from South Carolina, said after returning from a trip to South Vietnam, "My first impression was that our men and their officers felt they could win, and they wanted an objective. They could not understand why they were having to fight under wraps, and they don't like it."

Up to that point in the war, the ports at Haiphong and Hanoi and the surrounding facilities had been spared from American bombing raids, partly due to President Johnson's private concern that an errant bomb might hit a Soviet freighter. This, LBJ feared, would bring the USSR into the war, and it might then escalate into World War III.

Republican congressman Charles E. Chamberlain of Michigan noted, "In 1964, nations of the free world sent 401 vessels into North Vietnam. This was approximately twice the number of vessels that arrived in North Vietnam from all Communist nations. This is unpardonable. Yet the President has insisted that he have the authority to continue foreign aid to countries that are supplying North Vietnam. I cannot fathom the reasoning behind this. If the American people were aware of the extent of this free-world trade with North Vietnam, I think that they would rise up in anger."

Another sticky point was that the United States was cooperating with some of our allies in their boycotts of other nations. "I am a little fed up, frankly," said Democratic congressman Wayne Hays of Ohio, "with the State Department's attitude on Rhodesia and Vietnam. We are going along with the British blockade of Rhodesia—cutting off its oil and all that. But what about the British ships and the ships of other nations that are hauling stuff into North Vietnam. I think this ought to be a two-way street. . . . When I see the President, I am going to recommend that we bomb the port of Haiphong and blockade it. If that means a declaration of war, then let's have it."

A survey of 272 members of Congress indicated that 226 believed that the survival of South Vietnam was vital to the United States and 213 favored bombing North Vietnam into submission. Only 33 wanted the United States to accept its losses and get out of Vietnam immediately.

During the bombing halt, the North Vietnamese had increased funneling additional troops and supplies into South Vietnam along the Ho Chi Minh Trail through Laos and Cambodia. As a result, President Johnson said, after grounding the American bombers for thirty-seven days, "The evidence available to this government indicates only continuing hostility and aggressiveness in Hanoi." The bombing was resumed, although Hanoi and Haiphong were still exempted. They would be bombed later.

"The resumption of the air strikes," Hanoi shrieked, "once again divulged that the Johnson peace initiative was a fraud."

In February, the Senate began public hearings into the conduct and legality of the war. Eighteen months earlier, Senator J. William Fulbright had helped move the Tonkin

Gulf Resolution through Congress, but now he was having second thoughts about the war and Johnson's ability to win it.

Fulbright believed that Congress had to reevaluate its position on the war. "For God's sake," he said, "this is becoming a major war! I assume that this is still a democracy, that the Senate has a role to play in foreign affairs. The hearings are part of that role."

The committee hearings had a noticeable antiadministration bias. In addition to Fulbright, who chaired the hearings, the committee also included Democratic Senator George McGovern of South Dakota and Wayne Morse. McGovern said, "I think it is entirely possible that we could bring the Vietcong to their knees militarily and still see an anti-American government emerge in South Vietnam—perhaps even a Communist government."

Proponents for the public hearings contended that Americans were being asked to send their children to possible death and injury, and they had the right to know why. However, some Americans already had sons and daughters in Vietnam, and opponents feared that the information released during the hearings might help the enemy. This dilemma was never resolved.

A former Pentagon planner testified, "I was startled to find in the budget request figures for fiscal 1967 we are going to put $10.5 billion in Vietnam. . . . Is Vietnam at this point worth this investment of our natural resources with all the other commitments we have world-wide? Are we not being mesmerized with this? Are we not losing sight of the total global picture?"

Democratic Senator Albert Gore of Tennessee added, "We have escalated to the point that events are controlling our actions rather than the United States being in control of events."

One of the witnesses called to testify before the committee was former Army Chief of Staff Gen. Matthew Bunker Ridgway who, after the defeat of the French garrison at Dien Bien Phu by the Viet Minh in 1954, had ordered a special study to answer questions about the feasibility of U.S. intervention. In his earlier memoirs, Ridgway had written:

> . . . Soon I was deeply concerned to hear individuals of great influence, both in and out of Government, raising the cry that now was the time, and here, in Indo-China [Vietnam], was the place to "test the new look," for us to intervene, to come to the aid of the French with arms.
>
> At the same time, the same old delusive idea was advanced—that we could do things the cheap way and by going into Indo-China with air naval forces alone.
>
> To me this had an ominous ring. For I felt sure that if we committed air and naval power to that area, we would have to follow them immediately with ground forces in support.
>
> I also knew that none of those advocating such a step had any accurate idea what such an operation would cost us in blood and money and national effort. I felt that it was essential, therefore, that all who had any influence in making the decision on this grave matter should be fully aware of all the factors involved.
>
> To provide these facts, I sent out to Indo-China an Army team of experts in every field: engineers, signal and communications specialists, medical officers, and experienced combat leaders who knew how to evaluate terrain in the terms of battle tactics. They went out to get the answers to a thousand questions that those who had so blithely recommended that we go to war there had never taken the trouble to ask. . . .
>
> Their report was complete. The area, they found, was particularly devoid of those facilities which modern forces such as ours find essential to the waging of war. Its telecommunications, highways, railways . . . were almost nonexistent.
>
> Its port facilities and airfields were totally inadequate, and to provide the facilities we would need would require a tremendous engineering and logistical effort.

The land was a land of rice paddy and jungle—particularly adopted to guerrilla-type warfare, at which the Chinese soldier is a master. This meant that every little detachment, every individual that tried to move about the country would have to be protected by riflemen. Every telephone lineman, road repair party, every ambulance and every rear-area aid station would have to be under armed guard or they would be shot at around the clock.

If we did go into Indo-China, we would have to win.

We would have to go in with a military force in all its branches, and that meant a very strong ground force —an Army that could not only stand the normal attrition of battle, but could absorb heavy casualties from the jungle heat, and the rots and fevers which afflict the white man in the tropics. We could not again afford to accept anything short of a decisive military victory (as with Korea).

We could have fought in Indo-China. We could have won if we had been willing to pay the tremendous cost in men and money that such an intervention would have required—a cost that in my opinion would have eventually been as great, or greater than that we paid in Korea.

In Korea we had learned that air and naval power alone cannot win a war and that inadequate ground forces cannot win one either. It was incredible to me that we had forgotten that bitter lesson so soon—that we were on the verge of making that same tragic error.

. . . That error, thank God, was not repeated. As soon as the full report was in I lost no time in having it passed up the chain of command. It reached President Eisenhower. To a man of his military experience its implications were immediately clear. The idea of intervening was abandoned, and it is my belief that the analysis which the Army presented played a considerable, perhaps a decisive, part in persuading our Government not to embark on that tragic adventure. . . .

. . . when the day comes for me to face my Maker and account for my actions, the thing I would be most humbly proud of was the fact that I fought against, and perhaps contributed to preventing the carrying out of some hairbrained tactical schemes which would have cost the lives of thousands of men. To that list of tragic accidents that fortunately never happened, I would add the Indo-China intervention.*

When asked to appear before the committee, Secretary of Defense Robert McNamara initially declined, fearing it would "be giving aid and comfort to the enemy." However, after Senator Morse said that Americans might "die by the millions" and they had the right to know, McNamara reluctantly relented. Other high-ranking administration officials and supporters followed.

During Secretary of State Dean Rusk's testimony, Senator Fulbright charged that the United States had been demanding from the Hanoi government nothing short of unconditional surrender. Rusk replied, "We are not asking anything from Hanoi except to stop shooting their neighbors in Laos and South Vietnam. We are not asking them to give up a single acre of territory. We are not asking them to surrender a single individual, nor to change their form of government."

The squabbling continued, and, in a later exchange with the former ambassador to Saigon, Gen. Maxwell Taylor, Senator Morse said, "I happen to hold the point of view that it isn't going to be too long before the American people will repudiate our war in Southeast Asia."

General Taylor responded, "That, of course, is good news to Hanoi, Senator."

When Taylor was asked about how many American troops might ultimately be needed in Vietnam, he wouldn't put an upper-level limit on the potential troop strength. He did dismiss, though, eight hundred thousand as "fantastic." He did say that there were built-in limitations for the

---

* Matthew B. Ridgway, *Soldier: The Memoirs of Matthew B. Ridgway*, (New York: Harper and Row, 1956), pp. 276–278.

enemy who, he estimated, were suffering seventeen thousand casualties a month from deaths, injuries, and defections. "They will theoretically run out of troops by the end of 1966," General Taylor told the committee and the television audience.

When the February hearings concluded, public approval of the president's handling of the war had plummeted from a prehearings 67 percent to 49 percent. However, the majority of those polled opposed Johnson's handling of the war, not the war itself. They felt that LBJ was being too timid.

Georgia Representative Howard Callaway said,

> My people are close to the war, they know the people who are fighting there. More than 2,000 families of those men are living in Columbus, Georgia. There were 35 death notices from Vietnam in one week in Columbus, but in my district people don't say, "Get out of the war." They say, "Support our men in Vietnam."
>
> Now I think we made the right decision to go into Vietnam. But I think it's not right to send those men to fight and die without taking the steps that are needed to back them up.

Callaway's constituents were conservative and traditional, but elsewhere there were others—mostly young men of draft age—who were less supportive of the war effort. The televised Senate hearings and the questions they raised about the war's relevance and the ability of the Americans to fight it confused many draft-age men who were being asked to put it all on the line.

Psychologists tell us that there are three stages of pain —the anticipation, the realization, and the memory. By the spring of 1966, many young men in the college graduating class were being subjected to this first stage—predraft stress.

"My draft board tells me not to worry," a University of Utah senior said, "but all the time you know they've got your file in front of them with their little 1-A stamp in their hand."

While the overwhelming majority of these young men were patriotic and conscientious Americans, they were puzzled by this new slow-to-escalate conflict. A California college student said, "If they were drafting a lot of guys for a crisis in Berlin, I'd feel different. I'd feel different about a situation where you knew who the enemy was. It seems over there that the soldiers don't know if the people standing behind them are with them or against them."

Another student who was debating whether or not to seek a draft deferment to attend graduate school said, "If I were deferred, how could I justify my position here when others are being sent there? I will go if I am called, but if I died there, I don't think I would have died for the right cause."

Another summed it up for a generation: "I'll go, but without enthusiasm."

The first contingents of returning Vietnam veterans were just as confused because of the reception some received. One battalion sailed into San Francisco Bay after a tour of duty in Vietnam, and antiwar protestors showered the combat veterans with paper bags filled with dog feces as they sailed under the Golden Gate Bridge. Other veterans who returned home via major commercial California air terminals were spat upon and cursed. As a result, more than one of the draft-age men who merely questioned the relevance of the war were pounded by angry veterans. Other veterans—the majority—simply felt alienated and withdrew.

On April 1, 1966, a boisterous, intoxicated civilian began harassing customers at a California tavern. A hefty bouncer quickly hustled the drunk outside, but he returned and shot the bouncer, who staggered to the men's room and collapsed. A table of Vietnam veterans laughed the incident off as an April Fool's joke, but when a patron was shot going to the aid of the bouncer, they realized that it was no joke.

Everybody in the bar was frozen except for the gunman, who kept scanning back and forth looking for a target. Slowly, quietly, the veterans slipped under the table. A minute later a hand emerged from under the table and slithered across the tabletop until it reached a full pitcher of beer. With diligent care and a deliberate motion, the hand and the pitcher disappeared under the table.

BERNARD FRANCIS FISHER

Rank: Major
Unit: First Air Commandos
Birthplace: San Bernadino, California

Place: Pleiku
Date: March 10, 1966
Birthdate: January 11, 1927

"We were flying propeller-driven planes out of Pleiku. Most people don't realize it, but we were involved in a two-day battle, not one.

"The first sergeant of the Special Forces camp in the A Shau Valley with the South Vietnamese forces was in the hospital in Da Nang—he had a bad wound—and he knew what was going to happen. As a result he felt he had to get back to the camp. He just got his clothes, went down to the flight line, and got somebody to fly him back to the camp.

"He should have been in the hospital. I can't remember his name, but I met him later. He was a big fellow, a big scrapper. That brought the camp up to 450 people. At that time we didn't know anything about the A Shau, which was a terrible place—up in the mountains, in a boxed canyon, and it was always fogged in or it was raining.

"On that morning they started mortaring the camp. The weather was rotten, below air minimums for flying. I guess the enemy got a forecast from their weatherman: 'It's a good day to keep the planes off of you.'

"There were from two to four thousand North Vietnamese in there. A lot of people had moved into the valley. Just a sidelight—they dug two and a half miles of trenches in two days. A lot of people.

"They struck before daylight on that first morning. An AC-47 out of Da Nang, a Puff airplane, got in under the weather. The ceiling was down to three hundred feet. He got the airplane in there over the camp and he could see what was happening. Right away they hit him and knocked out one of his engines. He went a short distance and he lost his other one and crashed. He put out a May Day before he went down, so we scrambled birds in Pleiku, Qui Nhon, and Nha Trang.

"I was flying a mission when it began. I had just returned and got a plane that was loaded and ready to go. We'd been briefed by Intelligence and were going out when we got the word—'Scrub it. Take your birds to A Shau as quickly as you can.' That was just after the AC-47 had gotten knocked down. 'That's it. Jump off and go and do the best you can.'

"The weather was terribly rotten. As we approached the area, the mountains rose up around the Da Nang area, and we started probing the canyons. We'd start up a canyon and run out of visibility, so we'd drop down, go back, and try another canyon. We probed several of these canyons and knew we were pretty close to the A Shau because of the radio traffic. But we couldn't find it.

"We had three radios—FM, VHF, and UHF—and they were going a hundred miles an hour. Suddenly, I came by a Marine helicopter out of Phu Bai that was flying support for the camp. It was almost a midair. ZOOOOOM! He went right by me.

"I said, 'Criminy! Do you know where the A Shau is?'

"He said, 'I just came from there. I've got some of the wounded. Just keep going, and you'll come to a saddle. Go over the top and you'd be in A Shau.'

"That was all of the instruction we got. We pressed on. It was raining, miserable. We came to the saddle, went over it, and came down, and there it was—the A Shau.

"The camp was burning, they were really taking a beating down there. Militarily, we accomplished more that first day of the action than the day of the rescue. That first day we were really successful, militarily, but that does not come out because of the rescue.

"When we got down to the camp, our first instruction was to destroy that AC-47; it had three mini-guns on board. We didn't want them to fall into the hands of the enemy.

"Usually when you drop a hard bomb, you roll in at five thousand feet, drop it at twenty-five hundred feet, and away you go. Sometimes you are going to get hit with your own bomb at that altitude. When you've got weather down to three hundred feet, you know you are going to get hit with your own bomb. Bruce Wallace was with me—he was flying wing—and he backed off, got a head of steam, came right over the AC-47, and just pickled it—ping, ping, ping —and ZOOM, went over the top and out through the clouds. He couldn't get back down, so he was orbiting up there.

"We were doing a lot of things like trying to get the helicopters down. We had an ELT-type system in rescue work, and when they'd transmit, it would point to them. These guys were circling and would key their mikes. Then they'd line up with the canyon.

" 'Head one-two-zero and descend.'

"That takes a lot of guts, but everybody realized the seriousness of the situation, so they'd throttle back and down they'd come.

"We bombed and strafed and fought real hard that day. It lasted for quite a while. We carried about six hours of fuel and when we got down to an hour of fuel left, it was time to head back to Pleiku. But the camp called and said, 'Can't you stay just a little longer?'

"Up with Bruce were two C-123s that had medical supplies and ordnance. They had been waiting to get down and get the supplies in before we ever got there. But there was no break in the weather and they couldn't get down.

"We decided to stay another forty minutes and recover at Da Nang, which was only twenty minutes away. With that, we decided that maybe we could get those other birds down. While I was flying under the clouds, I looked up and could see a light spot indicating a break or hole in the cloud cover.

"So I told Bruce, 'What I am going to do is punch up through one of those holes, break out on top, flip over, and come right back down through the hole. If you spot me and follow me back in, you won't hit the mountains on either side. You'll be clear.'

"That's what we did and it worked out fine. I went out through the hole, rolled over, and came back. He spotted me, and he and the two C-123s followed. Just like a couple of fighters, the C-123s rolled over and down they came. I'm sure they damaged the airplanes—overstressed them and bent the wings.

"But they got down. They circled, made one 360 and into the camp. They were taking hits going in, but they dropped about fourteen bundles. I can remember those guys turning in the canyon after they dropped their supplies. You could see the bottom of their wings in the trees and the top of their wings in the clouds. That's how low the cloud cover was. It was really tough to do, but, bless their hearts, they knew how important it was to get those supplies in.

"After they dropped their bundles and headed on out, Bruce said, 'I've got to go.'

"He was lower on fuel than I was and I said, 'As soon as we get the last of the '23s out of here, I'll follow you on out back to Da Nang.' When they left I was getting ready to check out when two B-57s checked in.

"I said, 'You guys can't come in. It's too low.'

" 'We've got wing-to-wing napalm.' You can drop that at thirty-five feet. Their call sign was Yellow Bird and out of the Philippines. Bless them, we needed it so badly. We were able to get them in. They were just beautiful. They did a tremendous job.

"By then I was really low on fuel and I said, 'I've got to go,' and I pulled out. I got on top and headed for Da Nang. The radar at Da Nang said they would give me a GCA—a ground-controlled radar approach. The weather there was down to about eight hundred feet.

"I had pushed it as far as I could and I hoped I could stay

up for those twenty minutes. I said, 'I don't have the fuel for a GCA.' What they would do was back you off and bring you right down the glide path until touchdown. That takes fuel, and I didn't have it.

"I said, 'Just bring me down opposite of the air strip and I'll make my own landing.' They brought me down out of the clouds and the runway was right there. I dropped my gear and declared an emergency.

"The guy in the tower said, 'You're number two in the emergency pattern.' It was really unusual to have two emergencies at the same time, but one of the C-123s was on final approach and cleared to land. He was all shot up and his gear was damaged. He was really sweating it.

"I told the tower, 'I'll land on your runway, your taxiway, or the grass in between, but I'm not going around over the bay, because I'm out of fuel.'

"I could see the 123 so I pressed on and landed. I got criticized for it later, but there was nothing I could do. I was out of fuel.

"They refueled our airplanes while Bruce and I went over to the club for a sandwich. We headed on back to Pleiku and got in about ten thirty or eleven. They had the lights out and were loading the airplanes for tomorrow. Everything we had was going back to A Shau.

"We went in and sacked out.

"The commander up at Da Nang called at about five in the morning and said, 'We've lost A Shau.'

"Basically, that hurt. It was an emotional thing. We put so much into it. We went ahead on our regular mission at seven o'clock in support of one of the infantry units. Just before we checked in, we got a call on one of those emergency channels and they said, 'Hey, take your birds to such-and-such latitude.'

"I looked at the map and said, 'Is that A Shau?'

" 'Yes, that's A Shau. We made some contact with some troops and they need some help very badly.'

"What had happened, there had been some mutiny with

the South Vietnamese forces during the night. Their own people had cut down their telephone wires. They had been fighting all night and were hanging on just by the skin of their teeth. When morning arrived, they got their phones back up and contacted the Special Forces camp at Nha Trang. They got the word out that they were still in there and needed some help.

"The weather had raised a little and we knew we had to get there in a hurry. We opened them up and went as fast as we could go. It took us about an hour and when we got there we could see the peaks of the mountains through the clouds. Everybody was trying to get down.

"The Forward Air Controllers were doing the yeoman's job. They knew the area, but were having a difficult time because of the weather. Their transmission went something like: 'I think it is in this canyon.' Then they'd down full flaps, throttle back, and ease down through the clouds. 'Well, it's not in this canyon, but I know it is over here.' Then they'd probe another canyon.

"The thing that was interesting was that they diverted everything that was available to the fight. The Navy was in there, the Marines, the Air Force. What would happen, a flight of four would come in from a carrier. The weather was starting at about six or seven thousand feet and they would just hold them in the stack. The next flight would come in and they would stack them about a thousand feet higher. We had birds stacked up to twenty thousand feet.

"We had all of the forces in the world, but we just couldn't get in. The Navy did send an F4A pilot in, but he turned into a box canyon and hit a mountain. The jets just wouldn't turn that tight with ordnance. Empty they were fine.

"In the meantime, I flew over a break in the clouds and recognized the terrain. I said, 'Hey, I know where we're at.'

"Paco Vasquez was my wingman that day. He was a new pilot going on an easy mission with the infantry until we were diverted. I went down through the hole and of course he was right on my tail. Another flight of A1s—two of them—on its way to Laos spotted us, turned, and the four of us went down through the hole and into the valley.

"The weather was up to about eight hundred feet. It was nice for the North Vietnamese because they could hit us. The day before we hadn't taken too many hits because they couldn't see us. But since the weather had lifted a little, they really opened up on us.

"We had gone a mile or two and the number-four man was hit. We dropped him and the three of us went on to the camp. We had an FM radio and we could talk directly to the ground. I called and said, 'We are the A1s who just went over you. What do you need?'

" 'We've just been overrun. We've lost two of the mortar bunkers and have one left. We have the COMM shack and a place where we've put some of the wounded. That's all we've got left.'

"So the three of us decided to hose down the camp. Usually we would bomb first and clear the bombs off the racks because you don't want to bomb at thirty-five feet off the ground. Then we would fly underneath each other to make sure there were no bombs left. Then we would drop napalm and strafe.

"However, because of the urgency, we went in and strafed first. I went down the east wall and with twenty-millimeter high-explosive rounds, you either dig in or get hit. Paco Vasquez was right behind me and over twenty feet and he made a run. Jump Myers was about twenty feet over and he made a run too.

"We'd strafe this lane and pull up to the left, strafe this lane and pull up to the left. I guess the NVA knew we were going to be breaking left after the strafing run because just before Jump Myers was going to pull up, they got him.

"He caught on fire, his engine quit, he lost his air speed, and he had no place to go. We didn't have ejection seats in those A1s because it takes between five hundred and seven hundred of altitude to jump out of an airplane. By the time you jump, clear the airplane, pull your rip cord, pop, and it catches you, it takes five or six hundred feet.

"If he put that burning aircraft into the jungle, he wasn't going to make it either, so he didn't have any other choice but to take her down.

"There was a PSP—pierced steel planking—runway down there. The Caribous were a real short-landing airplane and they resupplied the camp on this runway, but now it belonged to the North Vietnamese. Initially, he was burning and the cockpit had filled with smoke. He opened the canopy to get rid of the smoke and the fire came over the glass. He called out, 'I'm hit! I'm on fire!'

"I was on my second strafing run when he pulled out, so I was right behind him. The A1s had an emergency handle to clear the racks and I reminded him he had a full load of bombs. He released everything into the jungle, and just before he touched down I told him the runway looked awful short.

"It had been our experience that the Navy A1 was a pretty sturdy airplane. But they could go off the end of a short runway like that and flip over on their backs, and if you were already on fire, you weren't going to get out. So, I reminded him to pull the gear.

"He pulled the gear and slid for about five or six hundred feet on his belly sideways and fell off on the right side. He hit the bank and was just a big ol' ball of fire. I watched for a moment. He didn't get out. I called the command post and told them a plane went down and the pilot was killed in the crash.

"But just after I called, the wind blew away some of the smoke and here he comes running out. I went over the top of him and put a wing next to him. I thought he was on fire; the smoke was trailing after him as he ran.

"The Marines were flying resupply out of Phu Bai, and I called and asked if they could get a helicopter in there to pick him up. They said they could.

"We went back to the fight, and by this time the South

Vietnamese were in there on a different frequency and going in the wrong direction. There were a lot of close calls. Guys going this way and that way, wing-to-wing passes, and in such a small area. I don't know how many had joined us, but everything that was available.

"After about ten minutes I called and said, 'Where are the choppers?' They said it would be another twenty minutes. However, the NVA were within about twenty feet of him.

"Well, I felt real strong about going in and trying to pick him up. There was a lot going on, and at a time like that you can get quite spiritual. I said, 'Heavenly Father, I'm in trouble, but I feel that this is what I ought to do.' Then I went in. I credit my success to Spirituality. I always will.

"It was a terrible thing to try and take that airplane in there. I didn't know what the runway was like or anything, and if I did get in, he might be dead.

"I felt so relaxed. I called John Lucas, who took over the rest of the flight when I went in, and said, 'John, I'm making a one eighty and land. I'm going to try and pick him up.'

"He said, 'I'll cover you.'

"I had a map in the airplane, but was flying so close to the ground that it was difficult to take out and look at it. I called the command post at the camp and they said the runway was thirty-five hundred feet. However, it was twenty-five hundred and that created a significant problem.

"I made my approach and came in from the south, but there was so much smoke and fire, I couldn't see the runway. Finally, I broke through the smoke and was over the runway. I stalled her in and hit the mat. With the flaps down, you have a tendency to bounce when you cut your speed. So I had the flaps up to get more braking action.

"That steel planking had been mortared and there were three-foot prongs sticking up. The Marines had been dropping rockets in there, and there were rocket pods cluttered all over, fuel barrels were on the runway, and Jump's airplane was burning on the runway. It was just a mess.

"When I came in I skidded and skidded and skidded, and I braked and braked and braked. The brakes were red hot and I'm sure they were smoking. I could feel them fading. When I got to the end of the runway, I thought, if I stand on these brakes, I'll probably bust something. So I backed off and went off the end of the runway into the fuel storage dump area.

"The Caribous would come in, roll off the fuel barrels, and take off, and there were quite a few of those barrels. I hit several of them and did some damage to the airplane—the wings and the tail—but I didn't damage the prop or the engine.

"I got her turned around and back up on the runway, and headed back. Jump was about eighteen hundred feet down the runway. When I went by his burning airplane, he jumped up and waved. I stopped right there. He says I went by him two hundred feet, but I don't think I did. We still argue about it.

"I waited for a minute and nothing. They nailed me; they got me about three times right there. Then I got a sick feeling that he might have been hit trying to get to my airplane. So I unstrapped to go get him.

"The A1 was a two-seat, side-by-side airplane. After I unstrapped, I started to go out over the right side, and there he was on the trailing edge of the wing trying to get up. But he couldn't make it; the wind from that four bladed, fourteen-foot prop was just too strong. I thought I had it back to idle, but I didn't have it quite that far back. And with the wind blowing over the top, he couldn't make it up.

"If the engine would have stopped on the runway then, I'd have had a real difficult time restarting. It probably would have caught on fire before I'd have gotten it restarted. So I jumped back in and eased back the throttle to idle.

"After I cut the engine back, he was able to get up the wing and he fell halfway in. I reached over, grabbed him, and pulled him head first into the seat. We didn't even strap in.

"John was still up there and he said, 'Denny, let's make another strafing run. Bernie's getting ready to take off.'

"Denny Hague came back and said, 'John, I'm Winchester.' Out of ammo.

"John replied, 'Denny, I'm Winchester, too, but they don't know that.'

"They were just beautiful, right down on the ground. Denny told me—he's a great guy; he lives up in Kellogg, Idaho—he said, 'Bernie, if one of them had stuck his head up, we'd have got him.' They had those big ol' props right down in the grass.

"I'm sure on the ground they didn't know they were out of ammunition. They'd been strafing all of this time, and by then other birds had joined them.

"Initially, I thought I was going to need a little more runway, but by then they had really zeroed in on us, so I just spun around and opened her up.

"Jump said, 'Keep her down. There is a lot of ground fire there.' So, I held her down until I got to the end of the runway, and pulled. She came off beautifully.

"I took her up to about ten thousand feet on the way home and looked her over. And, boy, they'd gotten to me. The cowling around the engine was peeled back; they'd opened up the wings and the fuselage. I pulled a manifold pressure check—it's a test you run to see what kind of performance you're getting from the engine—and it was 100 percent.

"It was turning just beautifully. I knew they hadn't gotten the engine or the prop.

"I initially should have gone to Da Nang to get him to the hospital, but I knew they really needed that airplane home at Pleiku, so I overflew Da Nang. When I was leaving, I called the fellow on the ground and said, 'What do you want? What can we do to support you?'

"Bless his heart, I don't remember his name, but there was a Marine lieutenant colonel in charge of the unit at Phu Bai. He had had his helicopter shot out from under him and he'd crashed inside the camp. He said, 'We just need more ammunition and more men. We're staying.'

"In my own mind, I knew he couldn't do that. They had gone from 450 men down to 150. What I didn't know was that the only way out of the camp was slipping two or three guys out at a time at night. They'd crawl through the grass and de-de on out. He was in the camp for three days and he led the troops out of there.

"It was successful and I felt great."

Reflections

The guys in the infantry really had it hard; they really were tough. It was a bad mission. I didn't have to do that. The feeling among the Air Force people was extremely high, the morale was good. There was always tragedy when you'd lose somebody, and difficulty being away from your family, but we recognized that. Everybody did.

We thought we were doing the best we could, pretty high-caliber people. I do know this: People who are fighter pilots are mighty proud of it. I've seen it time and again. A guy will stand up in a bar and say, "I'm a fighter pilot and I can lick anybody!" (And he gets licked.)

I know how difficult it is to ever get to be a fighter pilot. Very few people ever achieve it. So, I feel quite proud of it; that I flew fighters.

When we moved to Pleiku, we built the hootches we lived in. Ice cream was unheard of then, you just didn't have it. The group commander had a C-47 and when he flew to Saigon one time, I went with him. On the way back from town we went by the back of the PX and there, sitting with nobody around, was an ice-cream maker—a Dairy Queen type.

He said, "Hold it; back up to that." We backed up, loaded it onto the truck, and took it to the airplane. We also got some mixes.

It was some of the best ice cream, and I don't think they ever realized what happened to that machine.

When I came home, I went to the Pentagon and was told by a general in the Office of the Secretary of the Air Force, "You are going to be asked a lot of questions and talk to a lot of people."

I said, "Yes, I realize that. I've been involved in some classified things."

He said, "You talk about anything you were involved in. That's okay. But if you weren't involved in it, leave it alone."

That's good advice.

People ask me about the drug problem. At the time, we had no drug problem in our unit. We monitored it ourselves. If you have a buddy who is on drugs, you wouldn't want him flying with you. Your life depends on him so much.

I don't have any firsthand information on drugs.

I know there were other problems people were having, but I wasn't involved with them firsthand. I didn't have any problems at all.

I didn't do anything I was ashamed of, and I can't remember anyone ever being caustic toward me. I came home to this area, and the people are really neat people. They don't have a lot of means that some people have.

I had just gotten home on leave, and this old beat-up pickup truck—bashed a little bit—drove into our driveway. A guy came to the front door and knocked. He had just butchered seven or eight chickens, and he had a big cooker of fresh chicken.

He said, "There was nothing I could do, I couldn't get into the military. But I would like to do something. Would you accept these?"

I could never express my gratitude. I know who he is

and I'll always remember that. That was the attitude I received.

I have never met a bad child, only bad parents.

I'm a deputy and work with a crisis center for young people. One time a father and stepmother came in with a fourteen-year-old boy and said, "Here, take him. We don't want him." It was obvious that the father had to choose between his son and his wife, and he chose his wife.

He said that right in front of the boy, and I felt like popping the father right in the nose. I went to where the boy had been taken and told him that I was going to be his guardian. We live on a farm and get up before dawn. I told him that there were some chores he would have to do, and if he did them, we'd get along just fine.

He was in the choir at school and needed a white shirt and black slacks. He said he had them at home and if I called, his father would bring them out. I did and the father came out to the farm with them. When I answered the door, the father and stepmother were there.

The father asked if he wanted anything. No greeting, no hug, no closeness, and the son said, "I'm singing in the choir. Will you come hear me?" It was obvious he wanted his dad's approval.

The father said no.

Because we live on a farm, I'd take the boy to school when I went into Boise after the chores and pick him up after school in the afternoon. Early one morning I was awakened by a hand on my shoulder and the boy, bless his heart, said, "You can sleep in. I've already done the chores."

Operation Kansas

In the late spring of 1966, the First Vietcong Regiment had taken up positions in the Que Son Valley northwest of Chu Lai. It had been joined by two regular North Vietnamese army regiments, the Third and Twenty-first. Control of this valley was crucial for both sides because the Que Son Valley contained some of the finest farmland in Vietnam as well as rich salt deposits. A former Vietnamese commander in I Corps described the area as one of the keys in winning the fight in the northern provinces.

The American marines had been planning a reconnaissance-in-force in the valley, but when it was learned that regular NVA units had joined the Vietcong, the plan was aborted. Instead, General Walt and his staff decided that a more limited reconnaissance of the region was needed before large-scale units were sent into the valley. The concept of the operation—code-named Kansas—called for the insertion of six thirteen- to-eighteen-man teams from the First Reconnaissance Battalion and one thirteen-man team from the First Force Reconnaissance company (paratroopers) into the Que Son Valley at strategically located positions.

The North Vietnamese and Vietcong had massed by the thousands in the Que Son Valley, but because of the buildup of American forces at Da Nang and Chu Lai, the enemy refused to concentrate his forces and risk a premature confrontation. Instead, the enemy moved in squad- and platoon-sized patrols while staging for a future assault. The Recon Marines were to frustrate this procedure by calling in artillery and air strike when these small units were observed.

On June 13, the First Reconnaissance Battalion's command group, which was to control the operation, and a thirteen-man reconnaissance team was heli-lifted to Hui Loc Son, a small mountain in the middle of the Que Son Valley. The same day, an eighteen-man team, under the command of Staff Sgt. Jimmie Howard, was landed ten miles to the southeast on Nui Vu, a fifteen-hundred-foot hill that provided an excellent observation post. The Marines knew this. So did the enemy.

On June 14, the remaining recon teams were heli-lifted to their observation post around the valley and the force recon team made a parachute drop onto Hill 555, ten miles west of Nui Vu.

JIMMIE E. HOWARD

Rank: Staff Sergeant   **Place:** Nui Vu
Unit: C Company, First   **Date:** June 16, 1966
Recon Battalion, U.S.M.C.
Birthplace: Burlington,   **Birthdate:** July 27, 1929
Iowa

Lt. Col. Arthur J. Sullivan, commander of the First Reconnaissance Battalion of the First Marine Division, had set high training standards for his men. Each had received individual training in the techniques of forward observing and reconnaissance patrol procedures. As a result, when he was ordered to recon the Que Son Valley, he was confident his men could carry out the mission successfully, despite the obvious dangers. However, the training was only a part of it.

"The Vietnam War," Sullivan said, "has given the small-unit leaders—the corporal, the sergeant, the lieutenant—a chance to be independent. The senior officers just can't be out there looking over their shoulders. You have to have confidence in your junior officers and NCOs."

One such NCO was Staff Sgt. Jimmie Howard, acting commander of the First Platoon, C Company. In the Korean War, Howard had earned a Silver Star for bravery and three Purple Hearts. In Vietnam his men liked him, liked to work for him.

At dusk on June 13, a flight of helicopters landed Howard and his men on the slope of Nui Vu, twenty-five miles west of Chu Lai. Also known as Hill 488, Nui Vu dominated the terrain for miles, making it an ideal vantage point. Three narrow strips of ground ran along the top of the hill. From the air they resembled a helicopter rotor blade. After climbing to the top, Howard chose the northern blade for his command post and he established his observation teams on the other two blades.

Enemy foxholes about two feet deep dotted the area, indicating that the North Vietnamese and Vietcong were well aware of Nui Vu's observation potential, too. Since there were no trees or other cover on the mountaintop, Howard let his men use the one-man fighting holes during the day to avoid the hot sun and enemy detection.

For the next two days, the recon Marines on Hill 488 saw many small enemy units and called in fire missions regularly. However, not all of the fire-mission requests were granted, because Lieutenant Colonel Sullivan was concerned that the North Vietnamese would become suspicious if too many strikes were being conducted around Nui Vu. The Marines' position was too conspicuous and vulnerable to risk an enemy attack.

As a result, most of the fire missions were conducted only when an observation plane was circling in the area. After two days, though, Sullivan became increasingly apprehensive about leaving Howard and his team any longer, but since they had encountered no problems, it was decided to leave the platoon on Hill 488 for just one more day.

The North Vietnamese and Vietcong had long claimed to have absolute control over the Que Son Valley, but the reconnaissance teams' harassment and disruptive tactics challenged that assertion. In an effort to demoralize the recon Marines, Lieutenant Colonel Sullivan theorized later, the North Vietnamese wanted to wipe out one team. They selected Howard's Marines on Nui Vu.

On June 15—the additional day Sullivan had pondered leaving the First Platoon on Hill 488—the North Vietnamese began their preparations for assaulting the mountaintop. They moved a well-equipped, highly trained infantry battalion to the base of Nui Vu in small units, and late that afternoon began climbing up the three blades. The NVA expected to annihilate the eighteen Americans with a single surprise attack.

At the same time two Army Special Forces soldiers were leading a platoon of CIDGs on a patrol around Nui Vu when they saw the NVA battalion creeping toward the hill. After radioing this information to their base camp at Hoi An, the Americans began making plans to attack the North Vietnamese from the rear, but the irregulars refused. Howard's radio was set on the same frequency as the two soldiers', and he later described their reaction to the CIDGs' refusal to fight.

"The language those sergeants used over the radio when they realized they couldn't attack the PAVMs [People's Army of North Vietnam]," Howard remembered, "well, they sure didn't learn it at communications school."

Even though the two Special Forces NCOs were unable to provide any ground support for the Marines, their warning enabled Howard to develop his defenses before the North Vietnamese launched their assault. Howard briefed his team leaders about the situation, selected an assembly point to where they should withdraw at the first sign of the enemy, and told them of the need to remain on full alert. The corporals and lance corporals crawled back and instructed their men as dusk began to fall. The "Hide and Watch" game began.

At 2200 Lance Cpl. Ricardo Binns and his three fire-team members were whispering their sergeant's instructions and warnings in a shallow depression forty yards in front of Howard's position. Binns silenced everyone when he casually put his rifle to his shoulder and fired. Twelve feet away a "bush" fell thrashing to the ground. The three other Marines each tossed a grenade, and Binns and his fire team scrambled up the hill to the assembly point. The grenades burst and the North Vietnamese opened up with automatic weapons—the battle for Hill 488 had begun.

The other two outposts along the blades pulled back immediately to the main position on a tiny rock-strewn knoll. Howard put his two radios behind a large boulder and set up a tight perimeter defense about twenty yards in diameter. He then selected the best firing position for each

Marine. The North Vietnamese had made no audible noise in their climb, and when Binns killed one of their scouts, the NVA were less than fifty yards from the top.

The Marines were surrounded, and from all sides the enemy began lobbing in grenades. The next day the platoon corpsman, Billie Don Holmes, said, "They were within twenty feet of us. Suddenly there were grenades all over. Then people started hollering. It seemed everyone got hit at the same time."

Holmes crawled forward to help the wounded, but a grenade exploded between him and one of the injured Marines. Holmes was also wounded and rendered unconscious by the concussion.

The North Vietnamese had set up four .50-caliber machine guns to provide support for their ground assault. The tracers from these weapons and from light machine guns pinpointed the Marine positions for the NVA reinforcements in the valley. After a barrage of 60 mm mortars, the enemy launched a well-coordinated attack directed by whistles and snapping bamboo sticks. Firing automatic weapons, hurling grenades, and shrieking loudly, the North Vietnamese charged.

Howard later confided that he hadn't been sure how his young, inexperienced troops would behave. They had been surprised and confused by the withering enemy fire and the screams of their wounded buddies. He received a partial answer when the first wave of enemy soldiers was cut down by the savage Marine rifle fire seconds after the NVA stood to charge. At no place around the perimeter did the enemy gather sufficient momentum to continue the assault, so they went to ground and probed the Marine lines, looking for a weak spot to exploit.

The NVA crawled forward, hoping to overwhelm individual Marines, but the enemy was often met with American grenades, which were twice as powerful as the Communist Chinese grenades. In addition, the accuracy of the Marines had a telling effect. After howls of pain and confused jabbering were heard around the perimeter, the

North Vietnamese pulled back and regrouped for another attack.

During this lull, Howard called Sullivan on his radio and informed his battalion commander that his preplanned escape route had been cut off by the encircling North Vietnamese. "You've gotta get us out of here," Howard said. "There are too many of them for my people."

Because of his detailed planning for extraction of his teams and fire-support contingencies, Sullivan was a familiar figure at the air-support center of the First Marine Division at Da Nang. He called the center shortly after midnight and didn't mince words: he wanted flare ships, helicopters, and fixed-wing aircraft sent to Hill 488 immediately. The response was, unfortunately, delayed.

Meanwhile, the enemy forces assembled and mounted a second attack against the First Platoon. The Marines threw the last of their grenades and fired their rifles semiautomatic. The accuracy of the defenders' fire suppressed the NVA assault, but by this time every Marine had been wounded or killed.

Ammunition was becoming critical; the living took the ammunition from the dead. They waited for the next charge. Howard didn't tell anyone, but he doubted that the Americans would be able to withstand another determined charge by the enemy. There were so many of them.

Combat experience had taught Howard that the enemy would, after two severe maulings, be listening for indications that the American force had been shattered and demoralized before launching another attack. From the darkness of the moonless night, enemy soldiers taunted the outnumbered Americans: "Marines, you die tonight. . . . Marines, you die in one hour."

This seemed to have annoyed the Marines more than it frightened them because they wanted to know if they could answer the threats. "Sure," Howard said, "go ahead and yell anything you want." The Marines hurled back curses and invective that, like those employed by the Special Forces NCOs, weren't learned in communications school.

The NVA continued to scream back their death threats and one Marine said to Howard, "Ain't that a laugh, Sarge." Howard agreed and he instructed his men to do just that— laugh at the NVA. With raucous guffaws and horse laughs, the Marines demoralized the North Vietnamese, who were listening for a sign of weakness. Captured NVA and VC soldiers would later tell interrogators that the laughter had destroyed their confidence—how could these Marines laugh at certain death? Surely, there must be more than just eighteen.

The North Vietnamese did not mount a third attack, but the fight on 488 wasn't over. At 0100 an Air Force flare ship arrived and dropped its first flare. The mountainside lit up and the Marines peered down the slopes. "Oh, my God!" one lance corporal said. "Look at them!"

North Vietnamese reinforcements filled the valley below. A Pfc. vividly recalled later, "There were so many, it was just like an anthill ripped apart. They were all over the place."

Attack jets and helicopter gun ships had been circling overhead, but because they had lacked light, had been un-able to assist Howard and his men in their fight. When they got light from the Air Force flare ship, though, the aviators swarmed in. First, the jets loosed their rockets on the valley floor and the approaches to Nui Vu. Then the gunships came in—the Hueys—at altitudes as low as twenty feet, and they swept the mountainside with machine-gun fire. The Hueys then pulled back and let the jets back in to drop their bombs and napalm. The Hueys came back and picked off enemy stragglers who were scurrying for cover.

Four Hueys took up alternating stations over Hill 488 then, and although the North Vietnamese tried unsuccess-fully to bring down the choppers by ground fire, the heli-copters remained all night. Howard flicked his flashlight on and off for the aviators, and the Huey pilots strafed within twenty-five meters of the Marine positions. Because of the flickering light caused by the flares, the pilots were afraid to strafe any closer, fearing they might hit the Marines.

They just had to leave that gap, and into that gap crawled the North Vietnamese.

What ensued was a deadly game of hide and seek. Besides being out of grenades, the Marines were critically low on ammunition. Howard passed the word to only fire at identified targets: Don't waste any ammo. Since they had no grenades left, the Marines threw rocks at the enemy and, surprisingly, it was very effective.

When a Marine heard a noise, he would toss a rock in its direction. Fearing it might be a grenade, the enemy soldier would dive for cover. The Marine would then slither forward, sight in, and wait. When the enemy soldier raised his head to see why the "grenade" hadn't exploded . . . one shot.

When Corpsman Holmes regained consciousness—his head still ringing from the grenade blast—he saw an enemy soldier dragging away the dead Marine beside him. Then an NVA soldier reached over, grabbed him by the cartridge belt, and began tugging at him. From behind a nearby large rock, Lance Cpl. Ralph Victor watched as the North Vietnamese tried to pull the Americans away. Victor had been wounded twice by grenade fragments himself, and he could barely move. However, he was still able to deliver deadly accurate rifle fire.

As the NVA soldier was pulling at the fallen Marine, Victor sighted in and fired, killing the enemy regular. Then he took aim at the one tugging on Holmes and fired again, striking the North Vietnamese soldier between the eyes. Holmes pushed the dead soldier away and crawled back to the friendly lines.

Holmes's left arm and face had been peppered with shrapnel, and for the rest of the night he crawled around the perimeter bandaging and encouraging the wounded Americans. At the same time, he was also firing on the advancing enemy soldiers.

When the flares went out, the American aircraft were forced to break off contact to avoid crashing into the slopes of Nui Vu. Artillery crews manned by the South Vietnamese and controlled by the American Special Forces at Hoi An, five miles southwest of Hill 488, took up the slack when the planes withdrew.

"If you can keep Charlie from sending another company up here," Howard radioed to the Special Forces camp, "I'll keep these guys out of my position."

The South Vietnamese crews replied with concentrated 105 mm artillery fire that helped keep the North Vietnamese from amassing for another assault.

"Howard was talking on the radio, he was cool," the Special Forces commanding officer, Capt. John Blair, recalled later. "He stayed calm all the way through that night."

During these periods of darkness, each Marine fought, and sometimes died, alone. A relief force later found one dead Marine propped against a rock, and in front of him was a dead NVA—their rifle muzzles touching each other's chest; two American entrenching shovels were found covered with blood near a group of mangled NVA bodies; and one dead Marine with bandages around his head and chest was found with his hand still grasping the hilt of his knife that was buried in the back of a North Vietnamese soldier.

At 0300 a flight of H34 helicopters tried to land and extract Howard and his men, but the enemy ground fire was too intense. While Howard was being told that he would have to fight on until dawn, he was hit in the back by a ricochet. He was on the radio and his voice faltered and faded out. Everyone listening—the Special Forces personnel at Hoi An, the pilots, Lieutenant Colonel Sullivan at Nui Loc Son, the First Marine Division staff officers at Chu Lai—all thought the end had come.

Then his voice came back booming over the radio. His legs were rendered useless by the wound in his back, so Howard pulled himself and his radio from foxhole to foxhole encouraging his men and helping to direct their fire. He refused to let Holmes give him any morphine to ease the pain, fearing the drowsiness it might induce.

Binns, whose initial shot signaled the beginning of the battle, was also crawling around the perimeter despite his own severe wounds. After urging the men to conserve their ammunition, Binns began gathering up enemy weapons and grenades for the Marines to use.

The time slowly ticked by. "I'll tell you this," Howard said later, "you know that movie *The Longest Day*, well, compared to our night on the hill, *The Longest Day* was just a twinkle in the eye."

Finally, the night passed and the dawn began to break. At 0525, Howard shouted to his men, "Okay, you people, reveille goes in thirty-five minutes." At 0600, he announced, "Reveille." The perimeter had held.

As the Marines peered out of their positions, they saw enemy bodies and equipment scattered everywhere over the battlefield. Normally, the North Vietnamese would have scoured the hillside clean, but the Marines' suppressive fire was so devastating, the enemy left behind many who had fallen near the American lines.

Although they were badly mauled, the North Vietnamese continued to fire on the Marine positions they still had encircled. Stubbornly, the NVA slipped into foxholes and bomb craters to await nightfall when they could resume their attack. Bursts of light-machine-gun fire whizzed over the American heads, and two of the NVA .50-calibers continued to pound away.

When med-evac helicopters came in to attempt a withdrawal of the Marines Howard frantically waved them off. One chopper had been shot down already. Howard didn't want to lose another. The jets and gunships roared in and crisscrossed the hillside, daring the NVA to shoot at them. When the enemy .50-cals complied, the American pilots swooped in and destroyed them.

First Lt. Richard E. Moser was monitoring Howard's radio frequency and later reported, "It was like something you read in a novel. His call sign was Carnival Time and he kept talking about these North Vietnamese down in holes in front of him. He'd say, 'You've gotta get this guy in the crater because he's hurting my boys.' He was really impressive; his whole concern was for his men."

On the southern slopes of the mountain, a relief company from the Fifth Marine Regiment was landed. Machine guns were detached and sent up the steep fingers along the flanks of the hill to support the company's advance. When the lead platoon got to the recon patrol's position and crossed the perimeter, Howard welcomed them. "Get down!!" he shouted. "There are snipers right in front of us."

Another recon Marine shouted, "Hey, you got any cigarettes?"

One of the first to reach the recon Marines' position recalled, "One man told me he never expected to see the sun rise. But once it did, he knew we'd be coming." When the relief force arrived, Howard's Marines had eight bullets among them.

Enemy sniper fire continued to rake the hilltop, and an infantry battalion commander in Chu Lai called over the radio and asked the relief company commander, Buck Darling, "Is the landing zone secure, Buck?"

First Lieutenant Darling paused and then replied, "Well, not spectacularly."

Back at the base, two NCOs were listening to the conversation and the junior sergeant said, "I wonder what he meant by that."

An older, veteran sergeant replied, "What do you think it means, stupid? He's getting shot at."

Despite his own severe wounds, Holmes was busy helping the corpsmen from the relief company administer to the wounded. While the wounded were being moved to the south slope for medical evacuation, Holmes roved back and forth, making sure all of his buddies were accounted for. However, one Marine he had seen die was missing, and only after repeated assurances that they would not leave without the body were the infantry able to persuade Holmes and Howard to leave the hill.

The medical evacuation site on the south slope was still

taking incoming sniper fire, but the wounded and dead had to be extracted. "For the medical evacs," one pilot noted, "a pilot had to come in perpendicular to the ridge, then cock his bird around before he sat down. We could get both main mounts down. First the tail, well, sometimes we got it down."

Howard and his men—living and dead—were all evacuated. At noon the hill was quiet, and Lieutenant Darling declared the objective secure. Darling's company lost two men and the gunships also had two killed. Of the eighteen Marines in the First Platoon, C Company, First Reconnaissance Battalion, six were killed and the rest wounded. Fifteen were recommended for the Silver Star, two—Binns and Holmes—were nominated for the Navy Cross, and Staff Sgt. Jimmie E. Howard was recommended for and later awarded the Congressional Medal of Honor.*

Operation Kansas officially ended on June 22, but Marine artillery and reconnaissance teams remained in and around the Que Son Valley until June 27. During that period the teams made 141 sightings of 763 enemy troops and, exclusive of the fight on Hill 488 (it was impossible to determine how many enemy soldiers had died there), the North Vietnamese suffered 85 killed. Forty elephants and ten water buffalo used to transport enemy supplies were also killed. All of the 10 Marine KIAs and 14 of the 20 WIAs during Kansas were the result of the NVA attack on Nui Vu.

More significant than the casualty ratio was the fact that the reconnaissance teams had prevented the North Vietnamese from massing for an assault on the Que Son Valley in strength. Lieutenant Colonel Sullivan said, "Whatever his [the enemy's] intentions for forming in that area, this recon effort supported by fire broke up his for-

---

* Adapted from "Howard's Hill" in *Small Unit Action in Vietnam Summer, 1966.*

mations, caused him to move, and inflicted casualties upon him and his logistic buildup. . . . He is particularly vulnerable to observed fire and air strikes."

Usually, it fell on the infantry to trudge through the rough terrain in large operations and small unit patrols to seek out and destroy the illusive Vietcong and North Vietnamese regulars. The experience derived from Operation Kansas by the First Reconnaissance Battalion and the supporting artillery and air units provided a more effective and less costly method.

★ ★ ★ 4 ★ ★ ★

In the spring of 1966, Edgar Z. Friedenberg, a University of California professor, noted that society deserves the children it gets, and if those children are a disappointment, then it is because the world that has been created for them is an even greater disappointment for the adults who created it.

The Free Speech Movement at Berkeley and the subsequent growing student dissatisfaction on other campuses raised perplexing questions for many adults. In reviewing the underlying cause of the unrest, one thing became apparent: many college students were angered by the depersonalization of the "multiversities"—the mammoth schools that were swallowing up freshmen and spitting out classes. "They [the demonstrators] had suddenly become not just numbers in a punch-card alphabet," *Today's Health* explained, "but rather, individuals proclaiming a desire. They were fighting . . . a feeling of 'alienation,' a term as pertinent to the 60s as 'anxiety' was to the past decade."

This alienation manifested itself in protests on the campuses, and was becoming increasingly apparent in the precollege set—a group collectively called "teenagers." A Poughkeepsie, New York, boy realized the problems facing him when he said, "High school is either the beginning or the end." The fortunate went on to college, the less fortunate went to Vietnam.

"I've flunked the college-entrance exams," a seventeen-year-old Texas boy gloomily remarked, "and I don't have any money, so I've had it."

The problems of the world and the country had grown more complex for the young, and many had become contradictions. The war in Vietnam, where many of the poor and academically mediocre were headed, was a perfect illustration. On the one hand, their government was saying that the United States had to stand by the South Vietnamese during their struggle for freedom from Communist domination. On the other hand, they could turn on television and see the same government expressing serious doubts and reservations about sending American boys and girls into the growing war.

Another contradiction was the civil-rights movement at home. In high-school classrooms, students were being taught that, according to their Constitution, all men are created equal, but television revealed that some of those who sought that inalienable right were often beaten, tear gassed and set upon by vicious police dogs and bullying mobs. The hypocrisy of the adult world turned off many young people, and they withdrew into their own world with their own kind.

"The adolescent years bring a different search for identity," *Today's Health* observed. "In this period of life, fancy uniforms, secret societies, code names, and militaristic urges have great appeal. In his search for identity, the individual becomes part of the herd." Most important, they hadn't become numbers yet.

This herd sometimes terrified the adults. At times it seemed to be meandering aimlessly and harmlessly. Suddenly, it could explode and stampede out of control. At a posh debutante party in New York, four hundred affluent, socially prominent youths wrecked the host's mansion for no apparent reason; in Times Square a rampaging herd of less affluent youths broke shop windows and looted stores; some middle-class children were smoking marijuana and using heroin (some as young as fourteen were already addicted to the stuff). These and other reports from around the country were becoming more frequent. "They have become the enemy," wrote one adult.

"*Teenager* is a dirty word," said one teenager. "It means the same as juvenile delinquent. . . . If you walk down the street with a group of friends, you can sense it—the hostility. People look at you kind of funny, and step out of your way. It doesn't matter how you're walking. If you are laughing, they think you're hopped up. If you're quiet, they think you're going to mug them. White or Negro, it doesn't matter—you're a bunch of kids, so you're dangerous."

This generalization was often shared by the police, the group of adults young people had always been told to trust and to turn to when in need of help. "If they see a group of four or more," said one boy, "the cops assume you're a gang and you're out for trouble. What's wrong with walking down the street with a group of friends? They've got this 'stop-and-frisk' law now, so you're lined up against the side of the car and frisked. It's humiliating."

This New York youth had lost his respect for law-enforcement officers as well. "I've seen cops getting paid off by the local bookmaker, the local pusher, and the local madam . . . I've seen them walk into grocery stores and walk out with an armload of groceries [without paying]. There's one cop on our beat that gives the local numbers runner a lift to his drop. I'm not saying all cops are crooked, but plenty of them are."

This alienation between the teenagers and the authorities was not restricted to the major metropolitan areas, either. In one New Jersey hamlet, a police car pulled up to a teenager during daylight hours and the officer shouted, "Get off the street, punk!"

"Maybe my hair wasn't combed," the seventeen-year-old youth said later, "but I think I was dressed okay—in my YMCA sweatshirt and khaki pants."

The current fashion for boys was sloppy, but a carefully groomed sloppy. If they wore cut-off jeans, there was just the right amount of fraying which had been carefully worked with a pocket comb; if the shirt tails were worn out, they were wrinkle-free; if the socks were white, they were brilliantly so; if it was jeans and a sweat shirt, they both were ironed meticulously; and if it was a disheveled Beatle haircut, each lock was carefully placed.

Contrary to the collegians and the budding hippie movement in California, *Holiday* magazine reported, "American adolescents are obsessed with personal cleanliness. No other girls in the world devote more time to washing their hair. For boys, fashion may decree loafers without socks, but ankles must be clean."

If their bodies were clean, some parents reasoned, then teenage minds must dwell on "dirt." "My parents sort of forced me to cheat on them," one boy said. "I know they want me to be interested in girls—my God, they'd think I was abnormal if I wasn't. But a few months ago my mom found lipstick on my handkerchief, and she hit the ceiling. So what I do now is carry a little pack of Kleenex in my pocket, and throw the used ones out on the way home from a date. She thinks I'm very pure, but she's turned me into a litterbug."

Parental distrust was also reflected in rock-and-roll music. One song, "Louie, Louie" by the Kingsmen, had lyrics that were impossible to understand because of the singer's twangy style. Since the parents couldn't understand them, then some believed that the words must be "dirty," and as a result, the song was banned on several radio stations around the country. In court the song's author showed that there was neither profanity nor suggestive words in "Louie, Louie." Nevertheless, some stations refused to lift the ban. Some even played the record backward in an attempt to find the dirt that they knew was there. There were no dirty words, though, only dirty minds.

Singers Peter, Paul, and Mary poked fun at the contro-

versy around "Louie, Louie" when they sang "I Dig Rock
'n' Roll Music"—

> But if I really say it,
> The radio won't play it,
> So I must lay it,
> Between the lines.

The teenagers twisted and shouted to the rock-and-roll
music and harmless songs about holding hands, summer
breezes, downtown, and up on the roof. The folk-rock
music of Bob Dylan, Joan Baez, and P. F. Sloan was popular
on the college circuit, but the high schoolers preferred the
simpler music of The Beatles, Petula Clark, and Neil Se-
daka.

"People my age," said eighteen-year-old Herman of Herman and the Hermits, "want fun. We don't look a long way
ahead. As long as tomorrow looks good, everything's okay.
Of course, I have plenty of serious thoughts, but I prefer to
face growing up tomorrow. It will come soon enough—and
I don't want to rush it."

While they shunned the serious problems of the adult
society, teenagers tended to turn to each other for support
and validation. "There are few periods in life," a sociologist
noted, "in which associations are so strong, intimate and
all-encompassing as those that develop during adolescence." However, once the teenager entered the adult world
—the "Real World"—he or she was forever banished.

In the summer of 1966, two nineteen-year-old Marines
tried to get into a dance at Newport Beach, California. Ad-
vertised as being exclusively for teenagers, the dance was
being promoted to show that the vast majority of young
people were not the troublemakers depicted by television
and periodicals.

The two had just gotten back from Chu Lai, Vietnam,

and even in civilian clothes they didn't look like your average teenager. They had short hair and were cadaverously thin (one had dropped from 178 pounds to 138 pounds), and they looked more tired than tough. Yet when they tried to buy tickets for the dance, they were stopped by an anxious-looking adult. He feared that somebody inside might say something offensive about the Marine Corps or Vietnam, and try to start a fight which would destroy the whole purpose of the dance.

"I can't risk that," the adult explained. "I hope you understand."

A teenage girl meticulously dressed in Levi's jeans and a sweat shirt was leaning against a nearby wall. The young girl's age allowed her to remain inside the haven; the veterans' experience kept them out. They were no longer teenagers and, yet, neither were they adults.

The two veterans left the dance and bought a pint of Jim Beam (one of them had a phony I.D.). They sat in a Ford station wagon near the beach and sipped bourbon and Coke from a paper cup while listening to the radio.

As they stared blankly out over the Pacific Ocean, a police officer tapped his baton on the window and ordered them out of the car. When he found the liquor, he arrested the two Marines and charged them with drinking under age.

Both subsequently returned to Vietnam. Not because of any heroics, but that was where their friends from their youth were. That was where their dreams were, too. It might have been a little more dangerous, but it was much simpler over there, and age really didn't matter.

A lieutenant was flying back to his base near Da Nang and on the deck of the chopper was the dead body of a young Marine. The officer stared at the youth's body and said to nobody in particular, "God, he looks so young."

An ageless gunnery sergeant looked over at the lieutenant who was barely older than the dead teenager at his feet and said wearily, "The man's dead—that's as old as you get."

Operation Hastings

While the Vietcong were picking up the tempo for the war in the districts in the Central Highlands, the North Vietnamese army was raising the ante in the northern provinces. By the first of July, Marines from the Third Reconnaissance Battalion operating near the DMZ began observing increasing numbers of NVA regulars. A recon patrol from Company A began patrolling eighteen miles west of Dong Ha (eighty-five miles north of Da Nang) in the vicinity of the Rockpile, a seven-hundred-foot tall toothpicklike hill whose sheer cliffs dominated the terrain immediately south of the DMZ. During the next two weeks, the Marines sighted more than three hundred enemy soldiers from their perch on the Rockpile.

Two captured NVA soldiers revealed to interrogators that they were members of the 324B Division, whose tactical mission was to infiltrate Quang Tri Province from the DMZ, the three-mile buffer zone that separated North and South Vietnam. Off limits to military operations according to the Geneva Accords that ended the French-Indochina War in 1954, North Vietnam had long been funneling supplies across the zone and now for the first time was sending across a whole division.

The 324B, consisting of the 90th, 803rd, and 812th Regiments, was entering South Vietnam using five basic trails, the two most important of which lay northwest and northeast of the Rockpile. These two main trails converged four miles south of the DMZ and from there, the two captured soldiers said, the North Vietnamese planned to move east, attacking South Vietnamese government positions at Son Lam, Can Tho, and Dong Ha. Simultaneously, NVA elements would proceed south from the Rockpile into Ca Lu and the Ba Long Valley, long a Vietcong stronghold, and link up with the VC units there.

Seizing these areas was preparatory, the enemy soldiers said, to "liberating" the provincial capital of Quang Tri, eight miles southeast of Dong Ha. The 803rd Regiment would attack to the east and the 812th to the south. Meanwhile, the 90th Regiment would attack and prevent any ARVN (Army, Republic of Vietnam) reinforcements from relieving the region.

After analyzing this intelligence, Third Marine Division commander Maj. Gen. W. B. Kyle requested permission to move his Marines "north to try and get them [the NVA] out of there and drive them back." Third Marine Amphibious Force commander Lt. Gen. Lewis Walt approved the plan and so advised General Westmoreland, "who needed little persuasion."

The battle plan—designated Operation Hastings— called for the formation of a combined American and South Vietnamese force with the Americans engaging the bulk of the NVA division near the DMZ while the ARVN forces patrolled to the south, keeping the insurgent Vietcong forces pinned down. While formulating his attack plan, General Kyle moved headquarter elements to Dong Ha and Cam Lo, forty-five miles north of the main division headquarters at Phu Bai. On the afternoon of July 12, after activating Task Force Delta, Kyle named his assistant division commander, Brig. Gen. Lowell English, as its commander.

The core units for Task Force Delta were four infantry battalions—Two/One, One/Three, Two/Four and Three/ Four—and one artillery battalion—Three/Twelve. Other infantry units which would participate in the operation were Three/Five (the Seventh Fleet's Special Landing Force), One/One, and Two/Nine. The First Marine Aircraft Wing would provide both fixed-wing and helicopter support for Operation Hastings.

General English's plan was to take the enemy by surprise and attack the key infiltration trails behind the NVA lines above the Rockpile and "smash and destroy him before he had a chance to regain his balance and momentum." Three/Four, according to the plan, was to land a mile south of the DMZ and five miles north of the Rockpile, where it would establish a blocking position across the main infiltration trails of the NVA division. An hour and a half later, Two/Four was to land three miles to the east at the entrance of the Song Ngan Valley and proceed west to Three/Four's position. There, the two battalions would combine and sweep and clear the region of North Vietnamese troops. The remainder of Task Force Delta would attack enemy positions to the south. A coordinating operation, Deckhouse II, would include the landing of Three/Five on the coast east of the main area of Operation Hastings.

ROBERT MODRZEJEWSKI

Rank: Captain
Unit: K Company, Third Battalion, Fourth Marines
Birthplace: Milwaukee, Wisconsin

Place: Helicopter Valley
Date: July 15–18, 1966

Birthdate: July 3, 1934

A helicopter reconnaissance of the Three/Four landing zone, LZ Crow, was attempted prior to the battalion's landing, but with little success. "Every time we attempted to get down low," Bob Modrzejewski recalled later, "there was heavy ground fire on the helicopters. So we made a reconnaissance from about four thousand feet. As a result, the density of the jungle and the difficulty of the terrain was underestimated."

The first Marines from K Company, Three/Four, landed at LZ Crow at 0745 on July 15. Although there was no initial enemy resistance, subsequent small-arms fire and the difficulty of the terrain began taking their toll on both men and machines. A couple of Marines were decapitated when they attempted to exit their C-46 Sea Knight helicopter after it had collided with another Sea Knight in the small landing zone. A third helicopter crashed trying to avoid the other two, and the Song Ngan Valley was later dubbed Helicopter Valley by the Marines.

"Not a very auspicious start," Modrzejewski recalled later.

When its remaining elements landed, K Company assembled and proceeded toward its blocking position along the infiltration trail on the other side of the valley. Modrzejewski and his men soon found evidence that the enemy was in the valley and in force.

"Along the way, we saw hundreds of fighting holes only two or three feet apart on the surrounding slopes. They looked as if they had been scooped out by machines. We were receiving steady sniper fire from the bush and we killed two snipers. Underneath the jungle canopy, we found a complete two-hundred-bed hospital in a bamboo building about thirty yards long and twenty yards wide. One man was guarding it and we shot him. Inside we found twelve hundred pounds of small-arms ammunition being guarded by three men. We shot them, too."

After this brief skirmish, the company continued southward. A half mile ahead of the main force, the second platoon killed ten North Vietnamese in a two-hour firefight. K Company then made its first attempt to cross the Song Ngan River at a point twenty feet wide, but was stopped by crisscrossing enemy machine-gun and small-arms fire. Three Marines were killed and five wounded. While searching for another place to cross the river, the second platoon heard voices and quickly set up an ambush. Ten more North Vietnamese soldiers were killed while two Marines were wounded.

In the meantime, Lt. Col. Arnold Bench's Two/Four was landing at LZ Dove at the eastern entrance to the Song Ngan Valley, and was proceeding west to Three/Four's blocking position. Although meeting no enemy resistance, Two/Four was having difficulty negotiating the terrain. By midafternoon of July 15, Bench's battalion had covered only two miles because, as one officer recalled in 1978, ". . . of the problems we were having negotiating the terrain, especially the vegetation. Though we knew our position, we could not see where we were going; trusting only to our compasses. The heat with no breeze and unlimited humidity was devastating."

After three attempts to cross the Song Ngan, Captain Modrzejewski ordered his company to backtrack a couple of hundred yards and set up night positions on a small knoll. The North Vietnamese then attacked the third battalion with small arms and mortars and it was quickly surrounded. Three/Four battalion commander Lt. Col. S. A. Vale put in a call for help from Two/Four, but because of the problems it was having maneuvering through the jungle, Colonel Bench was unable to provide any assistance. Bench suggested, and General Kyle agreed, that it would be best to wait until dawn before attempting to link up with Vale's Three/Four.

In an attempt to relieve some of the pressure the enemy was putting on Three/Four, General English tried to land elements of Two/One at LZ Crow, but the first troop-laden helicopter was shot down by North Vietnamese .50-caliber machine-gun fire, killing thirteen of the sixteen on board. As a result of the downing of this helicopter, further attempts to land Two/One at LZ Crow were aborted.

That evening, shortly after 7 P.M., a reinforced NVA company tried to overrun Captain Modrzejewski's company on the small knoll.

"We really were on a good piece of real estate, nice and high. We set up our perimeter defenses, had C-Ration meals and about seven thirty the show really started. It began when a huge North Vietnamese—he must have been six feet three—came walking up the trail like it was Sunday. He was probably hurt or sick, and trying to get to the hospital. We shot him, and almost immediately the NVA opened up with small arms and machine guns. You could feel it growing; a lot of bodies were stacking up.

"It was so dark we couldn't see our hands in front of our faces, so we threw out trip flares and called for a flare ship overhead; I kept the flare ship up all night.

"We could hear and smell, and occasionally see the NVA after that. When the firing stopped we heard them dragging the bodies of their dead away, but in the morning at first light, we found twenty-five bodies, some of them only five yards away, stacked on top of each other. On the basis of the dragging we heard and the bloodstains, we figured we got another thirty, which was listed as probably killed."

Three/Four suffered eighteen Marines killed that first day.

The next day, the third battalion again tried to cross the Song Ngan River, but was stopped by withering NVA machine-gun and rifle fire. When voices were heard in the nearby jungle, the Marines called in artillery and air strikes to within a hundred yards of their defensive positions. Several secondary explosions shook the jungle, indicating hits on enemy ammunition supply dumps. K Company was still under heavy attack, and Colonel Vale tried unsuccessfully to maneuver I Company to a position where it could provide support for its beleaguered sister company. Two/Four was also unable to advance to the aid of Modrzejewski's Marines.

That night K Company engaged an estimated NVA battalion in a four-hour firefight, often to within pistol and bayonet range. There was enemy contact three quarters of the way around the company perimeter. In attempts to confuse the Marines, the North Vietnamese shouted phrases like, "Pull back." The Americans weren't fooled.

Once a Marine yelled to a nearby corpsman, "Are you all right, doc?"

A few feet away, a North Vietnamese soldier aped back, "You all right, doc?"

During this phase of the fight, Captain Modrzejewski was wounded several times, yet, despite his painful injuries, he crawled two hundred yards through intense enemy fire to provide critically needed ammunition to exposed elements of his command. Surrounded by the NVA, the captain skillfully directed artillery fire to within a few yards of his lines. K Company successfully repulsed three waves of NVA soldiers which came within five yards of the American positions.

When the fighting slackened, sounds of bodies being dragged away were again heard by the Marines. The next day, July 17, a search revealed seventy-nine NVA bodies that had not been removed by the enemy. One of K Company's Marines had been killed and five wounded by gunfire. Another forty received minor wounds from grenades being tossed at close ranges.

Also on July 17, Colonel Vale abandoned his attempt to cross the Song Ngan River, and he ordered K Company to remain in its defensive positions on the knoll for another night. Late that afternoon, Two/Four finally established a tenuous link with Vale's battle-weary battalion. This linkup, shaky as it was, strengthened the Marine lines, and an anticipated enemy assault never materialized. Although there was no major enemy attack, minor probes and skirmishes persisted throughout the night as the North Vietnamese fortified and stabilized their own lines. They were getting ready for an all-out assault the next day.

With the North Vietnamese holding the high ground to the south of the river, Task Force Delta Commander English prepared to move the battalions out of the Song Ngan Valley to the east. Bench's Two/Four was to take the lead and clear the enemy out as it advanced to a blocking position astride the Song Ngan River about a mile south of the DMZ. Three/Four was to remain behind and destroy the captured NVA supplies and ammunition as well as the downed American helicopters at LZ Crow. It would then proceed to Hill 100, a mile south of Two/Four's blocking position.

Bringing up the rear of the column was K Company's first platoon under the command of Staff Sgt. John McGinty, a twenty-six-year-old Boston native. At about 1430, while the battalion was mounting out, the enemy attacked, first with mortar and then with infantry.

Vale recalled several years later, "Since we had already filled in our fighting holes there was nothing to do but clear out of there on the double to the east, which we did. Unfortunately, the rear guard did not move fast enough and it was still in the area when the enemy infantry attack started."

The first platoon took the full brunt of the NVA assault and, according to McGinty, "We started getting mortar fire, followed by automatic-weapons fire from all sides . . . they were blowing bugles, and we could see them waving flags . . . 'Charlie' moved in in waves with small arms right behind the mortars, and we estimated we were being attacked by a thousand men. We couldn't kill them fast enough. My squads were cut off from each other, and together we were cut off from the rest of the company. I had some of my men in the high grass, where our machine gunners had to get up on their knees to shoot, which exposed them."

In this bitter fighting, McGinty charged through intense automatic weapons fire and mortar fire to the most exposed elements of his platoon, and found twenty men wounded and the corpsman dead. Although painfully wounded himself, the sergeant cared for the wounded men and quickly reloaded their weapons. He shouted encouragement to his men and directed their fire so effectively that the enemy attack wavered.

When enemy soldiers tried to envelop his position, McGinty killed five of them with his pistol. Then he directed artillery and air strikes to within fifty yards of his position. Captain Modrzejewski tried to maneuver his other platoons to support the first platoon, but with little initial success. He recalled later, "We were getting mortars right in the landing zone and the bombs and napalm were landing only fifty yards away from us. At one point, the NVA were trying to get the ammo out of those three wrecked helicopters that were still sitting there. Napalm got about twenty of them and then another forty in the middle of the landing zone. I remember one kid shouting, 'Here come some more Marines!' But they weren't Marines

—they were NVA. And when they saw us, they ducked into the river on our flank.

"All we could see was their heads and rifles above the water—it was like shooting pumpkins."

Lieutenant Colonel Vale then brought up his command group, "particularly the radiomen, to reestablish communications and get things sorted out." He ordered L Company to attempt a link up with K Company at LZ Crow, and at the same time radioed Lieutenant Colonel Bench to come to his assistance.

Shortly before 1700, L Company joined up with Modrzejewski's company at the landing zone while Bench's Two/Four moved into supporting positions on high ground. Fire superiority was quickly attained over the North Vietnamese and the pressure on McGinty's platoon was eased. Under the covering fire, the first platoon was able to withdraw, evacuating its wounded.

Captain Modrzejewski remembered, "We formed a column of walking wounded to be carried, a security force for them, and then proceeded upstream, where the wounded were evacuated that night."

Lieutenant Colonel Bench applauded the efforts of the helicopter pilots who "on a pitch-black night . . . descended into an unlighted gorge, talked in by their exhaust glow, to have a flare popped when they were only a few feet off the landing zone."

On July 19, the remaining elements of K Company were withdrawn to a rear area for rest and replenishment of men and supplies. Both Staff Sergeant McGinty and Captain Modrzejewski were later awarded Medals of Honor for their actions during Operation Hastings.*

Reflections

We were up against a formidable enemy. Prior to that time we were involved in guerrilla-type actions, one or two

---

* Adapted from *U.S. Marines in Vietnam: An Expanding War,* 1966.

---

people, squads, those kinds of thing: civilian, during the day, soldiers at night. When we engaged the North Vietnamese regular army units—well equipped, well trained, and very tenacious—we found that it wasn't going to be an easy task.

The thing that really sticks out in my mind about Operation Hastings is the competence of the people in the foxholes. Here we were, in very close combat with the enemy and the young Marines—eighteen, nineteen, twenty years old—sticking it out, doing their job. They had a real "can do" attitude in spite of that adversity over that period of time, to be able to sustain themselves and keep going with very little sleep. Some suffered multiple wounds.

In addition, I felt that with the training, at least that I had had,—my lieutenants and my platoon sergeants—and my Marines in general, we would make out very well.

The anger comes afterward when you take a look at your dead Marines and your wounded Marines. You really don't have time to assess casualties during the course of a battle. When you speak of anger, I guess that is one of the things I noticed about Vietnam in general. I was never really angry in the sense that you could be angry with the Germans and the Japanese during World War II. The hatred that built up for the VC and NVA, I never experienced it.

I think that for the professional soldiers, it really doesn't matter much who we go and fight, whether it is in Vietnam, the Middle East, or Central America. To the careerist—the lifer—it isn't going to make that much difference.

In Vietnam, I don't think we ever had the war won. I don't think there was ever a point that we could have said, "One more guy in the ground will turn the tide of battle." I just don't think it was ever in the cards for us.

Those people had been at war for twenty-some years. It didn't take anybody long to realize that it was going to take more of an effort than we were willing to put forth. I just don't think it was ever in the cards for us to come out with a military victory as such.

Oh, we could have not gone there and let the place be overrun, but we have treaties, we have obligations. Quite frankly, I think what we tried to do was live up to some of those agreements.

I'm not sure we're not doing the same thing in Central America as we did in Vietnam—the similarities are there. I don't see the same type of involvement down there, though.

A short time ago in the early sixties, the Vietnam War started in the same way. There are parallels, and how are we going to deal with them? Are we going to win or withdraw? Should we go? Should we send advisers? Should we pour in money to governments that are corrupt?

Quite frankly, this time, if it came to Central America, I would go in to win and do whatever it takes and whatever is required to do the job. People have got to understand that if we are willing to go ten thousand miles away to help somebody, we'd better be ready to go the whole way.

The whole time I was there, I didn't see any atrocities. Most of the time I was at the DMZ—Dong Ha, Cam Lo, Camp Carroll. Our operations were battalion-size with company and platoon patrols. The guerrilla stuff the other guys down at Chu Lai and Da Nang were involved in maybe was different. I read most of that and saw most of it on TV after I had gotten back.

Also, I never once during my whole time in Vietnam experienced any problems with drugs or alcohol or fragging or people refusing to do their duty or follow their leaders. I never even heard of it; it was incomprehensible.

Now, I think we are making some pretty good progress in the drug-abuse area, and I think we will eventually be able to handle it, just as we did with the racial issues. A year ago our commandant came out and really put the word out to people involved with drugs. We've got those people on the run, and we're getting rid of them.

There are three sides. One, you have to treat it with very strict discipline; two, you have to dispense appropriate punishment; and three, it is also an educational process. We as leaders have to educate ourselves, too. I think the bottom line is that the staff NCO's and junior enlisted people have to turn it around themselves. They have to do it in their own ranks.

I could stand up and preach from now until doomsday, and that's not going to make a rat's ass. They have to do it themselves.

If you are a veteran of Vietnam, you don't deserve any special treatment. But I think the American people and the U.S. government have a responsibility to provide programs like counseling, medical care, employment, and the G.I. Bill, not as privileges but as something earned. It is not a question of special favors.

The Vietnam veterans have not asked for anything more, in my estimation, than what people from World War II or Korea or anyone else got. To give the Vietnam veteran anything less than is due him is not right.

I don't know your feelings on the Vietnam Memorial, but I think it looks pretty damn good. I saw a special about it on TV. It is really a remarkable effort.

The point, in my estimation, is not to have a grandiose, pretentious memorial that has to stick out. I am convinced that people who go to Washington and will want to see the Marine Memorial and Arlington National Cemetery are now going to put that Vietnam Memorial on that list of places they must see. And it is going to build and build and build and it will stand by itself.

I don't think the American people ever expected it to happen, and here we are, teaching them and making them aware of what the hell this country can do when its people stick together. It's just amazing that it could come to that.

★ ★ ★ | 5 | ★ ★ ★

T he Civil Rights Act of 1964 had stripped away the FOR WHITES ONLY signs from public accommodations and had made desegregation a national policy. The Voting Rights Act of 1965 had enfranchised many southern blacks for the first time since Reconstruction.

However, a White House conference on the problems confronting blacks in America reported that, "the national government's response to the compelling cry of the Negro American for justice and equality has not been matched by state and local governments, by business and labor, the housing industry, educational institutions and the wide spectrum of voluntary organizations that, through united efforts, have the power to improve society."

The victories for blacks regarding civil and voting rights shrank to insignificance when compared with the daily problems created by the tangle of poverty, crumbling family life, crime, inadequate schooling, and joblessness in the nation's slums.

In July and August 1966, racial violence again erupted around the country. In Omaha, Nebraska, the National Guard was called up to end the looting, vandalism, and rioting that had broken out, and quell what many were calling "the Negro Insurrection." It was a hot summer— record heat waves in the Midwest—and tempers were short.

In Cleveland, police attempted to disperse a large milling crowd in a supermarket parking lot, but were driven off by bricks and bottles. After the police retreated, the rioters turned on their own neighborhood and began looting and vandalizing local stores; some were white-owned, but most were black-owned. When the police and National Guard restored order, four blacks were dead and scores were injured.

In Chicago, sweltering temperatures produced the spark that ignited a black powder keg of anger and frustration. In an attempt to escape the heat, youngsters in a black ghetto turned on a fire hydrant and splashed in the gushing water. Police officers moved in, though, and turned off the hydrant, clubbing two teenagers in the process.

Blacks in Chicago exploded and, after three days of rioting, looting, vandalism, and sniper fire, over four thousand National Guardsmen (some of whom had joined to avoid combat duty in Vietnam) and over one thousand city policemen restored order. Two blacks had been killed.

A sympathetic white man said, "The day a Negro is born, someone says to him, 'You lose.' "

Many whites, on the other hand, felt that the blacks were demanding too much, too fast, and, after the rioting had ended, one white said, "The whites are getting tired of this. They have taken about as much as they can."

The governor of Nebraska met with black leaders in an attempt to alleviate the problems confronting the Negroes. After listening to their complaints about police brutality and a lack of jobs, the governor said, "We're having no truck with advocates of violence. We're not going to deal with these hoodlum elements or teenagers. We are not going to listen to a lot of grievances that have been chewed over and over again. Lawbreakers will be prosecuted to the full extent of the law."

After the riots of 1966, Democratic congressman Adam

Clayton Powell of New York said, "This unrest now comes from a group of young people who don't know what else to do and they are striking out against society . . . because society has rejected them. . . . Black teenagers, who already have a 28 percent unemployment rate, only got 4 percent of all new jobs in the last year.

"I hate to say that riots are inevitable," the controversial black representative added, "but one thing we must realize is that these young Negroes in the cities are leaderless. Nobody can control them, as was witnessed in Chicago when Martin Luther King was not only booed on the streets but was booed in church. These young Negroes have no leaders."

After the racial rioting in the urban areas and the one-sided, violent civil-rights confrontations in the South, a new movement with new leadership developed. The Student Nonviolent Coordinating Committee (SNCC) under the leadership of twenty-five-year-old Stokely Carmichael, bitterly opposed the passive nature of the National Association for the Advancement of Colored People (NAACP) and the Southern Christian Leadership Council (SCLC). SNCC preached defiance instead of deference and pride instead of submissiveness. "Black is Beautiful" was SNCC's slogan, and "Black Power" its goal.

Carmichael, a native of Trinidad who moved to New York when he was eleven years old, had helped organize blacks in the South and had been arrested twenty-seven times in civil-rights demonstrations. He also helped organize the new Black Panther Party, which advocated retaliation. "If Whitey hits you," Carmichael told his followers, "hit him back."

While addressing a racially mixed crowd, he said he'd never known a white person he could trust. A young white man who considered himself Stokely's friend rose and asked, "Not one, Stokely?"

Carmichael looked directly into his eyes and responded, "No, not one."

In a position paper on its goals and purposes, SNCC

linked the struggle of black America with that of the colonized peoples of Africa, Latin America, and Asia. "Whites are the ones who must try and raise themselves to our humanistic level," the paper stated in a report published in the *New York Times*. "We are not, after all, the ones who are responsible for a genocidal war in Vietnam; we are not the ones who are responsible for neocolonialism in Africa and Latin America; we are not the ones who held a people in animalistic bondage over 400 years."

He angrily asserted that there were 180 million white racists in America. "If we are to proceed toward true liberation," he stated, "we must cut ourselves off from white people."

This new black pride was being met by a new white anger. Many whites felt that the recent legislation would be enough to stifle black cries of injustice and inequality. And if they wanted improved economic and employment conditions, the blacks would have to wait their turn just as other immigrants had had to do.

After the racial violence in Chicago, a mob of three thousand whites threw rocks and bottles at peaceful civil-rights demonstrators who were protesting the housing discrimination in the Chicago suburbs. The whites were unable to distinguish the violent racial rioting from the peaceful march, and some screamed, "White power!"

Low-income whites, in fact, did not feel that blacks were being discriminated against at all. Yet, overwhelmingly, they said they would not feel comfortable mingling with blacks at movies, in restaurants, or on buses, according to results of a Harris poll. Fifty-four percent told the pollsters that they would object to a black family moving in next door.

In an August 1966 cover story, *Newsweek* reported,

[The white man] feels himself pressured by his government, goaded by Negro demonstrators and frankly scared by the ghetto riots. . . . The Negro can only reply that he has come too far to stop. He has won equality under the law and found it good—but the prize of equality in fact seems to be dancing around the next bend in Freedom Road. He doesn't like violence either, and his marching shoes are just as frayed as the white man's nerves. But he means to keep walking, talking and prodding until the prize is his.

The war in Vietnam was another area of friction for blacks. A poll conducted for *Newsweek* indicated that 35 percent of the blacks polled opposed the war because they felt they had less freedom to fight for than whites. "What are we fighting for?" snapped a black housewife in San Francisco. "I don't know. Communists? We should be fighting the white folks in Mississippi!"

Another 44 percent believed that the cost of the war meant less money for the War on Poverty and civil-rights programs. This could lead to more violent and widespread racial rioting. When asked if there was any hope of avoiding future rioting, Congressman Powell responded, "Not as long as we are engaged in the conflict in Vietnam. . . . It relates to [the war] because we don't have the money to fight an international war against communism and racial discrimination at the same time."

There were riots in Vietnam, too.

In Da Nang, Buddhists (long-time enemies of the Catholic-supported regime in Saigon) rebelled as they had in previous years. With the support of several hundred sympathetic ARVN soldiers, the rebellion rumbled through the streets of the city.

The monks who led the revolt were demanding that the oppressive dictates from Saigon be lessened, but the government had neither the time nor the manpower to waste on the tiny rebellion, and it was crushed brutally. Only eight soldiers and two monks were killed, but one grenade-throwing rebel was captured and immediately executed by a loyal officer.

After five days, the rebellion was put down, but shock waves quaked throughout the country. In Saigon, a Buddhist monk demonstrated his dissatisfaction with the Saigon government by pouring several gallons of gasoline over himself, kneeling in the middle of a street, and striking a match. It was reminiscent of the eight similar immolations in 1963 that had helped topple the Diem regime.

In the rice paddies and on the hills around An Khe, Pleiku, and the DMZ, few Americans knew about the aborted rebellion in Da Nang. Nor did they know much about the racial disturbances in Cleveland, Chicago, and Omaha, nor about black and white power. These were faraway things.

There were more immediate concerns.

Operation Deckhouse II

On the morning of July 16, while Modrzejewski's K Company was policing up the area of enemy bodies after the first NVA attack on the small knoll off the Song Ngan River, Lt. Col. Edward Bronars's Third Battalion, Fifth Marine Regiment, began Operation Deckhouse II in association with Operation Hastings. Three/Five's India and Kilo Companies landed unopposed across Blue Beach 2,500 meters north of the Cua Viet River, and L Company was helilifted 3,500 meters inland.

Although not technically a part of Operation Hastings, Three/Five's movement flushed out some NVA units to the west and its positioning served as a blocking force, limiting North Vietnamese movement to the south.

Later in the afternoon of July 16, thirteen members of the First Force Reconnaissance Company rappelled down from helicopters onto the top of the Rockpile with the purpose of gathering intelligence on enemy movement in the region. Within half an hour, the recon troops spotted thirty-eight NVA soldiers moving through the valley below in advance of units from Three/Five. The enemy soldiers were all killed by artillery fire directed by the Marines on the Rockpile.

The recon team remained in position on the Rockpile for the next two weeks and observed numerous enemy troop movements on the trails that converged in the vicinity. As a result of the observations, Two/One was landed west of the Rockpile to block the 324B Division's escape route back into Laos.

During the next few days, Two/One's contact with the enemy indicated that, indeed, the North Vietnamese had had enough and were attempting to withdraw back across the border. Except for one more vicious brief battle, there would be no more major encounters between the NVA and the American forces in Operation Hastings.

That last major battle would occur on July 25, a week after the fight in the Song Ngan Valley. India Company, Three/Five, had been ordered to establish a radio relay station on Hill 362, a mile south of the Song Ngan Valley and six miles northwest of the Rockpile. After a week of sporadic fighting after the landing on Blue Beach, India Company moved out to 362.

RICHARD A. PITTMAN

Rank: Lance Corporal

Unit: I Company, Third Battalion, Fifth Marines

Birthplace: French Camp, California

Place: Hill 362, near the DMZ

Date: July 24, 1966

Birthdate: May 26, 1945

"I was very impressed with President Kennedy, as most all of us were, and the Special Forces or Green Berets. When I was in high school I saw a commercial about the Special Forces, and that's what I tried to join first, believe it or not. I'm blind in my right eye and have been that way since I was five years old and, obviously, I couldn't get in the Army.

"So, I tried to join the Navy and the Air Force and I couldn't get in. I didn't try to join the Marines because once they told me I couldn't get in the Army, I figured I could never get in the Marines. That was the thing from that generation; we were expected to join the armed forces for a couple of years if we didn't go to college. I was classified 4-F and I just kind of accepted the fact that I couldn't get into the military.

"Then my younger brother graduated from high school and joined the Marines and went to Vietnam in June or July of 1965. Basically, I was embarrassed and hurt. I was the oldest and I should have been there first, and when he went to Vietnam, I just told myself, 'By hook or by crook, I am going to join the service and I am going to join the Marines.'

"I wrote a letter to my draft board requesting that my draft classification be changed from 4-F to 1-A so that I might enlist in the armed forces, and the damned thing came back in the mail changing me to a 1-A. I still had to take the physical. I took so many physicals for the other services I just knew I was not going to get in.

"When I went to the [induction station] in Oakland they stood me up in this big, long hallway with the eye chart at the far end. It wasn't the most effective eye test.

"They told me to cover my right eye and read the chart. So I covered my right [blind] eye with my right hand and read the chart. Then they said, 'Cover your left eye and read the chart.' I took my left hand and covered my right eye again and I read the chart.

"After I read it, they told me to follow the yellow line —the Yellow Brick Road—and that's what I did."

In 1966 Richard Pittman was sent to Vietnam and as-signed to the first platoon, India Company, Third Battalion, Fifth Marine Regiment, First Marine Division. On July 16, while Modrzejewski's Marines were slugging it out in Helicopter Valley, Pittman and the rest of India Company landed on Blue Beach, and after a week of sporadic action, proceeded a mile south of LZ Crow to establish a radio relay station on Hill 362.

"The aroma, the smell from Vietnam, you never forget it. It smelled—it might sound strange—like death. When I first got there I can remember everyone saying, 'What is that smell?' Steamy, muggy, funky, you just couldn't put it together. You smell the gunpowder and the deterioration of the vegetation and the rest, and finally it comes to you—it was death. It just smelled like death.

"The thing that stands out in my mind that particular day besides the action was the comedy of errors, the things contrary to all of the training and tactics we had learned that happened prior to the company being ambushed. There was a chain of events that happened as we were moving up the hill to establish the radio relay, and it should have told our leader—it told us—that something was getting ready to happen.

"We were supposed to recon the area by artillery; he called in one round and 'Ceasefire.' He didn't have time to do that; he had to get to the objective.

"We moved out and my platoon—the first platoon, India Three/Five—was the last platoon in the column. We spotted movement to our right and reported three North Vietnamese in khaki uniforms moving across a clearing. We reported it to the C.O. and he ignored it. 'Keep Moving.'

"The second squad of my platoon was ambushed—three or four rounds were cranked off at them—and our squad went to the front and killed two North Vietnamese and captured one. They were carrying mortar rounds and, except for taking the prisoner, this was disregarded. 'Keep moving.'

"I think the third platoon was point."

Shortly after noon on July 24, the lead platoon reached the crest of Hill 362 and moved down the other side and the trail to establish forward defensive positions. "A while later—I can't give you a time span—is when the shit hit the fan." I Company had been ambushed by a North Vietnamese battalion. The sixty- to ninety-foot-tall jungle growth provided excellent concealment for the enemy and the third platoon—also ambushed the previous night—was cut to ribbons.

"They had nine people who were not killed or wounded the next day.

"They were ambushed and we were still at the rear of the column. So we started doing what training dictated, which was to move forward as far as we could, establish a perimeter, get the wounded, start setting up a headquarters area, calling in artillery and supporting arms and all of those kinds of things.

"We weren't taking any rounds and were just sitting up there kind of helpless. You just can't believe it. It's hard to explain. All of your buddies are shot. You hear, 'This one's dead, that one's dead.' Guys are coming back all shot up and bandaged up, and I'm hearing people call for more firepower and more help. The word is going around that all of our machine guns are knocked out, no rockets, nothing.

"There was a 3.5 rocket guy—I guess they used to call them bazookas—and he's got a machine gun. I remember, at that time, a good friend and a member of our squad we all called Pops, a kid from Chicago, came back up the hill and his jaw was all shot up and he was wounded in a couple other places.

"We made eye contact and I just turned to the guy with the machine gun and asked if he was going to use it. I don't know what he said. The next thing I know I gave my rifle to him and started belting together machine-gun ammunition.

"I don't know how big a belt I put in the gun, but it

must have been seven or eight hundred rounds. I wrapped others around my body. I must have went down there with ten thousand rounds of ammunition.

"A corpsman asked if he could go with me. I said, 'Yeah, but I don't want you to move until I go down, hit the deck, and fire. Then you come up.' We started down the trail.

"I just felt that somebody had to do something. People are dying, getting the shit shot out of them and nothing is happening; no offense on our part at all. My squad leader had come back all shot up and then Pops came up, and when I saw Pops maybe I snapped. I knew at that time I was going down that trail, and I went.

"I remember the mortars coming in and the automatic-weapons fire. As we went down the trail about twenty or thirty yards, I got some automatic-weapons fire and I hit the deck and fired. I started to get back up and the Doc passed me, doing what I told him not to do. He got hit right between the eyes. Until I got down to where they [NVA] started their frontal attack, Doc was the last person I remember seeing and he was looking straight up as I went over him. From that time on, everything seemed to be in slow motion.

"I remember one of the NVA at a second automatic-weapons position falling out on the trail. Maybe I was still firing and my fire was keeping him up, but I remember he just came out in slow motion and hit the ground. I *know* it wasn't slow motion. I guess because of your adrenaline, it appeared that way.

"I got down the trail and there were other members of my platoon and squad. We were just getting the shit kicked out of us. I remember a kid from New York was throwing in magazines as fast as he could put them in. It seemed like he'd put one in, pull it out, put one in and pull it out. They tell us that an M-14 can fire seventy-five rounds a minute. I swear he was firing ten thousand rounds a minute.

"It wasn't like we were taking too much fire. It was like targets of opportunity. They were coming out everywhere and then all of a sudden we started taking it. I guess it was because I opened up with the gun. The kid behind me got hit in the chest and how I didn't, I don't know. We were surrounded.

"I remember [the kid from New York] got hit and turning around and the NVA were just everywhere. Then I can remember being pissed. From the time that I saw them is when I was just going to kill them. It was either them or me. That's it.

"There was no place for me to go and no place for them to go. They wanted to go someplace and I was going to do my best to stop them. And fortunately I was able to do that, but I had a lot of help down there until they all were killed or wounded."

After he learned that there were additional wounded Marines fifty yards down the trail where the ambush had begun, Pittman advanced under withering small-arms and mortar fire to where the point Marines had fallen. The enemy launched a bold assault with about forty soldiers, and Pittman established a firing position in the middle of the trail, raking the advancing NVA with his own withering machine-gun fire. While he was laying down this base of fire, his M-60 jammed. Calmly, he pulled the buffer group and cleared the gun of accumulated belt linkage. He then slapped in another belt of ammunition and continued firing at the advancing North Vietnamese. The gun jammed again but before he could disassemble and repair it, a bullet smashed into it, thus saving Pittman from taking the round himself.

His M-60 now useless, he picked up an enemy AK-47 and continued to fire into the advancing NVA, killing three. When the AK-47 ran out of ammunition, Pittman discarded it and picked up a .45-caliber automatic pistol and continued firing until it was emptied of ammunition. By this time the NVA had broken off the assault, and as they were withdrawing, Pittman took his last bit of ammunition—a hand grenade—and hurled it at the retreating enemy soldiers.

"I tried to get a couple of wounded out but couldn't move them. They were in too much pain. The [platoon] radioman had his intestines hanging out, so I did what I could, covered him up with brush after moving him off to the side of the trail. I crawled back up the trail back to the unit and tried to get people to go back down, but they wouldn't let me go back and that's when I got scared. I started crying and raising hell. I wanted to go back down the trail.

"They [NVA] harassed us and probed us all that night till about two in the morning.

"Seventy-six of us walked off Hill 362 two days later. It was three thousand meters south of the Rockpile. Most people have heard of the Rockpile, not many have heard of 362."

According to Lance Corp. Raymond L. Powell who survived the ordeal at the point, "The North Vietnamese came back in and began shooting . . . anyone who moved. It was darn near like a massacre. I pretended I was dead when they got to me. They took my watch and cigarettes, but they didn't shoot me."

Other helpless Marines were bayoneted by the NVA, including the one Pittman tried to conceal on the side of the trail.

"He was bayoneted a couple of times and how he didn't cry out, I don't know. They, meaning the North Vietnamese, shot our executive officer six times in the forehead. He was either already dead or wounded at the time. The wound on his body, we were told, apparently was not fatal. Definitely, the six times in the head was fatal."

Reflections

It's not fair and neither is it right for a professional soldier to assassinate a wounded member of an enemy force under any circumstances. It's just not morally right. It has nothing to do with whether it is war or not.

I have a lot of old, old beliefs. War, to me was the Knights of the Round Table, George Patton, General MacArthur, and those kinds of people. General Grant and General Lee believed in the codes that they had. I believed in those things. I'm not saying rules—because there can be no rules in war, but there must be boundaries. An individual must be bound by his own honor and integrity. If he breaks that, then he has to suffer the consequences, and if that is punishment by the law, then so be it.

People were prosecuted and kicked out of the service because they cut off fingers or ears, regardless of the reasons. I heard about one incident where a kid cut off a finger [of an enemy soldier], and the reason he did it was that the day before his buddy—a fire team leader—was killed on patrol. They had gone to high school together and joined the Marine Corps together. He found his buddy propped up against a tree with his penis and testicles stuffed in his mouth.

Can you imagine seeing your best friend in that position? Our laws and customs call that he be prosecuted and he is punished for it [cutting off the dead NVA soldier's finger], but nobody reads about what provoked him to do that. It is not fair, but it has to be that way.

They sent me to the transit facility at Chu Lai and I had to wait three days to go fifty miles to Da Nang. There was not one grunt there. People were running around in starched khakis, clean, really squared away, and I'm in jungle fatigues covered with red dust. I didn't know anyone.

A guy from Seventh COMM pulled up in a jeep and I asked where he was going, and he said back to Hill 35. I said, "I'm going with you."

He said he didn't know if I could go back, and I said, "I *am* going with you!"

He said, "Okay, corporal, whatever you say."

I went back to the hill and three days later they came and got me. My C.O. said, "You have got to go home." He thought it was time I got off the grunts.

I said, "I'm not going home. I'm staying with the company. I want to stay here."

If I wasn't on patrol, I used to go down to a bunker and just shake. I wanted to stay with the unit, but he told me, "I don't think that is a good idea . . . I'll go to the airport with you."

So he rode with me back to the air terminal, and stayed with me until I got on the airplane. The next thing, I was home.

Just after I left, the company went on Operations Union I and Union II. A lot of my people, my squad got killed. That really hurt. I felt I had deserted them. That caused a problem for me for a long time.

I remember my dad saying he was on a ship for sixty days coming home [from World War II]. All of the stories, the gambling, the winding down, stopping in Hawaii for fifteen days and raising hell, being in Seattle, and finally coming down to San Francisco.

We didn't get that.

We got out of the field, onto a plane, and the next thing into L.A. I remember walking down the long hallways and feeling insecure and alone. Nobody said, "You did a good job," or "Welcome home."

For whatever reasons, we went there because our country sent us. Eighteen, nineteen years old, young war babies, products of our fathers who were in World War II so, obviously, we are going to be pro-American, the vast majority of us.

So, when our country called, we went and when we came home, nobody gave a shit. Me and my friends went to Vietnam with one attitude and that was to do the best for this country. And we went there with the will to win, but we were never allowed to win. We did not lose in Vietnam, but we didn't win because of politics. I think—here goes, right on the line again—President Johnson lost his guts in 1968. We had their butts kicked at Khe Sanh. They took a beating. That's why they pulled out. They were sitting in those hills getting their asses kicked. We just wanted them to come on down. That would have been the end of the war right there. But I think the president, because of media pressure said "we can't do this." We had to pull in our horns, so to speak.

A combat soldier in Vietnam came to realize in a few months that we weren't there to win. There were just too many things you didn't do. After I was there a couple of months, everything the Marine Corps had taught me, we weren't doing. We weren't taking the beachhead, holding it, and moving out from there. We weren't being aggressive. We weren't even using effective counter-guerrilla-warfare methods that they had taught us, for crying out loud! They would not let us do it.

The American people didn't want to hear the truth. Every day they were seeing the names and pictures of somebody's son—maybe theirs—but they didn't want to hear that he might have died because he couldn't fire at the enemy first, or he couldn't load his weapon on patrol, or he couldn't fire primary supporting weapons, tanks, Ontos, artillery.

They didn't want to hear those kinds of things.

Outside our perimeter at Chu Lai the word was passed, if they've got a lantern, they can walk in and out of your lines all night long. No magazines in your weapons on the perimeter; not to shoot until fired upon. You put out crap like that and the guerrilla is going to be the one to get the word first.

That actually happened; that's a fact.

All of this trash about baby killers was probably the most painful. One of the things that always galled me was that I never understood how Americans could think so badly of their sons and daughters. They just didn't see the compassion of these kids. Squads would sit down and cry over children killed accidentally. To see a young Marine carrying a young child or baby who has been shot by the enemy or whatever; giving their last C-Rations to civilians; risking their lives putting wounded civilians on helicopters before wounded Marines. Nobody talks about those things —they're not newsworthy.

A Free Fire Zone? I'd never heard of it. We had a big joke in our unit. When we got shot at, we'd say, "Oh, this must be a Free Fire Zone and we're free." I've heard other veterans refer to them, but I do not know of a Free Fire Zone.

It got to the point that I did not want to put on my uniform in public. I did not want people to know I was a Vietnam veteran. I'd been in newspapers all over the country, and I did not want people to know. It got to the point where I would purposefully avoid any type of off-duty military function where I might be seen in public.

Somewhere, sometime, somebody asked me if I was ashamed to be a Vietnam veteran and I think that is what finally snapped me out of it and I said, "Wait a minute. I am not ashamed of anything I did or anyone I served with."

Once I was asked if I was ashamed of being a Vietnam veteran and I said, "No, I'm ashamed of how my country treats its Vietnam veterans." I didn't get censured, but it was close.

The veteran came home and he was ignored, scorned,

and shunned, and, subsequently, I think he assumed the country's guilt for Vietnam. I really feel the American people's problem with Vietnam is that they feel guilty that they even allowed Vietnam to begin. The second thing is that they kept it going and the third thing is they didn't allow their sons to win. They allowed them to die for nothing, not a damn thing. Fifty-seven thousand people and we didn't prove a damn thing.

The bottom line is that all *Apocalypse Now* did was prove to a lot of civilians what their opinions of Vietnam veterans were anyhow: they were drug-crazy, wouldn't follow orders, did what they wanted to do, and all that other garbage. I think *Apocalypse Now* proved it, or is a source of proof for a lot of those people and it reinforces their opinion.

I paid to see it one time and I walked out. By the time they got halfway through the movie with all of the clichés and innuendos and all of the drugs and that trash—not denying that drugs were in Vietnam—I walked out.

I think James Webb's book *Fields of Fire* was very, very good. I wish that he would have or could have made it fact and said this is autobiographical or biographical because it is true. I mean being a Marine infantryman at that time of the war and being there, well, that book is true. I know it is true and every combat veteran over there who has read it knows it is true.

After Hastings I was a squad leader and I trained my squad just like I was trained. We were good. I never lost anyone while I was there, nobody killed. I trained them all of the time. They didn't get killed.

But the first operation they go on when I wasn't there, four or five of them got killed. That really hurt. For a long time I felt that the reason they got killed was that I had left them. I wasn't there.

I talked to my brother and he said, "You'd have probably gotten killed too. You had pushed your luck far enough."

Within the last year, I have come to accept that my presence didn't change fate, one way or the other. It's just the way it is.

It is not easy for a Vietnam veteran to say, yeah, I was in Vietnam and, no, I'm not ashamed.

A question like that, "Are you ashamed?" creates so much pain. The minute it is asked, there is so much, emotion, feeling, and pain. It's not like "Are you a former professional baseball player?" or "Are you a former police officer?" It is not that kind of question and once it is asked, many veterans withdraw.

Our country is the one that set the policy for the direction the war took. We didn't do it, so what do we have to be ashamed of?

I was an American Marine and I was ordered to go to Vietnam. I went there because I felt it was my duty. My country had told me all of my life that it was my duty to serve.

I was at a community college in Sacramento one time, and someone asked me if I didn't feel I had to apologize to God and to the American people for all of the people I had killed.

I said, "No. In the first place, God understands; second, the American people should apologize for allowing all of those people to be killed for nothing; and third, you should apologize for asking such a *dumb, fucking* question."

I got a standing ovation.

6

As 1967 began, foreign correspondents reported that North Vietnam was suffering numerous civilian casualties as a result of the American bombing. President Johnson denied these reports, saying, "We have never bombed the population." A United States spokesman added that if there were any civilian casualties it was the result of the North Vietnamese antiaircraft gunfire and missiles falling onto populated areas.

However, when a *New York Times* journalist visited Hanoi and reported that he had seen evidence of American bombs falling on residential areas, the American government admitted that there might have been some civilian casualties and property damage that were the result of American bombs, but it was unintentional. Because the North Vietnamese were locating military targets close to populated areas, the Americans said, civilian casualties were bound to occur.

Nevertheless, this admission helped widen the credibility gap—the distance between what the American government was saying publicly and what was actually happening. *Le Monde* of Paris reported, "Hardly a day passes that even the most moderate American newspapers don't catch the President and his staff in the act of lying."

Mendel Rivers, chairman of the Senate Armed Forces Committee, responded, "Flatten Hanoi if necessary . . . and let the world go fly a kite."

Most Americans agreed, but a growing minority was drifting away from the president's policies regarding Vietnam. Student leaders from over one hundred American college campuses, including Harvard, Duke, Amherst, Stanford, and Tulane, expressed their concern in a joint letter to the president—"A great many of those faced with the prospect of military duty find it hard to square performance with concepts of personal integrity and conscience. Even more are torn by reluctance to participate in a war whose toll in property and life keeps escalating, but whose purpose and value to the United States remain unclear.

"Unless this conflict can be eased, the U.S. will continue to find some of her most loyal and courageous young people choosing to go to jail rather than bear their country's arms, while countless others find means to avoid their legal obligation."

Many of these young people were opposed to the Selective Service system which was based, in part, on grades and class standings. To them grades had become a matter of life and death. Flunking out of school was equated with a one-way ticket to Vietnam, and this "crime" didn't seem to fit the punishment.

While lecturing at Howard University, Selective Service Director Lewis B. Hershey was hooted and heckled off stage by shouts of "Hell, no, we won't go," and "Draft beer, not students." Incensed by the students' rudeness, Senator Rivers said angrily, "Student deferments may become a thing of the past."

The war in Vietnam, however, was not the only thing pressuring students. In many instances, status-seeking parents were pushing their children to pursue careers in the professions rather than what the kids really wanted. "We have kids who are going to make lousy engineers," said a

Northwestern University professor, "but who would have made great mechanics. But daddy can't let his son be a blue-collar worker."

Also, due to advancing technologies, students were being required to learn more and more than their predecessors in the same amount of time. Progress was leaping forward, and some young people just couldn't keep up.

As these pressures continued to mount, an increasing number of students sought help. A Harvard psychiatrist estimated that 10 percent of the student body would require professional counseling. "They are desperately unhappy about their parents, about society, about authority generally, and about themselves," he said. "They see little hope in the future and little meaning in what they are doing."

This malaise was not restricted to the campuses. This was a quiet depression and it was to be found everywhere. In the *Saturday Evening Post* a journalist wrote,

It was a country of bankruptcy notices and public-auction announcements and commonplace reports of casual killings and misplaced children and abandoned homes and vandals who misspelled even the four-letter words they scrawled. It was a country in which families routinely disappeared, trailing bad checks and repossession papers. Adolescents drifted from city to torn city sloughing off both the past and the future as snakes shed their skins, children who were never taught and would never learn the games that had held society together. People were missing. Children were missing. Parents were missing.

It was not a country in open rebellion. It was not a country under enemy siege. It was the United States of America in the year 1967, and the market was steady and the G.N.P. was high, and a great many articulate [people] seemed to have a sense of high social purpose, and it might have been a year of brave hopes and national promise, but it was not. . . . All that seemed clear was at some point we had aborted ourselves and butchered the job.

A few couldn't take it anymore and they simply dropped out—copped out, some critics said—abandoning the established American society which they saw as dehumanizing, hypocritical, violent, and materialistic. Like lemmings they rushed to their fate. They were the hippies. They sought an Arcadian society based on pastoral tranquility and a pure, simple truth. But they found that truth is seldom pure and never simple.

The Hippie Era had begun two years earlier when the phrase "Flower Power" was coined. The hippies believed that hate could be defeated by beauty, love, peace, and freedom. Unlike their predecessors in the fifties—the beatniks of the North Beach region of San Francisco—the hippies did not want to change society; they totally rejected it. They felt that mainstream America would come to understand and then join them.

"The Establishment is falling apart," said one hippie. "Why fool with it?"

A sociologist at the University of Southern California suggested that the hippie movement had resulted from the relatively untroubled adolescence of the Baby Boom years. In other more primitive societies, teens were required to make their own way, but American teens, for the most part, had been spared the rigors of responsibility.

"The first [point] of interest about the hippies," wrote *The Atlantic Monthly,* "was that they were middle-class American children to the bone. To citizens inclined to alarm, this was the thing most maddening, that these were not Negroes disaffected by color or immigrants by strangeness, but boys and girls with white skin from the right side of the economy in All-American cities from Honolulu to Baltimore."

Due to their transient nature it was impossible to determine exactly how many hippies existed nationwide. Another factor that made an accurate census difficult was that "weekend" hippies would flood into hip areas wearing the appropriate garb, affecting the appropriate mannerisms, and adopting the appropriate philosophy on a part-time basis. However, they would return to the "Established Reality" after brief glances of "Hip Fantasy". They looked, but would not leap. At their peak, though, there probably weren't more than a quarter of a million hippies in the United States. "Weekenders" probably numbered two to three times that many. Seldom before had such a small group captured the imagination of the nation's media. Television crews swarmed into hippie havens from Haight-Ashbury in San Francisco to Greenwich Village in New York to televize the phenomenon while numerous establishment journalists donned hippie clothes and tried to enter the hip world.

"Hippies are easy to spot," reported *U.S. News and World Report.* "In most cases, he needs a shave, a haircut and a bath. He makes every effort to look bizarre." Their attire did seem, at times, a little absurd. They wore as much, or as little as they wanted. Cowboy hats, stovepipe hats, sombreros, police caps, military caps, bandannas, berets, and even leather shoes-strings could adorn their pates. Their headgear could be accompanied by aluminum ties, war paint, military uniforms, furs, feathers, denim, coveralls, boots, sandals, bare feet, rings, earrings, nose rings, bracelets, anklets, and slippers. And always beads, and buttons that could bear any slogan.

"I was as surprised when I first saw the hippies in their ecstatic dress," wrote a journalist for *Look,* "as I was when I first saw the topless waitresses in their ecstatic undress. Too much is as startling as too little."

A typical hippie—if there was such a being—probably had a year or two of college, but no political interests. He or she was not an activist in any sense of the word, and sought serenity through self-contemplation. And to the outside world, he was allergic to work.

"When we get enough money," said one hippie from England who was living in Haight-Ashbury, "we'll probably stop work. It's not because we're lazy, but because we think we have better things to do with our lives. We think that to waste life doing repetitive jobs is blasphemy, when to live joyously and creatively is to live close to God." Another said, "Human beings must be ready to give away the property they think they own but which no one really owns except God."

Panhandling, as a result, came easy to the hippies, and this begging incensed mainstream America. Not only was it against the American work ethic, which stressed hard work as a virtue, but it was against the law. This also created a dilemma for the police.

If arrested for panhandling, the hippies would be jailed because they seldom could post bond. This meant a couple of free meals and a place to crash, all at the taxpayers' expense. In other words, exactly what the hippie was panhandling for in the first place.

"Hell," remarked one hippie looking around the pad that he shared with his "old lady," "this isn't what we want, to live like this. This isn't the whole trip. We're out to bust up the concrete—to let the flowers grow. What we're really looking for is a new beginning."

One investigative reporter entered the hip world and found that hippies felt neither superior to nor wanted to force their way into the straight world. "Man," a hippie told the reporter, "you know, I feel everyone's my better half. Like we're all part of the same sideshow. I mean, there may be some who'd call you and me freaks, and maybe we are. But by whose standards?"

"I could never join the mainstream of society now," a hippie girl in Berkeley told a *Newsweek* reporter. "If you've been made aware, then you can't suddenly bury yourself. So society is just going to have to accept us. Either that, or this darned society is just going to collapse."

☆ ☆

Hippies had their own music—acid rock. It was a thunderous electronic sound that attacked the otic senses. Acid-rock lyrics often were bizarre and ethereal. The leading acid-rock bands in San Francisco were Big Brother and the Holding Company with Janis Joplin, and Jefferson Airplane with Grace Slick, and in Los Angeles it was The Doors with Jim Morrison.

This latter group seemed almost to advocate total anarchy. Anything that interfered with freedom—any freedom—was deplored, and The Doors advised that it was perfectly acceptable to break the rules and taste the Forbidden Fruit.

Ray Manzarek, twenty-five, Doors pianist: "There are things you know about and things you don't, the known and the unknown and in between are the doors—that's us. We're saying that you're not only spirit, you're also this very sensuous being. That's not evil, that's a really beautiful thing. Hell appears so much more fascinating and bizarre than heaven. You have to break on through to the other side to become the whole beings."

If there was one thing that underscored hippiedom, it was drugs, particularly hallucinogens. LSD, STP, psilocybin, peyote, and anything that might bend the mind were used to escape. They became almost like a sacramental wine.

In 1960 Harvard psychology professor Timothy Leary downed nine Psilocybe mexicana mushrooms and took off. "I realized," he later told a writer for *The Saturday Evening Post*, "I had died, that I, Timothy Leary, the Timothy Leary game, was gone. I could look back and see my body on the bed. I relived my life and reexperienced many events I had forgotten. More than that, I went back in time in an evolutionary sense to where I was aware of being a one-celled organism. All of these things were way beyond my mind."

He returned to the United States and with another clinical psychologist named Richard Alpert founded the International Federation for Inner Freedom (IF-IF). "The experience [of hallucinogens]," Alpert said in a 1963 interview, "is so wonderful, so intense, and so hard to talk about except to people who've had it that we like to be together and share our understanding."

Leary and Alpert were subsequently fired by Harvard, and they recruited a broad spectrum of society to join the Experience—ex-cons, junkies, alcoholics, Hindu seers, avant-garde theologians, psychiatrists, and artists. In February of 1967, the hippies held a convention—The First Human Be-In—where Leary advised the approximately ten thousand who attended the San Francisco happening, "Turn on, tune in, and drop out."

Young people sought refuge in Hippieland for a variety of reasons, including a place to hide from the draft. Law-enforcement officials often scoured hip communities looking for deserters from the military and draft dodgers. In New York two FBI agents searched the East Side for a boy named Johnson who had failed to register for the draft in his home state of California. The G-men walked up Avenue A showing Johnson's picture to people and asking if they had seen him. It was almost funny because the agents walked right by their prey, but failed to recognize him, because Johnson hadn't been Johnson for a long time. In Manhattan he'd become a hippie named Scuby.

"My father's a fink," Scuby told a reporter. "He'd turn me into the feds." While he didn't want to be drafted, he had no real pacifist convictions. "I got better things to do than get shot at by a bunch of Vietcong."

If the hippies formed communities in urban areas, it was usually the low-income and slum regions because of their near poverty. This caused friction between the local residents and the newcomers.

"Their whole attitude toward us," said one ghetto dweller, "is 'Look, your whole life is wrong.' But there's no right or wrong when you're working twelve hours a day in a factory. Everything they say and do threatens us—and the law of the jungle says destroy that which threatens you."

The "peace and love ethic" of the hippies was having a tough time in the jungle: in Manhattan two Flower Children were beaten to death for no apparent reason; in Central Park a fifteen-year-old Flower Bride was raped and her poet husband beaten viciously; in Denver a hip mother slashed the wrists of her crying two-year-old son; and in San Francisco an "acid freak" was arrested carrying the severed arm of a drug dealer in a shopping bag.

As the violence escalated, a hippie girl named Suzie lamented, "There's no love here anymore, Everyone is scared to death. Everyone carries weapons. Even I carry a knife now."

As Hippieland began to deteriorate, the North Vietnamese paraded two captured American flyers before the foreign correspondents in Hanoi.

"I sincerely acknowledge my crimes and repent having committed them," one of the American POWs said. He appeared to have been drugged.

LEO K. THORSNESS

Rank: Major
Unit: 357th Tactical Fighter Squadron
Birthplace: Walnut Grove, Minnesota

Place: Over North Vietnam
Date: April 19, 1967

Birthdate: February 14, 1932

"All of my missions were Wild Weasel Missions. Some called them Iron Head Missions. What it consisted of was that I had a Trained Bear—an electronic warfare officer [EWO]—in the back seat, and we had as much state-of-the-art equipment that was available mounted in that two-seat F-105.

"We would usually go in with a flight of four. You'd have a Weasel leading and a Weasel in the number-three position. They would become the alternate leader in case number one aborted, or was lost.

"Our job was simply to seek out and destroy SAM [Surface to Air Missile] sites. Once they [the North Vietnamese] realized that we had such an airplane equipped with whatever equipment was available at the time—electronically speaking and Shrike missiles that would home in on radar signals—it became a game, an interesting game.

"What seek out and destroy meant was to prevent the strike people from being lost to SAMs, to hold the SAMs down, so to speak. We'd come in just kind of trolling and their acquisition radar would come up and transmit. The Weasels would turn and home in on the SAM site. Well, once they understood what we were doing, they'd often shut down. That effectively eliminated that threat, and we would try to hold down two or three sites at the same time. Eventually, they would stay up and fire at us. The name of the game was to troll high enough to let them shoot at you, yet low enough so you could get down to the deck and outmaneuver the SAMs. Our loss rate was very heavy.

"What also made it dangerous was that we would go in first, ahead of the strike planes, and come out last. The strike pilot had a specific target—an intersection, a railway —and knew exactly where he was going. He knew that he would be in the target area for two minutes. When I first got there in October 1966, we were in the target area for five minutes for each of five flights. Also, we couldn't afford to use our afterburners for more maneuverability and speed if we were going to cover all of the flights.

"In the aviation business, a hundred missions completed your tour of duty instead of a year for the ground people. The Wild Weasel was a very high-threat job and few people completed a hundred missions.

"The strike people's advantage was that they could look at a map or chart and say, 'All right, I'm going to move from this point to this point at this altitude and that will eliminate most of the antiaircraft guns and SAMs. When I cross that railroad and that river at that bridge, I'm going to pop, roll in, turn left at fourteen thousand feet, and roll out.'

"The way we did it, we just trolled around up there until we rolled in on a SAM site. They would fire three missiles at us. They'd always fire three at six-second intervals, and we would have to take it down and evade them.

"The North Vietnamese would move their missiles from established site to established site. Of the two hundred sites, thirty or so would be active. ELINT [electronic intelligence] would plot where they would pick up signals, and if they were near a SAM site, EL IN would say, 'It looks like this one is going to be active today.' So, I'd be studying photographs while in loose formation with the tankers during refueling operations, and my back seater would be flying the plane except during actual refueling.

"Harry Johnson was a very good back seater, and we were well matched. I always felt sorry for those guys in the back seat because I think they were all cross-eyed, at least Harry was. He'd be looking at a scope between his legs and call out, 'We've got a three ringer at three o'clock, a two ringer at two o'clock, and one growing at nine.' At the same time he'd be watching the sky for enemy planes and he'd say, 'Leo, we've got a MIG at four o'clock.' How he could look in both directions at the same time, I don't know.

"On April 19, my wingman, who happened to be a Weasel, was shot down over the foothills west of Hanoi. While I was directing rescue efforts and trying to bring support aircraft in, we saw a MIG and it looked like he was going to attack the chutes. I shot him down with guns at very close range. It was so close that I was leaning on the trigger and pulling up at the same time because I was about to eat him up, my overtake speed was so great.

"It wasn't a particularly good shot, debris was coming off his left wing. I suppose shooting [an aircraft] down with a Phoenix or Sidewinder missile is challenging, but that is so mechanical, so impersonal. It is not quite the same thing as the old dogfight, outmaneuvering people with the skill of stick and rudder.

"After destroying the MIG, I was low on fuel and went to refuel from one of the tankers and to wait for the controlling agency to determine which flight to join and go back in. There was a mixup and no flight of four to go in with, so I went in alone.

"Old World War II Corsairs, single-engine propeller-drive fighters, were used to locate downed pilots, talk to them, and then bring in the rescue helicopters. They were armed with a lot of rockets and .50-cals, and they could take a lot of damage. Two Corsairs went in—we called them Sandies—and one Sandy was lost to a MIG. They were not used to engaging MIGs.

"I went in by myself and ended up in a flight of MIGs. I initiated an attack, damaging one and driving the others from the scene of the attempted rescue.

"The odds were that I shouldn't have made it out of there. Somebody said later that I'd taken on the North Vietnamese air force. Well, that wasn't my intention. I wasn't looking for any trouble. They started it.

"Many times situations came along where you should have been court martialed for what you did, depending on how it was viewed. I lucked out. I was risking a plane and two people. We had already lost two aircraft and three people. The North Vietnamese had all of the advantages when I went back in there.

"Finally, a flight of four was coming in and I went out —out of fuel, out of ideas, out of everything—when one of the flight of four said, 'Leo?' You never used first names over the air.

" 'Yes.'

" 'I'm lost from the flight and I'm not sure where I am. I've got seven hundred pounds of fuel [six minutes]. What should I do?'

"I ordered the tanker to come farther north and I had no authority to do that. SAC [Strategic Air Command] controlled those. We didn't want to lose one of them because they were very good and hung it out for us a lot of times.

"I planned to rendezvous with the tanker first, but told my back seater, 'I think we have enough fuel to glide across the Mekong and eject.' So I ordered the tanker to work with this guy critically low on fuel, and they hooked up just as his tanks read zero.

"We saved mine, too. It ran out of fuel just as we landed at a base in northern Thailand.

"I was flying again the next day, doing my best to finish my hundred missions."

On April 30, 1967, while flying his ninety-third mission as a sitting duck, seven shy of going home, Maj. Leo Thorsness and his cross-eyed back seater, Harry Johnson, were shot down over North Vietnam. They were captured and, as prisoners of war, joined the two airmen who Thorsness had directed rescue efforts for on April 19.

"I didn't know at the time because I lost track of time, but I was in interrogation for nineteen days and eighteen nights, and that was basically without sleep. A lot of brutality, a lot of torture and I was, well, uh, anyway, after six or seven days, I did lose track of time.

"The beatings: Oftentimes they would take a fan belt, cut it in half, and beat you with it. It's like a rubber hose, but, unlike a hose, the fan belt is solid. Finally, after so much the mind begins to hallucinate and that saves the body. The pain dissolves and you can't feel it anymore. You're beyond that point. The North Vietnamese didn't know when to stop as far as trying to get information. They were brutal, but they just weren't sophisticated. Oftentimes they didn't know when to stop. They either broke you, or you died.

"We often joked that they must have taken interrogation by correspondence. They'd ask you your name, rank, and serial number. Then they would ask, 'Are you married?'

" 'Yes.'

"Usually the next question was, 'Do you have a refrigerator?'

" 'Yes.'

" 'How many cars do you have?'

" 'Two.'

" 'What was your target?'

"They just hadn't been trained to get information from you clandestinely without you realizing you were giving it to them. And they had no limits.

"There was a Cuban team that came in 1968 and stayed for a year. We called them Fidel. There were three of them —obviously Cuban—and they taught the North Vietnamese how to extract information. They selected eight people —I only was on the periphery—and the name of the game was complete submission. They systematically tortured Earl Cobiel to death. He was struck along the brow with a hose and didn't blink. And they took a rusty nail and carved a bloody *X* across his back.

"With a wire, strap, or rope, the guards would pull your elbows together behind your back. Then they'd tie your hands together at the wrist and pull, cutting off the circulation. They would put a clevis around your feet and run a bar through it. It was hardest if they put the clevis behind because they'd bend you forward and put your head under the bar. Sometimes they'd hoist you off the floor and it felt like your sternum was going to break. Generally, you'd pass out. It didn't bother them if they dislocated your shoulders; most of us had our shoulders dislocated. We called it the Suitcase Trick.

"It was brutal, painfully brutal.

"My time in interrogation may have been a bit longer than average, but after they were done, I was put into a cell with another prisoner, and then into solitary.

"The most important thing to do when you became a prisoner was to get your name out. When someone knew your name and the North Vietnamese knew that someone else knew your name, your odds of being allowed to survive were better. If they wanted to torture you though and get what they wanted and if no one knew you were alive after being shot down, then they could kill you.

"We know of people who went into interrogation and never came out.

"People would take beatings to get your name out. You were already being subjected to beatings and if you were caught communicating with someone, it meant another beating. That was just normal for years.

"Occasionally we would be allowed to go outside of our cell and sweep the area with a little bamboo broom. You can do anything with a tap code and, for that matter, any one of your senses. For example, you can be locked in irons with someone else and you can communicate with him just by touch. You can sweep the tap code as well as tap it. When we found out a name, we would transmit it to the whole camp by sweeping. It took them a long time to figure that out.

"Sometimes you would tell a guard that you'd heard that your friend Major So-and-so was now a prisoner. You knew that it would result in torture for somebody if not yourself, but it was terribly important to get that name out and let the North Vietnamese know that you knew that name.

"There was humor, but what was funny over there wouldn't be funny here, and important things over there would be insignificant here. For instance, one might day-dream and say, 'If we get out of here. . . .' That was quickly changed to, 'When we get out of here, we'll sit around some day and have a drink and laugh about this.'

"Another one of the insignificant things was when the kitchen help would come along into the serving area and put out the dishes. There might be twelve POWs in four cells. They would come along and open the cells. You always hoped that your cell door would be opened first, because it meant that you got first choice.

"You couldn't control that, but within your cell it was important to take turns going out first to pick up your bowl of soup or rice. On rare occasions there would be a piece of gristle or a piece of hide off a pig or something else in one of the bowls.

"We kept a record of how many American servicemen were killed in combat according to their figures. Within a year they had wiped out everybody in all of the services. That was better than no news at all, because you could read between the lines. People seem to think that we lived in a dark hole when, in fact, anything that was negative to America, we were well informed about. Assassinations, floods, train wrecks, civil disturbances—everything negative was exaggerated.

"There was also a lot of quotes from the more influential antiwar people—the McGoverns, the Fulbrights, and all of the people coming over with the delegations. We had all of those statements piped into our cells, and we couldn't turn it off. Here, if you don't like bad news you can turn it off. There was a speaker in every cell whether you were in solitary or thirty or forty together in a big cell like we were toward the end. You had hours of that type of news every day.

"It took them three years to figure out the English language relative to what is singular and what is plural. For instance, they would say, 'Here are the news.' Or if they wanted to read just one item, they'd say, 'Here is a new.'

"I'm not knocking their intelligence. I'm just knocking their training. They are probably as intelligent as we are, but they were poorly trained.

☆ ☆

"There were delegations that came to Hanoi, American and otherwise, that you had to give the right answers to. The North Vietnamese officials would furnish the delegations with the questions and the guard would furnish the prisoners who would respond correctly to those questions.

"Then they would go to work on you—'bend on you' we called it. They'd bend on you until they had beaten you so badly that you weren't presentable, or you died—there were a few like that—or you agreed. Then you did your best when giving the answers to act strange like blinking your eyes or acting drugged. Anything to try to let the delegations know we weren't giving the answers freely.

"Over the years we did not allow ourselves to become emotional. We became less emotional as the years went by. As early as 1968, when Johnson put together the peace negotiations, we were convinced that no American president would stop the bombing, which was the only way he had to get us out. It was the last use of force or leverage he had.

"So after the bombing stopped, we knew without a doubt that we'd be going home soon. A commander-in-chief just wouldn't let his troops sit there without some sort of tacit agreement. We became very excited when we heard the news [about the negotiations] and we knew we were going home. That was in 1968.

"Six months later there were two days when they gave us a little better food, and we knew they were fattening us up to send us home. The first time they gave us bananas, we knew for sure that this time we were going home.

"We didn't.

"Same wife, same daughter, and I know at times it was harder on them than on me. I was there six years and, for me, three years were brutal and three years were boring. For them though—the wives and families—they imagined the worst. There were times when it wasn't that bad. You weren't free, but at least you weren't being tortured, you weren't being beaten, you were just there being kind of bored. But the families imagined the worst.

"After a couple of years, the decision was made by the families to go public. It was a difficult decision to make because they were being told by our government, 'If you make a big issue of the POWs, then they will become more valuable to the North Vietnamese, and it will make it that much more difficult to get them out. They also may be mistreated more because the North Vietnamese will value the propaganda they can extract.' The United States government really didn't want the families involved.

"Up to that point, the North Vietnamese were never really convinced that we were ever going home. I don't think they understood the importance that Americans put on the down-and-out. If a little kid falls in a well in West Virginia, the nation hears about it and no efforts are spared to get that child out. Yet one hundred people might die the same day in automobile accidents. The North Vietnamese didn't understand that mentality.

"When their people went south and were captured, their government just wrote them off. The North Vietnamese government didn't value its soldiers' lives as much as my government valued mine. The relatives of the North Vietnamese soldiers captured in the south didn't have any other choice but to accept their government's decision. They couldn't demonstrate, they couldn't have letter-writing campaigns, they couldn't do anything. That's the brutality of communism.

"Three years after I got there, most of the torture ended, and I credit a lot of it to the national awareness created by the wives and families.

"The Vietnamese didn't have much entertainment. They couldn't go down to the local bar and have a few beers with their friends after work. So, they had to entertain themselves. A high percentage of the guards were homosexual, a good chunk.

"The guards did have their rat races. They would each catch a rat—Vietnam was full of rats, especially in prison —and dip it in gasoline. Then they would light the rats and see which one would go the farthest before it burned to death.

"A few of the collaborators were occasionally allowed out of their cells to watch this sickness."

Reflections

I can't understand why the seven people who collaborated with the North Vietnamese weren't tried. To break is one thing, but to take special favors is something else. The seven collaborators condemned the war, said how we were the aggressors, and so on. They would say how peaceful the Vietnamese were, so humane and all.

After a while the Vietnamese got tired of bringing out the same seven for visiting delegations, so they'd try to find somebody else. Then they'd bend on you until they either scarred you up so bad you couldn't go, or you went.

When we returned we pressed and pressed for charges to be brought against the collaborators, but at the highest levels a political decision was made not to. I think that the rationale behind it was that America didn't have a victory to celebrate and the POWs coming home could replace that. The Hawks and the Doves, the Democrats and the Republicans, the Pros and the Antis, everybody could be for the POWs coming home; that was the only thing the country had to be happy about. So why take away that small thing we had to be happy about by court-martialing the collaborators.

However, that set a terrible precedent.

There was a major difference in attitudes between the late shoot-downs and the old-timers. Some of the late shoot-downs, some of the lieutenants were on the campuses in the late sixties. Their attitude about taking torture and holding out as long as you possibly could before saying, "It's a dumb war and we shouldn't be here," was completely different from ours, less resistant.

We—the old-timers—didn't accept that very well, but when we came home and were exposed to all of the change, we understood. We still didn't agree, but we understood.

I'm proud to be from a country that allows freedom to dissent, but there are some things you should not have freedom to do. Every free society needs some rules and regulations, otherwise that freedom will die in chaos. A hundred of us can go down to Beverly Hills and all buy a different-color car; we have that choice. But when it comes to national security we elect a national government—we are not a democracy, we are a republic—and those elected officials make the decision whether or not to go to war.

I felt that Jane Fonda and Tom Hayden should have been tried for treason because I think they prolonged our incarceration. It was all right to have been opposed to the war like a lot of people were—that's the choice they had. But in my opinion, they operated outside the accepted parameters of where Americans should operate. There are certain things that are black and white, and we have no choice about. They seemed to be antiwar, anticountry, antieverything.

There was a famous picture of Jane Fonda sitting on an antiaircraft gun in North Vietnam. I was shot down by the North Vietnamese, and my wife was very upset when she saw that photograph.

Tom Hayden is now my state representative and within the last three months, I've had two calls from him. One was on my answering machine and the other my wife took at suppertime. She answered the phone and asked who was calling. She said, "Just a minute," looked at me, and hesitated before asking if I wanted to speak to my assemblyman.

I said no.

Then he wrote me a letter saying that he had tried to contact me, and he suggested that we ought to sit down over coffee together. There are four billion people in the world, and he is about the last person I'd want to sit down and socialize with.

I'm a Christian and I've forgiven Tom Hayden, but just because I've forgiven him doesn't mean I have to be stupid. There is no doubt in my mind that if I did sit down with him, he could say, "There is that POW who lives in my district. He and I had coffee together the other day and, sure, we have our differences, but there are some things we agree on."

I worked very hard to try to stop his election. My employers don't know how much time off they gave me to walk sidewalks with my wife and other people I could recruit, but there was no way to stop him—the money and registration. Santa Monica is 80 percent renters and he supported the strictest rent-control law in California for Santa Monica for his district.

I can remember, I think it was 1969, him referring to us as war criminals on tape, and it was played over and over again into our cells.

(Leo and the other POWs returned to the United States in 1973.)

Gaylee Thorsness

It has happened to so many people and, oh yes, I knew when I saw them. That was your fear, to see people in uniform and a chaplain; it's that fear of having the blue car stop in front of your house. At least, I didn't have that.

I was doing substitute teaching in Las Vegas, Nevada, where we were living back then. The chaplain and another pilot came to the school and the principal said that there was somebody in the office to see me. That's when they told me that Leo had been shot down.

Initially, I had a hard time adjusting because the mail I

had initially sent to Leo would come back with "Deceased" written on it in Vietnamese. That happened several times. You go through all kinds of things.

I had decided when this happened that we were going to accept the fact that he was coming back. If we had to accept another fact at a later date, we would deal with that then. That pretty much helped, but there were times when you'd get a letter in the mail marked "Deceased," or in later years when you could send packages and you'd get one back marked "Deceased," you couldn't help but wonder.

There was one especially low time that I will never forget. It was eleven o'clock at night and a friend from church just happened to stop in. She never came at eleven o'clock at night before—no one came at eleven o'clock. I do have a strong faith in God and sometimes I'd have to pray for the strength just to make it another hour. It was at such a low time and she turned up for no earthly reason. I will always think that it was God working through her.

On October 25, 1967, six months after Leo was shot down, a letter came to my sister's house in South Dakota —my daughter and I moved back there to be near my family. It was a strange-looking letter. That's when I found out he was alive.

I suppose, initially, my constant thought was worry, what was happening to him. At first, when he was shot down, I couldn't eat his favorite foods, that just didn't seem right. My mother baked date-filled cookies and I thought, how can you do that? I wouldn't eat steak for a long time. It's funny how you react.

But what stands out most is being lonely, being a misfit, and being unable to see that it was ever going to end. The tunnel seemed so long. I can look at this a little differently now. We're talking about things that happened ten to sixteen years ago. Any resentment I may have may be more a result of all of the years we missed with our daughter, or the lonely nights I had when I was a young lady.

I do have a little bitterness to the Air Force, if you want my honest opinion. We were often treated as second-class citizens, as dependents. I wouldn't accept some of that treatment now. I wouldn't instigate problems, but I'm much more myself now, much more confident. I don't even like the word *dependent*.

It made me very, very angry when the Air Force came out and said that retirement pay would be exempt from being split as community property in the event of divorce. I feel they were patting the wives on the head and, there again, treating us like second-class citizens. Surely, we were supportive of our husbands and our husbands' missions. I just think they should have treated us with the respect due us.

I was teaching kindergarten when the bombing was stopped in 1968, and that was when I became very, very disillusioned with LBJ. There was no provision to bring the prisoners home; that was a great injustice that he did. Had he, in my opinion, made a provision to return the POWs as a condition to stopping the bombing, that would have made a big difference. That would have been four years of our lives that that man messed up.

War is hell and when you come right down to it, that was Leo's job. He was trained, as everybody in the military is trained, to fight a war. There was only a handful of prisoners, a very small percentage. And I felt very strongly that we should never forget our fighting men, and as a result we made the POWs an issue, a very important issue.

Our husbands, when they came home, were so patriotic, so gung ho. Leo still is, but I think he has realized that the wives did make a very important contribution to make the POWs a world issue, and their treatment changed at that time when the North Vietnamese thought the world was watching.

I probably had a reason to hate war more than anybody, but I was worried about the antiwar movement. Underlying that, I felt that it was our country's decision. What hurt me the most, was the people in the decision-making process who were dividing the country.

I had a bad feeling about Jane Fonda when I saw her on TV sitting on a North Vietnamese [antiaircraft] gun. I had a very bad feeling then and I probably still do. It is not as deep with me as it is with Leo. He is having to battle with that, too, because we are Christians and you must forgive, but I think Leo associates it with torture.

It seems that no matter how you felt about the war, everyone was happy when the prisoners came home. I remember when Jeremiah Denton got off the plane and said, "We've been privileged to serve under difficult conditions. God bless America." It was a great moment.

I knew that Leo had been awarded the Medal of Honor because we had a very close friend in the Air Force who gave me the information. I didn't tell anyone, not even my daughter, because if they [the North Vietnamese] would have found out, then it would have been harder on him.

I watched the Medal of Honor recipients who had been invited to sit in box seats at Nixon's inaugural. It was a great temptation to tell my daughter, "Dawn, if your Dad were back, he would be there." But, of course, I didn't. I can keep a secret. Well, you just don't tell a teenager.

Leo and Dawn are just alike. Leo's answer to raising a teenager is that there is no problem. He didn't have any arguments at all. She was eleven when he left and eighteen when he came home, and any friction they may have had when she was a teenager, Leo skipped out on.

Look at Cambodia. All of those people, first, who have been slaughtered and, second, who have been forced to flee. Leo and I sponsored a Vietnamese boat couple. They are a little older than our daughter, and we joked that they were better than our daughter because they did what we asked them and they said "thank you." They have been a real joy.

We found them jobs, helped them with their English. There were several people from our neighborhood and congressional campaign organization who helped them with furnishing their apartment with secondhand furniture, and driving and support.

They are doing well now.

I don't believe that we think about this all that much. It's sort of in the past.

I always used to think that probably divorce would be worse, because I had no feeling of failure. At that time my friends were either widowed or divorced. I was sort of a misfit. I used to talk to some of my friends who were divorced, and they had heavy feelings of guilt.

So, all in all, I think I had an easier time than they did. Theirs probably got over faster and they could make a new life for themselves. But guilt is such a terrible emotion—really, it is—it can destroy your self-confidence.

What we have to do, and have done, is look for the good times that have come from the experience. It did happen and there's no changing it. We did get some benefits from it. We probably matured a little more, our values are a little deeper, and we have a very close family. Right now we are very happy.

I've been married to the same man for thirty years and we've had a good marriage, better than good. He is a good man and he has been very supportive.

I've been very, very fortunate.

7

In the spring of 1967 the Arabs and Israelis began rattling sabers, and tensions in the Middle East began to mount. In April a major crisis began to develop when Israeli farmers crossed into the demilitarized zone separating Syria and Israel to plant a wheat crop. This had been an annual occurrence in the past, and, while the Syrians publicly denounced the yearly border violations, they had done nothing to impede the farmers' planting.

This year after the public outcry, however, the Syrians sent MIG jets to chase the farmers back across the border. Israel responded by scrambling its own jets. In the ensuing dogfights, six Syrian and four Israeli jets were reportedly shot down over the Golan Heights near the DMZ. A month later a terrorist mine exploded, killing several Israeli civilians, and the government claimed that this attack was the work of Syrian commandos.

Israeli General Yitzhak Rabin declared that the time might be right to topple the Syrian government and seize its capital at Damascus. The Syrians became alarmed and asked Egyptian President Gamal Abdel Nasser to come to their aid should the Israelis attack.

For Nasser to ignore their request would have been tantamount to abandoning one of Egypt's closest allies, so he ordered his troops to take up positions in the Sinai Peninsula. This military maneuvering, Nasser hoped, would be sufficient to dissuade the Israelis from attacking the Syrians.

The anxiety of the Egyptians (and to a lesser degree, the Syrians) was aggravated by the 1956 Mideast War. In that conflict, British, French, and Israeli forces launched a coordinated attack against Egypt after Nasser came to power and nationalized the Suez Canal.

Immediately, Israel had seized the strategic heights at Sharm El Sheikh on the southern tip of the Sinai Peninsula. The heights overlooked the Straits of Tiran that led into the Gulf of Aqaba, Israel's only access to the southern seas. After the war, Israel relinquished control of this important post only after assurances that the Egyptian Army would not return. After the 1956 war Nasser closed the Suez Canal to Israeli shipping. As a result, over 90 percent of Israel's oil supplies and all of her flourishing trade with Africa, India, and Japan passed through the straits under Sharm El Sheikh.

However, when Nasser sent his troops to the Egypt-Israel border in 1967, he also sent his forces into the Sharm El Sheikh position. "Under no circumstances," Nasser told his army, "will we allow the Israeli flag to pass through [to] the Gulf of Aqaba. The Jews threaten war. We tell them: You are welcome, we are ready. . . . This water is ours."

Israel replied that any threat to her shipping would be considered an act of aggression.

Because the Straits of Tiran flowed through Egyptian territorial waters, Nasser felt justified in exercising sovereignty. However, because the straits also bordered Saudi Arabia, Jordan, and Israel, the generally accepted principle was to allow "free and innocent" passage to all ships bound for all ports. Because Egypt and Israel were still technically at war since the conception of the Israeli state in 1948, Nasser reasoned that there could be no "innocent" passage of his enemy's ships. He had banned the Israeli flag from passing through the Suez Canal, so he felt justified in doing the same thing at the Straits of Tiran.

If the straits remained closed to her, Israel believed that her very survival was in jeopardy. This combined with the Syrian attacks in the north increased tension in the Middle East.

The crisis erupted into open warfare in June when the Israeli air force launched a well-coordinated air and ground attack against Syrian and Egyptian airfields and military installations. Israeli armored columns quickly plunged through the Sinai Peninsula to the Suez Canal and likewise overran the Golan Heights. The surprise air attacks crippled both the Egyptian and the Syrian air forces. With Israel in complete command of the skies over the Middle East, the outcome of the war was apparent to all.

While the Israeli planes streaked to their targets, a U.S. Navy communications ship was patrolling fifteen miles off the coast of the Sinai. Although in international waters, this American ship was attacked by Israeli jets and PT boats. Israel apologized for the attack, saying it had mistaken the Navy ship, the U.S.S. *Liberty*, for an Egyptian vessel. Nevertheless, some high ranking Washington officials suspected that the attack might have been deliberate. The *Liberty* had sophisticated communications equipment on board that enabled her crew to listen to radio messages being sent to and from the battlefields. The American officials believed that the Israelis might have wanted to eliminate this threat to her military secrecy.

Thirty-four American sailors died in the attack and seventy-five were wounded. One of the wounded, ship's captain William L. McGonagle, was later awarded the Congressional Medal of Honor for his actions during the one-sided fight.

The war lasted six days and left Israel in complete control of the entire Sinai Peninsula, the Golan Heights and, after Jordan entered the war on the side of her Arab allies, the West Bank region of the Jordan River.

The swiftness of the Israeli victory frustrated many

Americans. Here was a truly democratic country fighting for its survival against numerically superior enemy forces who were receiving communist support. Not only did Israel defeat these enemies on three fronts, but it did so without direct help from the United States. Many Americans shook their heads and wondered why South Vietnam with massive American aid and military forces couldn't do the same thing.

At an Air Force–Notre Dame football game in Colorado Springs, an Air Force colonel shouted encouragement to his team as it charged onto the playing field at the start of the contest. "Beat Notre Dame!" the colonel hollered from the stands.

A slightly intoxicated Fighting Irish fan took a slug of beer and retorted, "Beat Notre Dame? Hell, you guys can't even beat a bunch of goddamn gooks wearing pajamas. What makes you think you can beat Notre Dame?!"

GEORGE E. (BUD) DAY

Rank: Major　　　　　　**Place:** North Vietnam
Unit: U.S. Air Force　　**Date:** August 26, 1967
Forward Air Control Pilot,
F-105
Birthplace: Sioux City,　**Birthdate:** February 24,
Iowa　　　　　　　　　　1925

"I was striking a missile site near the DMZ when I was smoked. They [the North Vietnamese] had moved a missile, a trailer, and a radar to where the B-52s were bombing along the southern edge of the DMZ. What the SAM was doing there was to see if it could zap a B-52.

"I saw a plane from the Seventh Air Force land, and [the airmen] came over with a good picture of the SAM site, and I knew where it was. So I went after it. I expected it to be very well defended and it was. I started a pass coming in from the southeast to the northwest, and they were really shooting it up. I was doing about five hundred and absolutely full of fuel when I took a hit in the aft section. I stroked the burner [after-burner] and started for the water, but just as I got the nose up, the controls failed and I started to pitch over in an outside loop.

"I had a guy with me who was in the front seat for his first ride; that must have been a very exciting day for him. The sequence [for ejection] was that the back seat had to go first. I fired the canopy and told him I was going. I punched out and he followed almost immediately. We landed about a mile and a half apart. He was a little south, between twenty-five and forty miles north of the DMZ.

"A Jolly Green [rescue helicopter] picked him up. The V [Vietcong] had gotten to me about two minutes before the Jolly Green had got to him. They picked him up and by the time they came over in my direction, the V had me stripped and moved about a quarter mile.

"My left arm was broken in three places, twice in the forearm and once in the upper arm. I was blinded in my left eye for a long time due to a blood clot or a bruise. My left knee was dislocated, and I don't know how that happened; I hit the ground unconscious.

"I was captured by VC militia—kids really—and they took me to a holding camp near Vinh Linh. The camp was about halfway between Vinh Linh and the old railroad line that ran parallel to the coast.

"I got shot down on a Saturday, so they had me from then until the following Friday. By that time they had brutalized me and dinged me around, and I had the picture that I'd be damned lucky if I survived captivity. So, I thought I would give it a go, and see if I couldn't get away from them.

"They were very undisciplined and untrained, just kids, and I was able to delude them and fool them into thinking I was absolutely incapable of moving and couldn't do anything. They started out wiring my good arm up to the ceiling of a sort of bunker about four feet high. I had a lot of problems with my other arm and couldn't even lift it up. If I could get my other hand over to it, I could make the fingers in the hand work, but I couldn't get any [independent] movement out of it.

"They would tie up my feet with about twenty-five feet of a cotton clothesline rope. It was one of the funniest things you ever saw. They would wrap it around my legs about twenty times and then tie up to sixty granny knots in the rope. Damndest exercise I had ever seen. It was really kind of funny.

"After they stopped tying my hand to the ceiling, I started practicing and after a while I could untie the whole strand of rope around my feet in twenty or thirty minutes —it was a piece of cake. After I figured I could escape, it was just a matter of time—and that Friday was the time.

"My guard was supposed to sit on a kind of stool outside the entrance to my cage but he never did. He had a buddy who had the duty guard and he'd always walk up the road to his buddy. They'd be up there and grab ass and shoot the breeze just like all fifteen-, sixteen-, seventeen-year-old kids who are brainless will do, a lot of horseplay. They don't have anything to do, so there was a lot of horseplay. They got up there and began to giggle and scratch, and as soon as they started that, I began untying the rope around my feet. As soon as I got it busted loose, I bellied out of there and headed south."

At the time, Major Day was about forty miles north of the DMZ, and from visual sightings during previous flights, he believed that the region consisted entirely of rice paddies all the way down to the DMZ. However, four or five miles south of the camp, the paddies changed to hard, cleared land. After traversing the rice paddies, Day continued for about ten miles until he hit an area of light forestation at dawn. After making about twenty miles that first night, he stopped to rest near a North Vietnamese artillery position that was firing.

☆ ☆

"I didn't sleep that first day because there were a bunch of people and kids near that gun position. If anybody had been looking, they'd have seen me, but they weren't. Apparently, they [the Vietnamese kids] aren't like American kids who run all over the place playing cowboys and Indians, because they never got off the paths. I was in really light cover, and I was terrified to go to sleep. I figured if I snored or anything, the lights were out, so I stayed awake all day.

"I had a very close call with some bombs [from B-52s] when I first held up. Apparently, they were attempting to bomb the gun site, and they just about got me. I went in and bellied up and when I took out of there, I had to go through where they had just bombed. It was really bad going and I cut up my feet and didn't make much progress.

"It clouded up and started to mist and I lost all reference to the sky, so I slid under some bushes and went to sleep. I don't know if it was a round or a rocket, but after it stopped raining something landed very close to me, and I took a hit in the leg. The concussion picked me up off the ground and then crunch back down. My sinuses and eardrums were ruptured and I was really nauseated. I barfed and barfed and barfed and barfed until I thought I'd barfed my kidneys out.

"That really buggered me up and I had to hole up for about two days until I stopped barfing all the time and stopped being so dizzy. I lost my equilibrium and couldn't even stand up. I was bleeding out of the nose and some of the vomit was bloody. That really took the steam out of me. Hell, I hadn't gone four miles from where the B-52s had almost gotten me—I didn't have any stamina left.

"When I felt better I took off and was walking fairly well although my leg began to swell because of the shrapnel I'd taken in it. I knew it was a wound, but I couldn't see it that well. That day I lost about a mile because I started walking in circles.

"There was a lot of forestation and I was trying to do

everything I was taught, but none of it worked under those conditions. Walking through the brush was like walking through a brick fireplace—all the rattan, the little trees, the goddamn fifty-foot trees and those hundred-sixty-five-footers that reach up and wipe God's brow. I didn't know where the sun was, because in there there was no sun. I just couldn't stay oriented.

"I finally figured out that if I was going to make it I had two choices: either walk on the trails or go down the streams. That's what I started doing—moving down the trails very, very carefully, hoping that my senses worked.

"There was so much junk—bombs and crud ricocheting around—that there wasn't any fruit on the trees. The shock waves would shake the fruit to the ground and it would decompose real quick. I did eat a thing called a bale fruit. It looked like a tangerine with a real thin shell and inside was the world's largest seed. Between the shell and the seed was a thin pulp that tasted like marmalade. It was really tasty. I also had about two thirds of a handful of a mulberrylike fruit.

"I caught three frogs and ate them. If I'd been a little more agile, I could have made it on frogs. There were jillions of frogs, but those little buggers really move and I just could not catch them. Out of the hundred I tried to catch, I only caught three. The three frogs and the fruit—that was it.

"Somewhere about the tenth day I started running out of control. I began to hallucinate and talk out loud. I didn't realize what happens after you starve yourself. It would frighten me to hear myself talking out loud and the hallucinations were just wild.

"I had heard [an American artillery] gun firing from south to north for several days, and I tried to home in on it. I could just see the gun site in my mind, and apparently I thought it was just over the next ridge. I heard a chopper's whop-whop and I heard another one land. I figured the one was landing and dropping off supplies to the gun site while the other one circled overhead providing cover. The one that landed spent about five minutes on the ground—about the time it takes to drop off a couple of pallets of supplies —and hauled ass. Actually, they were two Marine helicopters, and what they were doing was picking up a patrol.

"Boy, I was higher than a wino on a quart of port. I had it all scoped out and I could almost see it—the guns, the positions, the observation towers, everything.

"When I was captured I was stripped of my flight suit and put in boxer-type shorts and by then I was all dirty and sunburned. I figured I looked like a gook, so I was concerned about approaching the gun site. I figured I'd take a lot of time, get the lay of the land, and make sure that some private didn't blow me away by mistake. So, I holed that night.

"Well, I went up there the next morning to take a look and there wasn't anything, just a grass spear that split off into the jungle. There was no position, no towers, no guns; there wasn't squat. Nobody was shooting. I'd gotten all charged up with adrenaline and my head just went tilt. I went back to talking to myself and that stupid stuff I hadn't been able to control.

"The body is kind of like a car: You can't run it without an energy source. Of course, I had never gone that many days without food. I hadn't read anything about anyone going that long without food and what happens to you. After that I couldn't get back into control, and I figured the gun had to be right over the next hill.

"I walked into an ambush, and I wouldn't have done it had I not been so out of brains. I had just evaded a couple of patrols and a kid washing clothes at a stream. I had a terrible decision to make—either I could go off to my right, which was a little longer, or I could go off to my left, where I had just gone by this gook washing clothes. He was down by a U in this little stream, and his AK-47 was lying up on dry ground.

"I'd seen two other kids about ten minutes before scrounging for bananas or whatever, so I knew there was a bunch of them around. This guy doing his laundry was in white tennis shoes and a decent brown uniform, so I knew he was a VC regular. I was having a lot of trouble thinking. I didn't know whether to sneak up, pick up the AK-47, and blow him away, or try to walk around him. In my condition —my leg was really huge by then and my feet were all sawed up too—there was no way I was going to be able to outrun them. I thought If they find this gook dead, they are going to fan out and start looking for me. There was no way I could move far enough away or fast enough to get away.

"So I decided to sneak around him, and I did. I went down the trail and past this burnt-out village. Apparently the Americans had been using the trail—probably the same ones that the chopper had picked up—because the VC were dug in along the trail in ambush positions.

"Here I come down the trail from the northwest almost stark-ass naked, and I'm sure their eyes must have gotten this big, because they didn't know what to make of me. One of them shouted and it sounded like, 'Hey, boy.' I thought, Wow, I think I've got me a South gook here. The uniforms were similar, both green, but what he was actually saying was, 'Ay, doi,' which means 'hey you.' All of a sudden I realized that he had a hold of his rifle with a pistol grip—VC.

"Well, I thought, I didn't come this far to surrender to this little son-of-a-bitch. I tried to take off running, but after the fourth or fifth step, they started firing.

"I got hit in the leg and hand, but I continued down the trail for about thirty feet before sneaking off it to the right. They didn't come far enough down the trail after me, because I was bleeding like a stuck pig and the trail of blood would have led them right to me.

"Finally, one walks up to within about a foot of me, looks down, and there I was.

"I never did know exactly how long I was out, and the V in reconstructing it, didn't know straight up. I was out somewhere between eleven and fifteen days, somewhere in there. They took me back to the same camp I had escaped from, but in about thirty-seven hours. I couldn't believe it. Those little bastards were just like billy goats.

"In October I had one interrogator who was the first one who could speak even faintly decent English, and he was terrible; I could barely understand him. There was a lot of brutality from him. My arm had partly healed, and he was the guy who broke it again.

"They had hung me up from the ceiling and paralyzed this [left] hand for about a year and a half. I could barely move my right hand. My wrist curled up and my fingers were curling. I could just barely move my [right] thumb and forefinger.

"The questions were absolutely brainless. If I remember right, the first question was what political party was my family. A lot of dumb, dumb questions. I was completely shocked, because I expected them to be looking for a lot of military information. But that was only part of what they wanted: They wanted your head.

"In some of the torture sessions, they were trying to make you surrender. The name of the game was to take as much brutality as you could until you got to the point that you could hardly control yourself and then surrender. The next day they'd start all over again.

"I knew what he was—he was obviously Cuban and had either been raised at or near [the U.S. Naval base at] Guantanamo. He knew every piece of American slang and every bit of American vulgarity, and he knew how to use them perfectly. He knew Americans and understood Americans. He was the only one in Hanoi who did.

"I had gotten to the Zoo on April 30, 1968, and he had already pounded Earl Cobiel out of his senses. No one knows exactly what happened. A young gook, whose name escapes me, and two other beaters beat him all night. They brought him out after a fourteen- or fifteen-hour session, and he obviously didn't have a clue as to what was going on. He was totally bewildered and he never came unbewildered.

"The gooks kept thinking he was putting on, so they would keep torturing him. The crowning blow came when one of the guards some people called Goose struck him across the face with a fan belt under his eye, and the eyeball popped out.

"The guy never flinched, and that was the first time the gooks finally got the picture that maybe they'd scrambled his brains.

"It sounds so savage you have trouble picturing it."

Reflections

The objectives in World War II were very clear. I enlisted in the Marine Corps in 1943 as a seventeen-year-old kid, and there was not a question in my mind—we were going to go and thump the Japanese and the Germans, and we were going to thump them good! Of course, the demand of both our leadership and the British leadership was absolute and unconditional surrender.

But with the Japs it was so incredibly brutal. There weren't any prisoners taken for probably a two-year period, particularly after the Japanese rape of the Philippines and the murder of the American airmen on the Doolittle Raid. There were no holds barred and the Marines were not taking any prisoners.

You heard stories about how dedicated the Japanese soldiers were. Well, there was a good reason for that: either it was fight and get killed, or not fight and get killed. That was it. Obviously, the smart money was on fight and get killed. The Japanese were very good soldiers. They were able to capitalize on a combination of the national spirit and a quasi-religious belief.

People thought that the Japanese were so brutal. They hadn't seen brutality until they looked at those Marines.

Firing flame throwers into those caves—there's nothing like that smell. Anybody who ever smelled it will never forget it. It was a horribly brutal, brutal war.

The point is that it was fought to a finish, and the real thrust was that unless you came back with something missing, you were going to stay out there and fight until it was over. The First Marine Division almost exhausted itself at Guadalcanal. It was so sick, so starved, so ridden with malaria, disease, and wounds that it was taken down to New Britain and Australia to rest. After it was sent down there, the walking wounded were sent right back to the line at Guadalcanal or wherever the division was at that time.

It wasn't like the kind of stuff we had in Vietnam where you did your tour and were home in a year. I think that, in itself, was sort of a mistake.

When I came home from World War II there wasn't any change at all. I left the United States in early '43 and got back in November of '45, and it was like going to bed one night and getting up the next morning. The only thing that had changed was that we had thrown the tremendous industrial capability of this country into high gear. Factories were booming.

Right after Truman put the troops in Korea after the invasion in June 1950, it appeared that the same clear policy that we had in World War II was going to be followed. Particularly after they started whipping up on us after MacArthur drove so far to the north and the Chinese came into the war. Then, all of a sudden the notion that we knew what we were doing and that we were going to win disappeared. The malaise, the unhappiness, the dissension started to rise back here at home.

Vietnam was Korea magnified by fifty. Zero direction.

I remember so well back during World War II, before I joined the Marine Corps, listening to Edward R. Murrow reporting from London. You could hear the bombs falling in the background, and this marvelous voice narrating what was happening. And you knew that that was what was happening.

Out in the Pacific we had a guy named Ernie Pyle who wrote about the point man. Ernie was out there with him, and it was so beautifully and simply written it was almost Shakespearean. [Journalist Ernie Pyle was killed by machine-gun fire while on the point with American soldiers on the Japanese-held island of Ie Shima in 1945.]

At that time, we had a very exalted view of the press. The press did not lie, the press did not distort, the press did not mislead. If there was a mistake, then it was an accident, a misprint.

They ambushed us in Vietnam because they sent in a bunch of reporters who reported what their editors wanted. They were not interested in the facts. They had already made up their minds that the war was wrong.

The perfect illustration is David Halberstam, who got a Pulitzer Prize for reporting that Vietnam was a civil war. The dumb bastard never understood that it was a war operated, manned, financed, et cetera, from North Vietnam. After the North Vietnamese told how they had run the war and fought it with North Vietnamese, no one went back to David Halberstam and said, Give us back the Pulitzer Prize. David never got up and said, I bare my hairy chest and show that I have feet of clay, because I screwed up. Never a word about that.

So anyone who ever read David's mispronouncements about the war believed that David knew about *The Best and the Brightest,* one of which was never him. He writes beautifully like poetry, but it's bullshit, because he didn't know what was going on. He had already made up his mind what was happening and never did what reporters are supposed to do—what Ernie Pyle would have done and what Edward R. Murrow would have done—which was to find out what was going on.

I sound overly hateful because I thought about it very

long and hard the first couple of years I got back. It is still going on, but has really backed off since Walter "Crankcase" left CBS and since Dan Rather, Mike Wallace, and Morley Safer were successful in creaming Nixon. They began to realize once they did that that there was a backlash and it would be provident to back off. Then I think a lot of the press who were not committed one way or the other made a strong shift back to the middle of the stream and realized that it was not the most glorious chapter in the history of the press.

The Vietnam War gave the press all of those years to pick everybody's bones and to hang out every worm to swing in the wind and let everybody see it wiggle around and die. People didn't want to sit and watch their televisions and see that. They wanted to watch "The Dukes of Hazzard" and all those no-brainers. Seeing hootches burning, people crying, and all the blood, people didn't want to see it. It was unpleasant.

I felt that the press had essentially manipulated the anticountry, antiwar attitudes into being. Instead of making an attempt to balance the reporting of the war, they committed themselves to the gooks winning. When I got back I was terribly surprised at how anticountry they [the press] were. For example, in the first interviews, they were so surprised that we [POWs] spoke so highly of the country, and that we were thrilled with America, delighted about coming home, and saying good stuff about it. They hadn't heard anybody say good things about America for so long that they didn't know what to think of it. The politicians were apologizing or bad mouthing the country themselves, and all, I shouldn't say all, but most of the press was bad mouthing America. That was my worst shock coming back home.

My second shock was the general apathy of the people about international affairs. They had lost all concern and didn't want to hear about war or international affairs. I don't think it was a matter of isolationism, but rather I think that the press had just so turned them off.

The news reporting in World War II was rigged, to put it to you straight. We sent the planes out and most of them always came back; the troops attacked the beach and there were a few casualties; and the subs went out and none of them were ever sunk. All they did was sink enemy ships.

It was that kind of news, all positive and manipulated, but I don't know how else you can keep the people's morale up and keep the casualties down, or how you keep the internal subversion down which would otherwise cook and simmer, without managing the news.

Grenada is a great illustration.

If we are going to fight a war, it shouldn't last more than a few days, and there is only one option and that is to control the press.

I heard about the My Lai Massacre on December 6, 1969. We had just had an escape and a massive purge. I had been in irons for three months and had been getting pounded around. I'd taken over three hundred strokes with a fan belt in a two-day period. I'd been on my knees in leg irons and my arms manacled behind my back. I was kept awake around sixty hours, and had taken an incredible beating during that time; they'd crippled my arm again.

I was in bad shape. They decided I needed a nurse [another POW] to clean me up and take care of me, because the policy had changed. We didn't know it but Ho Chi Minh had died September 1 and there was a new government. Someone had convinced them that we were right on the edge of a riot—which we were. They had wisely said, "We better back off a little bit, or these guys are going to revolt and we are going to have to kill a whole bunch of them which we don't want to do."

On December 6 they gave me the nurse and this guy came in and cleaned me up a little bit. I started talking to him about the My Lai Massacre, which we had just heard about. We had no idea it had gotten the big play back home that it had.

☆ ☆

I remember hearing how the war was going according to the gooks in a broadcast piped into my cell. This announcer was going through how many planes they had shot down, how many Americans they had killed, and how many tanks they had destroyed. It was so incredible that nothing they ever said from that time forward had the slightest bit of credibility. They had shot down more planes than the Air Force and the Navy had together; they had destroyed more tanks and weapons-carriers than the Russians probably had; and the staggering number of Americans they had killed was just mind boggling. It made you think that the guy doing the news was smoking marijuana and hallucinating, or whatever you do when you smoke marijuana.

A couple of days before I had heard Tom Hayden, who is Jane Fonda's husband, in another broadcast into my cell, and I thought it was one of the most treasonable things I had ever listened to. Because of those two things—Hayden's blast and that news broadcast—I got to the point where if they told me the sun was going to come up in the east, I'd wake up in the morning and start checking west.

It was kind of unfortunate.

Part of America's heritage is that you have the right to shoot your mouth off up to the point where you interfere with other people's rights. A soldier's rights begin when his government asks him to put his most precious thing on the line—his life. I think the very least his country can do is to back him fully.

One of the things I didn't like about Hayden, Fonda, and the rest was that they buoyed the V's morale. Every time it was really low, they were on the spot to give them some reason to think that things were going to hell in a hand basket in the United States.

The problem was that the gooks knew nothing about a free society. When Pham Van Dong speaks for Vietnam there is no doubt he speaks for Vietnam, because nobody else gets to talk. If anyone talks against Vietnam, there is a quick shot—end of speech. Therefore, if someone runs off at the mouth in one of those kinds of country, obviously he is speaking for the government.

So, when someone like Ramsey Clark, who is an ex-attorney general and as naïve as a six-year-old boy, and all the others spoke against the war, the V thought they were speaking for the hoi polloi. When their morale hit rock bottom, it never failed that Hayden or one of those crud would deliver the day for them. It caused I have no idea how many thousands of American kids to come home in a bag with no I.D.s.

I'm bitter about that.

JAMES ALLEN TAYLOR

Rank: First Lieutenant
Unit: Troop B, First Cavalry, Americal Division, U.S. Army
Birthplace: Arcata, California

Place: West of Que Son
Date: November 9, 1967

Birthdate: December 31, 1937

"It was probably the longest nine hours I ever spent in my life.

"I can remember portions of the action, and I view it as something I had to do. I come from a large family. My father was a strong disciplinarian. He always taught me, 'You've got to be an individual, but you can never forget your fellow man. You can't stand alone and never forget him. Anything you can do for him, do it.'

"It was just one of those things. I drew strength from God, but I also drew strength knowing that it was something I know my father would have wanted me to do. Also, I had a considerable amount of training, thirteen and fourteen years in the service.

"Of course being a Mustang—I came up through the ranks—I knew what those suckers had done. I had pulled K.P. and went up from a private. So, I respected them not only from their point of view as men and soldiers, but also what they were doing for their country. And they respected me for the same things.

"The guys I took to Vietnam were probably the best bunch of guys I ever served with, and I spent twenty-four years in the service. We trained them at Fort Hood, Texas, and we went to Vietnam together. So, I got a little closer to them than you normally would.

"When I was at Fort Hood with some of these guys, I had my doubts. I really did. But, by golly, these young whipper-snappers were good—there was nothing that you asked them to do that they didn't do. It amazed me later when some of the infantry companies had some problems. I didn't. When I asked my guys to do something, they did it. It showed me that these young men could do a hell of a job. You just had to believe in them.

"We were a reinforced armored cavalry troop of approximately 160 people, about the same as an infantry company. We had armored carrier vehicles—the ACAV 113—and nine tanks—the M48A1, the ones with the ninety-millimeter main guns. We got caught in a situation where my troop commander got hit (he recovered), and I had to take over the troop. We weren't getting our tails kicked, but we were pinned down pretty good.

"We were crossing this rice field, over a small creek to some high ground. There was only one place where we could ford. The NVA were smart. They set up a good ambush, well concealed. We couldn't see anything.

"We had one platoon on the other side of the high ground. We were receiving fire and were getting ready to assault the hill. The tracks were pulling over a rise with their noses in the air.

"What these son-of-a-guns had done was to dig tunnels and when we got our tracks up there, they would stick the barrels of their 106-millimeter recoilless rifles out, look down the breech, and, as soon as a track would pull in front, they'd load and fire.

"They waited until they had five of our tracks in their sights. When they got hit, they just lit up.

"I told the troops when we went to Vietnam, 'There's one thing about it: we are going in together and we are coming out together.' It was a team, and that was the way we operated.

"I was seeing guys that I had trained and had a certain respect and admiration for in a dangerous situation and I wasn't going to leave them to die there. If they were going to die, then they were going to die some place else.

"I acted out of instinct and knowing, 'Hey, I can't leave that guy there. Ain't no way. I wouldn't want to be left there.'

"I had some super guys, I really did.

"I will never forget one of my lieutenants, Bill Wheeler, who is a lieutenant colonel now. Bill's track got hit; I put him on one of the choppers and got him out of there. The next thing I knew a chopper came back and here was Bill coming out, ready to take over his platoon again.

"I was never so glad to see anybody in my life. I said to him, 'Get out there and get to work.' He'd taken some shrapnel, but it was more of a concussion than anything else. He was semiconscious when I packed him out. I was sure glad to see him.

"I think we had every type of aircraft that was in Vietnam at one time or the other over us. I talked to some Air Force guys later and told them, 'If it hadn't been for you guys up there, I wouldn't be here today.' We had F4s, A6s, Canberras, Skyraiders, helicopters, everything.

"General Westmoreland was upstairs watching, too. A couple of times when I was getting on some command guys' cases trying to get them off my channels, I'd hear somebody tell them to clear the air.

"I asked him later, 'Who was that up there?'

"He said, 'That was me.'

"Hell, I didn't know that. All I knew was that every time that voice came on, they all cleared out.

"That day we had over a 95 percent casualty rate, and a couple of KIAs. We were lucky in that regard. Everybody, it seemed, was hit at one time or another.

"I was yelling at the second lieutenant forward air controller sitting next to me when some jets were coming in. I looked back behind the track and he's lying there. He got hit right next to me.

"There was a lot of little things that happened, human things I call them. Everyone of those guys was doing so many things. Jesus, they were flawless. Most of these guys were young—eighteen, nineteen years old—caught in a situation where I never want to be again. And these young men were doing one hell of a job. They didn't buckle, or nothing. You had to be there to see them to believe it. It was fascinating what some of them did.

"I just wish that I'd had every one of those troopers with me when President Johnson put this medal around my neck, because they have a part of every little thread in that ribbon."

Reflections

Vietnam, personally for me, was the greatest confidence builder and the realization of faith in myself. It is just like a ballerina: you can practice and practice, but until that curtain goes up and the lights come on, you don't know how the hell you are going to perform. I was able to prove to myself that I was able to do a job under adverse conditions.

When I see people criticizing what went on in Vietnam, well, I would just like to have had them over there. When you have a trooper you know is going to die within minutes and he asks you, "Sir, would you light me a cigarette?" You light that damned cigarette and before he can take three or four puffs, he's dead. I'd like to have those people there with me.

Or when you have to sit down and write the guy's wife or mother or father a letter. Boy, that's tough. I don't ever want to have to go through it again. There were so many guys who lost their lives over there and so many commanders that had to write letters they did not want to write. I saw grown men, strong combat commanders with tears in their eyes. They told me, "You know, Jim, I'd rather go out there and get involved in whatever than to have to write this letter."

That's tough, that's really tough. People don't realize that a soldier has feelings, too.

I know, myself, that I went to Vietnam to do a job, and I was not going to let that stuff [demonstrations] going on back here get involved. We had a job to do. We had a mission. We did it. We served our country as others had in past wars.

One of the things that stands out in my mind is that damned Jane Fonda. We were in heavy combat risking our lives for our country when we got the word about her support of the North Vietnamese. I think that if I could have gotten my hands on her then, I'd have blasted her. It had such an impact on the morale of our troops. I saw their mood change. Their attitude was, "Whoa, wait a minute. What's going on? What's this gal doing there [in Hanoi]?" It had an immediate impact on the guys who were there.

I despise her. There's no way I'll see one of her movies.

Our Elks Club—what an excellent organization, it is a patriotic organization that helps so many people—holds a Flag Day ceremony every year. They put a lot of time and effort in the ceremony. This year it was held right in the middle of town, and only had forty or fifty people show up. Disgusting, they had several thousand show up for the rodeo that is held in the city of Livermore each year.

When I look at our flag, the Stars and Stripes, I see all the faces, all of the bodies from the American Revolution to now, and the blood that they shed for my freedom. That flag is important. It does not just represent a piece of cloth.

I tell my daughter, "Our flag is the greatest flag that has ever flown." That's what we have to do with the young people; we have to explain to them, we have to teach them.

I put my flag out every day and I take it in every night. I try to impress on all of the little kids on the block the importance of love for their parents and love for their country.

We've got to teach the young people that the Pledge of Allegiance and "God Bless America" are not just empty words, that they have a very important meaning. Our freedom, our rights were given to us through the sacrifices of our fathers and forefathers. We—they—have to stand up and serve this country when called upon to protect our rights; to ensure our freedoms and rights are protected for future generations.

I went to a veterans' function in Milwaukee a little while back, and the main speaker stood up and said, "I don't know why they asked me to speak here today. I was a draft dodger during the Vietnam War."

At first, I was going to get up and leave. Then Gary [Wetzel] and Sammy [Davis] looked at me, and we started to get up to leave. But I told Gary, "Now wait a minute. Let's think about this. It took a lot of guts for him to get up there and make that confession." Not only were six Medal of Honor recipients there, but there was also a roomful of Vietnam veterans.

When he first started to speak, there was a lot of booing and that sort of thing, but as he continued to talk, it began to settle down. He finished his little presentation—he did an excellent job—and he came over to me.

He said, "Jim, you don't have to shake my hand, but I

would like to shake yours and thank you for what you have done for my country."

That takes guts. I shook his hand and said, "Hey, buddy, I admire you for what you just did tonight. I can't forgive you for what you did years ago, but I admire you."

As he was reading the Medal of Honor citations and some of the statistics about the young men and women who lost their lives in Vietnam, he realized what a dreadful mistake he had made.

He's a guy in his early or middle thirties with tears in his eyes. Gary presented him with a Milwaukee Vietnam Veterans shirt. The son-of-a-gun turned around and asked us, "Can I put it on?" He did. I sat there thinking, "Decent."

I had never experienced anything like that before. It was really something.

My nephew Jerry is a Seventh Day Adventist. When Vietnam broke out he told me, "I'm not going to carry a gun, but I'll serve." He served honorably as a medic in Vietnam the same time I was there. He didn't carry a gun but he went and served his country.

Today I use him in my hometown every chance I get to have him stand in for me. He is a great young man, a man who did not run when his country called because of his religion—he found a way to serve.

The Vietnam veterans sat back and sat back and finally they got the horses together and the power behind them. Now he [the Vietnam vet] is getting organized. I think the country is opening its eyes and saying, "Hey, these guys ain't going to go away."

It's like any other civil-rights movement: we keep pounding away and pounding away. And we're saying, "Move over. We're coming in whether you like it or not."

The Vietnam veterans are going to move forward and

get out of the back of that bus. "I'm going to be your next senator, or your next congressman, or your next lawyer," he is saying, "and I'm saying, 'I'm a Vietnam veteran and I'm proud of it.' "

I do a lot of volunteer work at the VA when possible, and see some Vietnam veterans trying to use the system and get something from the government without any justification. They think the country owes them something. A lot of soldiers from the Civil War, World War I, World War II, Korea could have said the same thing.

Out of every conflict, every war we have had, the country owes a veteran something. But, I also believe that we veterans have to go out and do something for ourselves. You've got to contribute to society, to your country. You just can't sit back and complain, bitch and moan.

We've got one old boy up here, I think he's eighty or ninety, and the guy still can't speak English. He is from Mexico, and during World War II they picked him up. He thought he was going to work on a farm. Well, he ended up in Germany fighting the Germans. When he returned, because he couldn't speak English, they kicked him out of the Army. Now the country owes this man something. He's a pistol, an American.

I will not support the few Vietnam veterans who are trying to use Vietnam as a crutch. When we visited the VA hospital in Milwaukee, I had to leave because of the young guys who were there—triple amputees, paralyzed, blind. I just couldn't take it. These are the guys the country owes something to. It is so sad. I talked to some of the young guys who were in Vietnam in '67, '68, '69, and they've been in the hospital ever since. They'll be there for the rest of their lives.

There was one young kid who got hit in his third month over there. A lot of his relatives live right near by and they never go visit him. That's bad, real bad.

8

"We have endured a week such as no nation should live through: a time of violence and tragedy," President Johnson said, but he wasn't describing the horror of Vietnam. Instead, he was agonizing over the racial violence that exploded across the United States during the long, hot summer of 1967.

From Albany, New York, and Albion, Michigan, to Waterbury, Connecticut, and Waukegan, Illinois, black communities were ripped apart by rioting, looting, and sniping. Before the rioting started, Congress—ever conscious of the rising costs of the war in Southeast Asia—began rejecting new proposals aimed at upgrading life in the urban areas and drastically trimming existing ones.

Were these budget cuts responsible for the violence? It was hard to say, but impatience probably had more to do with it. During recent years, the Civil Rights Act, Supreme Court rulings, and Great Society programs led many blacks to believe that equality and prosperity were just around the bend.

Yet they remained elusive. A *New York Times* reporter noted, "Nothing is so unstable as a bad situation that is beginning to improve."

The young black militants seemed to be in the forefront of the trouble, and a black bartender in Los Angeles noted, "Older Negroes have a hell of a time with this new generation. Don't get me wrong. It's what the white man deserves for sitting on his ass for two hundred years. If he had taught these kids how to read and given them a job then they wouldn't be a problem."

In Detroit the black administrative assistant to the police commissioner climbed onto the roof of police headquarters and wept as he studied whole sections of the nation's fifth largest city that lay in smoking ruins. As looters and arsonists were still dancing in the street, the Detroit mayor said, "It looks like Berlin in 1945."

A seemingly insignificant incident sparked the riots in the Motor City. A paid informant told police that trouble was brewing at an after-hours nightclub in the black section of town. The tipster was a wino who had been given fifty cents for his information. "It's getting ready to blow," he told police officers.

Two hours later, the cops raided the nightclub and arrested seventy-three patrons and the bartender. While the squad cars and paddy wagons were ferrying suspects to the police station, a crowd gathered and began taunting the officers and "jiving" with arrested friends.

"Just as we were pulling away," a police sergeant remembered, "a bottle smashed a squad car window." The riot was on.

Rocks and bottles immediately filled the air. The few looters who began to pillage area stores soon grew into a frenzied mob that swept through the city's West Side and spilled over onto the East Side. After the stores had been picked clean, arsonists tossed molotov cocktails into the shattered businesses. Sniper fire cracked from the rooftops as firemen tried to quench the flames and policemen tried to restore order.

For five days, mobs looted, burned, and killed, as fifteen thousand local police, state troopers, National Guardsmen, and federal soldiers fought to end the violence.

Jittery and untrained, the Guardsmen often added fuel to the flames. Suspecting that there were snipers in a motel room, nervous Guardsmen poured a lethal barrage of automatic-weapons fire into one room. However, when they rushed into the room, they found no weapons and three dead black teenagers.

An unexpected pop or flash of light could result in phenomenal bursts of fire from police and Guard rifles, shotguns, pistols, and machine guns. In one instance, a black man struck a match to a cigarette and lawmen poured concentrated gunfire through the window, thinking it was a muzzle blast. The man's four-year-old niece was shot dead.

When it was over, Detroit lay in ruins. There were forty-one known dead, three hundred forty-seven wounded, thirty-eight hundred arrested, five thousand homeless, thirteen hundred buildings razed and twenty-seven hundred businesses ransacked. A black nationalist commented, "No pain, no progress."

H. "Rap" Brown, successor to Stokley Carmichael as head of the Student Nonviolent Coordinating Committee, told a black rally in Cambridge, Massachusetts,

Look what the brothers did in Plainfield. They stomped a cop to death. Good. He's dead. They stomped him to death. They threw a shopping basket on his head and took his pistol and shot him and then cut him . . . Detroit exploded. Newark exploded. Harlem exploded. It is time for Cambridge to explode. Black folks built America. If America don't come around, we're going to burn America down, brother. We're going to burn it down if we don't get our share of it.

A black motel owner in Detroit stood in the smoldering ruins of his business and cried, "I'm broke, I'm beat, and my own people did it. It's all gone because of a bunch of hoodlums. I spent a lifetime building this up, and now it's all gone." Across the street, his brother's grocery store was in ruins, too.

In Cairo, Illinois, tracked vehicles from the National

Guard patrolled the streets of the small hamlet of five thousand. When they rumbled up to the black project area, an elderly lady hobbled out and with a rusty shotgun that couldn't fire said, "All right white folk, if we can't git along, then let's git it on."

In Detroit a young black said to his friend, "You know, we made big news. They called this the country's worst race riot in history."

"Yeah," his friend responded, "My kids goin' study about that in school and they'll know their old man was part of it."

"We got the record. They can forget all about Watts and Newark and Harlem. This is where the riot to end all riots was held."

"That little girl that got shot, man, she shouldn't have been shot."

"That's the breaks, brother. We in a war. Or hasn't anybody told you that."

After a young black man had joined the Army and had come home, he felt that his military service would help him land a good job. After all, he had risked everything for his country, and now it was his country's turn. But it didn't work out that way.

"I couldn't even land a job driving a cab," he said angrily. "The lowest job in the world and I couldn't even get that. You know, now I feel I made a great mistake going to Vietnam. Over there I fought with the white guys and I was considered a man. Now I'm nothing but a lousy dog."

WEBSTER ANDERSON

Rank: Sergeant First Class
Unit: Battery A, Second Battalion, 320th Artillery, U.S. Army
Birthplace: Winsboro, South Carolina

Place: Tam Ky
Date: October 15, 1967

Birthdate: July 15, 1933

"This happened twenty miles from Tam Ky in a place we called Death Valley, a little bit above Chu Lai. The Marines were in there first, but they couldn't make any headway. They just pulled out and left their barbed wire up and put booby traps in there. We had an E-8 who was going to hang his pack on the fence. Shoot, it blowed him all away. He was scattered all down through there.

"At the beginning of this crisis we were in, we had an undetermined number of NVA—that's North Vietnamese troops—in a valley. At the time we didn't even know how many people we had down there, but we found out later that we had something like a division cut off.

"We set our artillery pieces up on this mountainside overlooking the valley. With the artillery pieces, we had cut off all avenues of escape for the North Vietnamese. We intercepted their calls for help, and the only way for them to get out of the valley was to destroy the artillery battery. That was the only thing keeping them in. They could escape from the infantry, but not from the artillery.

"In setting up a howitzer position, you dig it in and put up sandbags so you can fire your howitzer and be protected from enemy small-arms fire. The position was about twenty-five feet in diameter, to give you room to traverse the weapon all the way around. It was connected with interlocking bunkers and the ammo dump. One little area housed to operate that one howitzer. That's what I called my perimeter.

"We were supposed to have had 120 plus men in the battery, but we were fighting with 67 personnel. We had been hit with sniping, we had some fragmentation and some had jungle rot. That was the reason we had Vietnamese personnel on the perimeter. To a certain extent, that was SOP [standard operating procedure]. The infantry units would go out during daylight hours and patrol. Then they would come back to the battery area and sit on the perimeter. That way we could secure each other; they had the artillery pieces for their defense while they were on patrol, and they actually sat on our perimeter when they returned.

"However, in many cases they would drift so far out that they would either get pinned down or not be able to make it back by night. That was the other guy's best time for fighting. When they did get pinned down, they'd give us their position and we'd fire on their perimeter to keep the Vietcongs and NVAs off of them. That was why we would ask the Vietnamese to be on our perimeter. We were supposed to have seven men to a howitzer section, but we were operating with three and four, and if we were firing at night, we'd need everybody on the pieces.

"I wasn't even in the battery at the time. Because of my rank, they didn't have a job for me. I was back in the rear area and the battalion commander called and said, 'I want you to go take over this battery.'

"I said, 'Heck, you've got more ranking personnel up there.'

"But he said, 'I know, but you've got to go.' So I went.

"When I got to the battery I had direct communication with him and I told him, 'I don't have enough men.'

"So we had about forty-five South Vietnamese citizens sitting on our perimeter. We would give them a dollar a day, a weapon, and a meal to sit on the perimeter. Some of them were good people, but if we'd get into a firefight, they'd go over to the winning side. They didn't give a darn who it was. That made me angry.

"My first sergeant came up to me and said, 'I swear I saw one of the Vietnamese on the perimeter signaling to the valley.' I think he was right because the NVA knew exactly where everything was. They knew where the FDC [Fire Direction Center] was, and that was the first thing they hit with mortars.

"To some degree, we allowed this to happen, because we did not anticipate a suicide attack. I never ever thought I'd see a suicide attack like that, not on an artillery position. It was something that never crossed my mind. They had tried it during the daylight hours but quite naturally were very unsuccessful.

"At night when the attack began, they started with

mortars, bazookas, and grenade launchers to pin us down. Then they came in under their own fire. Our SOP said that when we came under attack like that to get into your bunker and lay low. Let the other batteries fire on your perimeter and cut them back.

"But this time, they were already in the area. I knew they were in the area because I could hear the small-arms fire underneath the explosions of the rockets and mortars.

"I had just gotten off watch and I got everybody up and we defended the position. We were using the 105 howitzer, hand grenades, and anything we had. One kid said, 'Sarge, the Vietnamese personnel are firing on us!' They were just standing there firing at us while these cats come up a big drop off.

"So I said, 'Kill them.' But they were already in the position and it was actually hand-to-hand combat. They hit right between the FDC and my position, and between the FDC and the ammo dump. They were concentrating on the howitzer pieces themselves because they knew if they could destroy the pieces and the personnel along with them, they could have gotten away by the time we could have those howitzers replaced.

"If we would have retreated back and given them any room, they would have annihilated the whole battery. It was a very treacherous situation. They knew exactly where the bunkers were. They just went in and dropped satchel charges into them.

"I needed a rammer staff because I had a round hung in my howitzer and I went over to another section to get the guys to help me. I knew the section chief and when I went into his section his head was gone. They had blowed him away.

"We were fighting during this time and I said, 'Damn!' That kind of got me. So I ran back to my position and I could hear someone running in behind me. As soon as I got back to my perimeter, I turned around and fired like hell. It was an NVA and he was coming in with me. He was going to get into my area. He was a smart dude. I just turned around and blowed him away. He had a satchel charge and he was going to blow the hell out of all of us. I guess if he had spoken any English I'd have probably let him in because it was dark.

"They were throwing grenades in and we were picking them up and throwing them back. Some of my personnel got hit, and I got hit, too. My legs were gone. A lot of people don't understand, but with all of the concussion, once you are hit, you are not really hurt. You just don't have those limbs.

"I took a live grenade off of one of my younger troops—the one who told me the Vietnamese personnel were firing on us—and it blew my right hand off. That still didn't stop me. I was encouraging my personnel to continue to fight. We were going to be killed anyway.

"A guy named Whitehead came over and said, 'The COMM Section left a machine gun over there.'

"I said, 'You've got to get that machine gun.' If they could have gotten that machine gun, they could have mopped us up, because they came to mop us up.

"So he went down and grabbed the machine gun. He got shot through the groin, but he came back with it.

"The Vietcong and NVA fought pretty good, but they ran to the other side of the battery area and were, more or less, on the perimeter themselves. They had just about knocked out all of our communications. By the time we did get some communication into the other batteries that were under attack—well, they could see it anyway—they started firing on the perimeter.

"We fought for something like three hours. It started at about three thirty in the morning and lasted until six or seven. I was up on the helicopter pad for about forty-five minutes, and Pat Brady flew in and got me out."

Reflections

I have to say that I don't believe the government should have taken kids right out of high school, put them into the military with a minimum amount of training, and sent them into the jungles of Vietnam. They were not equipped for that. I think they should have had the type of training that I received. The jungle training that I had was very good.

Some of those young kids didn't have any of that. They'd been on bivouacs, but never in a foreign country. In Vietnam, the infantry units would go out on patrol and through some of the villages. Maybe they'd go out a little too far and come back during the hours of darkness and get pinned down. Here again you'd have young lieutenants and young captains and they'd be afraid too.

They'd call in artillery fire on these villages. We would fire and after we ceased fire, there would be all of this crying and hollering from the village. That was pretty hard on some of these young kids. That you would have to kill people to save your own life. Guns firing, their buddies dying, and people calling out for help.

I had a good way to look at everything when I got to Vietnam. I had been an instructor in Airborne School in the United States. After I got to Vietnam, I had a helicopter to pick up stuff in the field and I got a good look at what was happening.

We weren't fighting a civil war in Vietnam. We were there to help the Vietnamese people to help themselves. We were dragged into the war by the NVAs and Vietcongs. If you could have gotten into a helicopter like I did and flown over Vietnam, you could have seen what the Vietcong had done to those villages. They would blow up the bridges and roads to each village and cut them off. Then they'd have control over these villages.

Each village was working their rice paddies and the Vietcong and NVA would get in the neighborhood of 90 percent of their crop to feed their own troops. Any time that you get a person hungry and if he has no other way to survive, you can pretty well talk them over to your side. That's what the NVA and Vietcong were doing.

Now that is why we had gone in there—to remove that isolation, to help the people help themselves—not to get in there and help fight a civil war. We were fighting Communist oppression. That's where we needed to fight the Communist threat, not here. I could see that.

But a lot of people didn't see it that way. We had a lot of guys go AWOL over there because this was not their fight and they left. You had the same type of thing here in the United States; all types of protesters against the war. I can understand that too, in my own way.

I remember back when Hitler was making threats—I was very young—and the things that he had done. The way he was burning and killing Jews. I wanted to be part of suppressing Hitler when I got to be old enough. People were saying that Hitler would be in New York in so many days, and I was going to protect my mother. People looked at that war differently. Boy, everybody was for it because that was the threat.

But there wasn't that threat in Vietnam and not too much of a threat in Korea, so Vietnam wasn't a popular war. But if there had been a great threat like Hitler, everybody would have supported the war and would have wanted to fight. We wouldn't have had people running away to Canada.

We never treated it like a war. We didn't fight it to actually win. It was more like a police action. In many cases we were told not to fire unless fired upon. If we'd have said, "Okay, we're going to call this a dad-blamed war and use everything we have—our Army, use our Marines, use our Air Force, use our Navy to win it," we could have mopped it up. And not retreat and leave those people all of the equipment that we left behind.

It was necessary for us to be there. It was just the way that we left. The protesters of the war didn't understand it. If it had been to the interests of the United States, I don't think there would have been any protesting. I believe the protesters were demonstrating that they didn't want to see young men killed. There were a lot of men being killed over there, but the protesters didn't understand that it was very important—and still is—that Communism be stopped.

Communism must be stopped.

It was depressing for myself to be in a hospital after being in another country and losing my limbs while Martin Luther King, Jr., was back here fighting for the rights of black people. Then somebody killed him. It was very depressing.

You know, I could have said, "I should have been fighting for my own freedom here rather than to be in a foreign country." It was depressing to be several thousand miles from home and getting blowed up fighting Communism when maybe I should have been back here.

This is what I'm telling you: we as soldiers in a foreign country especially during wartime get along like brothers. We fight in another country and be buddy-buddy, and come back here and cut each other's throat. There is no reason why we in a free country have any business fighting among ourselves. That doesn't make any sense at all.

I guess that is part of us, we are brought up with it, it's part of our system in the United States. We are born that way. I think it will change, but it will take generations. We have done a lot to better our relationships with each other in the last fifteen years, but there is more to be done. We have got to understand that we are here and we have to live together in such a way as to help each other.

I go to a lot of high-school football games and I see the teamwork between the kids. It will take time, but it will work out.

☆ ☆

SAMMY L. DAVIS

Rank: Private First Class
Unit: C Battery, Second
Battalion, Fourth Artillery,
Ninth Division
Birthplace: Dayton, Ohio

Place: West of Cai Lay
Date: November 18, 1967

Birthdate: November 1,
1946

"General Westmoreland was on one of his famous drop-in-out-of-nowhere inspections. All of a sudden there he was. Of course everybody went nuts—'My God, there's General Westmoreland.' All we had on were our trousers, boots, and steel helmets, no shirts.

"We were on an operation and couldn't just stop firing, but as he stepped up to a gun, it would stop firing and another would take up the slack. When he stepped up to our gun pad, we all snapped to attention. He went down asking, 'You getting your mail, son? . . . How's the food? . . . Is everything okay?'

"When he came to me it was, 'Yes, sir . . . yes, sir. Everything is fine, sir.' Well, he looked down at my feet and both of them were hanging out of the ends of my boots.

"He said, 'Is that the only pair of boots you have?'

" 'Yes, sir!'

"He looked around to my captain who had on a brand-new pair of boots and he said, 'Take those boots off and give them to that boy.'

"The captain sat right down in the mud and took them off and gave them to 'that boy,' and I put them on.

"That was just a few weeks before the November 18 action, right around my twenty-first birthday.

"My gun didn't even go out on that operation. Gun Three got to go and it was short one guy. My gun was supposed to stay and protect the base camp. We were all buddies so I said, 'Hell, I'll go with you. No problem.'

"The infantry had formed a big horseshoe on the Plain of Reeds, and we were closing off the end of the horseshoe. The idea was to push the Vietcong through the artillery fire, a very devastating tactic. We were supposed to be put down at our position at eleven o'clock in the morning. A half-hour before we were to land, there was supposed to be an air strike and, fifteen minutes after that, there was to have been a sixty-round artillery prep of the area.

"We got there an hour before everything was supposed to have started. They set us down and said, 'You ain't getting no fire, so everything must be all right.' Well, they had set us down right in the middle of a reinforced battalion of North Vietnam regulars.

"Everything went pretty well for a couple of hours. A guy in tiger cammies [camouflage uniform] came walkin' through, and we just took it for granted that he was ARVN. At that time, we were supposed to be really nice to the ARVNs. He just came strollin' through bummin' cigarettes. He said, 'Thank you,' and went on down the trail.

"He wasn't gone fifteen minutes and he came back with two buddies. They wanted cigarettes, C-Rats, and anything else they could get. We loaded them up and they left. The next time there were six of them and they wanted M-79 rounds, M-16 rounds and everything else; you name it, they wanted it.

"That was more than we could handle because we didn't have many M-79 rounds ourselves, and they *wanted* their 79 rounds. Our captain got on the horn and called our liaison and said, 'Hey, get a hold of the ARVN commander and get these guys off our back. They're begging, borrowing, and stealing everything that we've got.'

"The liaison called back in ten minutes and said, 'We don't have any ARVN within a hundred miles of that area.' We looked up and they were already gone, and they never came back. Evidently, they had been receiving our radio.

"We'd been firing on and off all day charge fours—set pretty close with less powder—for the infantry. Late that afternoon a major with intelligence reports flew in and said,

'The probability of you guys getting hit tonight is *real good*. We suggest you get everything squared away.'

"In that area you couldn't dig but about a foot without striking water, so we put up another line of sandbags and broke out the bee hives [antipersonnel shells that fired thousands of cotter-pin-like projectiles] and stacked them up.

"I was supposed to go on watch at 0200, but Marvin Hart woke me up at a quarter to and said, 'Boy, Dave, [Davis's nickname] I can't stay awake any longer.' The skeeters were bad anyway and I couldn't sleep, so I said, 'Yeah, I'm ready to go on.'

"I lit a sandbag and shoved it down a shell canister, and the smoke chased off a few mosquitoes. It was also a way to heat water for coffee. I lit a cigarette and heard a mortar sliding down the tube. Once you hear that sliding down and 'thump,' you never forget it.

"I said, 'Hell, when did they move in mortars?'

" 'I don't think they did,' Marvin said.

"We listened and didn't hear them hit. 'Hmmmmm.' Well, the North Vietnamese were right across the river and shootin' straight up. It seemed like it took twenty minutes to hit—I don't know how long it takes for a mortar to go up and come back down—but, boy, they had us.

"Each gun had about five bee hive rounds, but my gun had ten or fifteen because I was the type of fella who always wanted a few more of what I could get. They knew where everything was. They hit our ammo dump first where our main cache of ammunition was, and they hit my gun's ammo, too.

"They had a fifty-cal [heavy machine gun] set up about seventy-five yards from our gun, which was overlooking a river, and they were shooting at us the most. A mortar hit our stack of powder charges—they don't blow up when hit, they just burn—and that lit up the area for a while. Just about the time they went out, we got light [illumination] from some 155s.

"They mortared us really hard for what seemed like an

hour; realistically, it was probably closer to half an hour. Being that it lasted more than five minutes, we figured what was going to come, so we was tryin' to get our shit together.

"Sergeant Gant, a black guy, was our section chief. At that time, I didn't care for colored people. Anybody that was black was bad. Sergeant Gant was the same way with whites; anybody white he didn't care for either.

"Sergeant Gant said, 'Okay, boys, let's get it.' We got the gun turned around and fired three rounds across the river as a crew. I was the A.G. [assistant gunner] and when I pulled the lanyard on that third round they [the enemy] fired an RPG [recoilless rifle round] at our muzzle blast and hit the [protective] shield I was standing by. The round didn't explode and went on through the shield and hit the recoil mechanism of the howitzer. I got some shrapnel on my right side, and it hit Sergeant Gant right in the middle of the chest.

"It knocked me unconscious and blowed me into my foxhole. I was half in and half out, and when I woke up I rolled over completely in my foxhole. I thought I was in a bed of red ants because of the burning on my back. I had thrown on my flak jacket and that was the only thing that saved me, because I'd gotten hit with a bee hive. The North Vietnamese had already started swimming across the river and were going to turn our gun around. Our guys thought I was dead and they fired a bee hive right over me.

"The first thing I can remember was all of the pretty colors. Our tracers were red, and theirs were white, blue, and green, and I said to myself, 'Wow, it's just like Christmas.'

"Then I started getting my shit back together, and I tried wiping off the ants. A flare popped and I looked at my hand after trying to wipe off the ants; it was covered with blood. I said, 'Aw shit, man, I've been hit.' I decided I must not have been hit real bad because I could move all over and I had my hands and feet. I took my flak jacket off, which was real hard to do because if I would just stick my finger up, those sandbags would start to disappearin'. When I did get it off, I remember running my hand over the back of the inside and the bee hives were sticking through. I thought, 'Oh, that's what I got in me.' I started pulling what I could of those damn bee hives out of me. When I got to the hospital, I still had twenty-three in me.

"I laid there—not too long I don't believe—and started peeking up to see what was happening. I could see them swimming across the river, and our guys were still firing the bee hives at them; they still didn't know I was alive.

"The river was from here to the door [ten feet] and there were several North Vietnamese behind a little rise our guys couldn't get with the bee hives; they were getting ready to come out on the bank. I thought, I better do something. I had a sixty and my sixteen in the hole with me, so I grabbed the sixty and fired it until it either quit or ran out of ammo. I threw it in the river thinking, 'I don't want them to get it' —the weird things that go through your mind. I grabbed my sixteen—I think I had eighteen clips—and fired it until it quit or ran out of ammo. Then I threw it into the river.

"They kept comin'.

"By that time our guys saw that I was still there and not giving up so easy, and they stopped firing the bee hives. But they were still firing H.E. [high-explosive rounds] right by me and, man, let me tell you when one of those 105s with a charge seven comes across you, it about sucks your guts right out of your mouth. But that was much better than the bee hives.

"Here them suckers kept comin'. I had to do somethin'.

"I looked at the gun and it was a-burnin', the tires, and in bad shape, but that's the only thing I had. I couldn't go back to the next gun because by that time I was drawin' a lot of fire; they were really trying to get rid of me. That fifty-cal was really a-thumpin'.

"I thought if I could get some rounds off with that cannon, I could do some good. The recoil mechanism was blowed off, and it was in bad shape. I found a bee-hive round and put the projectile in. The canisters were scattered everywhere, and I was crawling around looking for one that was still good and not burned. I had to pick them up to see if the firing mechanism had been exploded, and finally I found one that hadn't.

"All of the powder bags had been blowed to hell, but there was loose powder. I started scooping up the powder with my hands and putting it in the gun. They always said, 'You've got to fire a bee hive at a charge seven to be effective.' So I filled that sucker plumb full with loose powder, which was probably a charge twenty; a seven is the max. I loaded the canister and closed her up. By that time I was drawing a lot of fire, and that ol' fifty was just a-thunkin' into that howitzer. He was at an angle shooting at me, and I was hiding behind a wheel.

"I couldn't move the cannon by myself, so the only direction I could fire it was straight across the river where they were almost standing in line waiting to get in the water. They were standing on the bank probably from here to that house [thirty yards]. I waited until a good number of them were standing there and I pulled the lanyard. With no recoil mechanism and overcharged, that cannon rolled right over me. That broke the third vertebra in my back and some ribs. We were on sort of a little peninsula with the river in front and a little creek behind. Well, it rolled right back into the creek.

"I looked over there and, 'Boy, that done some good; I need to do another one of them.' But this time I didn't charge it up quite so much. I kept firing the cannon, and it kept sinking in the mud—you know how it was in the Delta—till I was loading it under water. I don't know how it could do that, but it was actually going off under water. The barrel was about to come off, so I decided I better not fire it anymore.

"What helped me make that decision was that I heard somebody calling for help from the other side of the river. It was pretty well known that the North Vietnamese and the Vietcong did that quite a bit to keep you from firing. Pretty soon a flare lit, and I saw a black guy over there.

There ain't many black guys fighting for the North Vietnamese, so I figured he must be one of ours. The gun was shot and I couldn't fire it anymore.

" 'Well, I've got to go get the guy.'

"I didn't figure I could swim with my body in the condition it was in, so I grabbed an air mattress. It had been hit by that fifty-cal and had a big hole in one end. I grabbed it and blowed into the hole and held on to it.

"I was swimming across the river to get the guy and that fifty-cal came down on me. That sucker makes a lot of racket when it hits; it seemed like water was a-flyin' a thousand feet in the air. So I said to myself, 'I'll just dive under the water. I've seen it done on the TV and it works good!' I was a-swimmin' under the water still hangin' on to that air mattress.

"Later, I found out the guys got a big kick out of that, because they didn't know what had happened to me. All of a sudden, they heard the fifty-cal open up and all they could see was an air mattress standin' straight up on end a-goin' across the river; what the hell was happening? Well, that was me; I was underneath the water. He never hit the air mattress.

"I got over on the other side and stuffed the air mattress in some bushes and made my way down the jungle to where I'd seen that guy. I was crawling, running, whatever, but I came as close as me to you to the North Vietnamese. It didn't seem to bother them much; they were just as scared as I was. I was really grateful 'cause I didn't even have a rock in my pocket to throw at 'em.

"Finally, I found that guy. He was looking around a bush and I saw him. I worked my way over, but when I got to him, there were three guys. I said, 'Shit, what am I going to do? The only thing—I've got to get all three of them back.' One guy was shot in the back [the black], one was shot in the head, and one had his foot blowed off. I threw the guy that was shot in the head over my shoulder, and the other guys just held on and we kind of helped each other back to the bank.

"I used their weapons—a seventy-nine and two sixteens —to fight off the NVA. I ran out of ammunition, but by that time I was close enough to throw their weapons into the river. The indoctrination you get: 'Don't let the enemy get your weapon.' That keeps runnin' through your mind.

"I took the guy shot in the head across first. When I got to the other bank, there was a guy waitin' on us, and he helped get him off the air mattress. I went back and got the other two guys. Coming back I was pretty close to the bank and I realized I couldn't go any farther; I didn't have anymore left. I was hanging on to the air mattress and I just let go. I kept sinking down and the water felt so good. The water was about fifteen feet deep. We'd been throwing shell casings into the river all day, and when my feet hit bottom and touched those shell casings, I said, 'Wake up.'

"I came to the top and said, 'Hmmm, that felt pretty good,' so I laid there a minute and started floatin' back down. This time I came up and there was a face about this close [a foot].

"I said to myself, 'Aw shit, man, I don't know if I've got the strength to do anything about it.' A flare popped and all I could see were these big blue eyes. 'Thank God.' I can't remember his name—I wish I could—but he took the two guys on in and he left me in the river. I guess he figured I could make it back to the bank on my own. I stayed out there and kind of pollywogged up and down getting my breath. The cool water felt so good.

"I finally made it over to the bank and crawled up. I think I fired one or two more rounds from the cannon, but I'm not sure. By that time it was just getting light; you could just see the sky lighten.

"We had whooped 'em. We had whooped 'em good!

"Sergeant Gant was 100 percent military; that man was responsible for saving a lot of lives. He kicked our ass every step of the way, and he trained us what to do. I mean that guy was military. After I came back across the river I found him; they had just dragged him up and left him. He was hurt so badly—he had a big sucking chest wound—that he couldn't do anything, he couldn't even talk.

"Up until that point I didn't talk to black people; black was different. I'd never really thought that much about it. It's stupid that I didn't, but that was the way I was raised. That night changed my whole outlook.

"Sergeant Gant held up his hand and with the flares I could look right down into his soul; that's what it felt like. I just laid there beside him, holding his hand and looking into his eyes. His eyes were talkin' and—my God, I've remembered it a million times since then—it came over me, the answer was there: He's a people just like me.

"He was cold, and I wanted to get a poncho liner. I crawled all the way back where my bag was because I wanted to cover him up with *my* poncho; the stupid things that you do. It was all full of holes, all shot up, and I took it back and wrapped it around him. I don't know if he made it or not. He was one of the first that was Dusted Off, but he was still alive that morning.

"Sergeant James Gant.

"An air strike came in with twenty-millimeter cannon fire, it came right down through our position. Hell, they didn't know where to shoot; I think they figured we were all wiped out. If I remember right, the twenty-millimeter cannon fire got one or two of our guys. Then Spooky came in with the mini-guns and chased the VC away.

"By that time it was daylight and we went across the river and started stacking up gooks. There were three hundred in front of my gun, which I guess the bee hives blowed away. Did you ever see bee hives at work? There were gooks stuck to trees, weapons were stuck to some and others were stuck together. You'd pick up one and another would come with him."

☆ ☆

The three men Davis got back across the river were part of a squad that had been sent across the river to provide security for the fire base.

"They'd been out on a big operation for about two weeks. Any time you guard an artillery outfit, why that's a pud job because nothing ever happens to the artillery. Like I said, they'd been out for two weeks. They dug their foxholes and, hell, I don't blame them; I wouldn't have done it, but I understand why they went to sleep. When we went over there that morning, there they were with their throats slit. These were the only three guys that made it out of the squad.

"We came back and began dragging up all of our buddies. The first relief helicopter arrived at 8:02 A.M., and there was a damn major who jumped off with his camera taking pictures of the big action he was in. He doesn't know how close he came to getting blowed away. These were our buddies; we had laid them out getting the dirt out of their mouths, and here comes this son-of-a-bitch taking pictures.

"It infuriated us.

"I was told there was another Medal of Honor that was received that night, a Spanish guy. I can picture his face in my mind, but I can't remember his name. Hell, to 90 percent of the guys over there, I was Dave; the people didn't know my name. That makes it awful hard to look up your buddies.

"He was on the other side of the perimeter; he was one of the infantry. His legs had been blown off, and he had crawled inside our perimeter. He got a sixty, somebody stacked ammo around him, and he stood there on his stumps firing that machine gun, sweeping it back and forth.

"He didn't make it.

"But I don't remember his name.

"We called him Mex.

193

"After I was hit I went into the hospital and I was out for quite a while. The first thing that I can remember after I had left the field—I don't remember anything else till then—was someone a-shakin' my arm and talking to me. All of a sudden I opened my eyes, and I could see and hear everything; it was General Westmoreland.

"I thought, Boy, something must really be wrong if General Westmoreland is here; of course, I didn't know where here was. It was kind of like I was in a fog and trying to come out of it. The first words I can remember him saying were like echoing down a long hallway. He was looking down, pointing to my feet, and saying, 'But where's your boots?'

"I think that that was one of the things that gave me the strength to make it. All of a sudden I felt important, because the general remembered me.

"I got real bad after that. One of the bee hives had penetrated my kidney and I got a real bad kidney infection. At the time they told me I'd caught malaria. Now we find out I never had malaria; what I had was like a toxic shock syndrome due to dioxin [from Agent Orange]. My liver and kidneys were so bad I almost died—the dioxin almost wiped me out. With the fresh wounds I got a big charge of it.

"I ran a temperature of 107 for six days, and it almost completely dehydrated me. They would give me a transfusion and in twenty-four hours I'd be right back where I started. The doctor said my blood was just like buttermilk. That was during a really, really big push, and there were a lot of boys who were wounded. They ran out of whole blood.

"They couldn't get my fever down and I was pretty well messed up anyway, so they put me out in the hall. The doctor said, 'We've done all we can. With that temperature if he lives he's going to be a vegetable anyway.'

"One of the guys I swam across the river to get was in

the same hospital. They told me later he got hold of the doctors and told them, 'Take the blood out of my arm and put it in that boy's arm. If he needs it, here it is.' Well, hell, he was shot in the back, but I guess he laid down beside me in the hallway, and they did it. He was the black guy I'd seen on the other side of the river.

"When I got that good rich blood, my fever snapped like that and they brought me back into the ward. Two days later they decided I was going to make it and they shipped me to Japan. When I was in the hospital I received a letter from his parents thanking me for saving their son's life.

"By the time I got to Japan I couldn't walk, but I could get up on crutches and move, which I wasn't supposed to do. They were going to send me home. I didn't want to go home, I wanted to go back to my guys. There was only twelve of us left out of forty-two and I just felt a responsibility; you know how close you are to your friends. After losing so many of my friends, I didn't want to be sent home.

"I was in a panic and I called General Westmoreland's office in Saigon—don't ask me how, but I got him. I told him who I was and related the boot incident to him. I didn't know this but at the time the Medal of Honor papers were sitting on his desk. I told him that I wanted to be back with my people and he said, 'Son, I understand.'

"The next day I was headed back to Saigon, but I had to stay there until I could walk down the ward and back again, probably a hundred feet. I had General Westmoreland's paperwork in my hand and I was waving it at them all the time, 'He said I could go back to my unit.'

" 'We aren't going to let you go until you can negotiate under your own power.'

"Finally, they let me go and I went back on crutches and all bandaged up. They let me off from a helicopter at the end of a little dirt road. I had to walk a couple hundred yards, and that was the longest walk I think I ever made in my life. It was worth it.

"They didn't know I was coming; they thought I was dead 'cause they hadn't heard from me. I came walking up the dirt road and everybody came out to see me.

"Everything was okay.

"I stopped in Ohio a couple of years ago and saw one of the guys that was with me that night (Bill Few) and he said, 'Do you still have that ol' harmonica?'

"I said, 'Yeah, I do. Why?'

"He said, 'You know, I didn't realize what that harmonica meant. A few years ago I was laying in bed thinking and it dawned on me: As long as we heard that harmonica playing, we knew everything was all right.'

"I used to sit right out there on the line and play my harmonica. The captain got in my shit a thousand times if he got in it once—'You can't play that harmonica on guard duty. They're going to know where you are.'

"I said, 'Ah, don't be stupid, man. I'm sitting out here in a bunker and they know where that bunker is.' I'd go ahead and play it anyway; that kept me awake.

"I'd sit there with my legs crossed and play that harmonica—my eyes were a-workin' all the time. Everybody knew that as long as they heard that ol' harmonica a-floatin' out there, everything was all right because I didn't lay it down unless something was happening. When that harmonica stopped playin', everybody grabbed up their sixteens and started lookin'.

"It was real peaceful to the guys 'cause as long as that harmonica was playin', everything was all right."

Reflections

The irony to this whole thing is that after making it through Vietnam and recuperating from the wounds, I find out that Agent Orange is going to be my demise. Fifteen years later, one of the nation's leading toxicologists—Doctor Bertram Carnow in Chicago—confirms that Agent Orange is going to get me. It rather pisses you off.

For years I'd get to feeling bad and go to the doctors. They'd run all kinds of tests and end up saying, "There's nothing wrong with you. You're a big strong lad; it's all in your mind." Pretty soon I got to thinking, maybe it is in my mind. At the time, I was feeling good about three weeks out of a month, but I couldn't figure out why. Dr. Carnow answered my questions.

He said that if I was to erase my age off my medical history and hand it to another doctor, he'd look at it and say, "This guy isn't in bad shape for an eighty-year-old man." The fact is, I am thirty-seven years old, but my body functions just like that of an eighty-year-old man. My heart still works, my kidneys still work, my liver still works, but they are just burnt out by dioxin. That's one of the things dioxin does; it makes you very, very old.

I always wondered why these old dudes would walk down the street all bent over. I know why, I know why they walk like that. They just hurt so damn bad they can't do any better. There are a lot of days that's the way I walk. There are some days I've got to get my cane out—that's the only way I can function.

Usually when I'm sick, I don't like to go out, because I don't like people to see me when I'm sick. It just hurts your pride a little bit. Being on a speaking tour—I'll talk to anybody who will listen—there are some days that I don't do too well, but I've got to go out there and give them my message. Usually, I feel that I get it over pretty good. I'm not a fancy talker, but I've learned that instead of trying to impress people with facts and figures, just tell them what you feel, tell them how it really is.

Most Vietnam veterans—and I'll bet you're as guilty as anybody else—say, "That Agent Orange is really bad, but it ain't never going to happen to me." That was always me, but now it's got me by the throat, and nothing gets you involved and be damned serious about something as when it's got you around the throat. That's what I'm involved in. Agent Orange has taken over my life in more than one aspect.

The majority of the money that comes into the house is spent for travel to go to these speeches because I don't ask for any money.

We got calls from Washington, D.C., telling me what was going to happen if I pursued this issue: they were going to tap my phone, audit me and my family for the rest of my life—all of the things the powers could do would happen to me if I didn't drop the issue. That convinced me that what I was about to embark on was right. Up to that point I thought, Well, this is Uncle Sam—he is going to take care of us.

When I was threatened, that made me determined to see this thing through. There are a lot of good people in the government that want to help us. I am thoroughly convinced that there is just a handful who have had their pockets lined by the chemical companies behind the threats.

It came to pass. Me and Mom were followed all the way to Washington, D.C., and back by the same car. At first, I just thought it was my paranoia, but that same big green Lincoln followed me out there and back. I'll just keep fightin' till I can't fight no more, and then somebody else will pick it up and carry it on.

On June 12, 1983, former Army Pfc. Sammy Lee Davis took the Medal of Honor awarded him and appeared before the U.S. House of Representatives Committee on Veterans' Affairs in Washington that was considering legislation that would benefit veterans suffering from dioxin poisoning that resulted from being subjected to Agent Orange. After presenting the detailed medical report on his condition by Dr. Carnow he testified before the committee:

Gentlemen, I am a country boy, and I was raised with a country boy's love for this nation and belief in what my government was doing. In 1966, I joined hundreds of thousands of young men who voluntarily enlisted in the armed forces because we were convinced America needed us to serve her, a step I would take again today without hesitation. On a November night in 1967, good fortune and determination delivered me from a most difficult set of circumstances and I was awarded the honor I humbly display today. Throughout the darkest night in my life, although there was no one immediately present at my side, I never for a moment doubted that America herself was standing next to me. I come here today to join you, once again standing alongside America, seeking to serve her best interests.

Upon my discharge from the service in 1969, the state of my health began to lead me on a journey that, in many respects, is not unlike my travels through a jungle on the other side of the world. I have walked miles of hospital corridors while in pain; seeking answers, fearing the worst, but pressing on because I believed it to be my duty to my family and myself. While there was always another prescription, additional speculation, and what I believe to be a sincere effort to find the cause, the supreme question—why —could never be answered. And the pain could never stop.

The pain continues, the fear grows worse. But in March of this year, I broke through the jungle into the light. One man, Dr. Bertram Carnow, was able to tell me what both he and I believe to be the cause of my suffering. While I have suspected for some time that Agent Orange, and the dioxin contained in it, may be responsible for the illnesses that have cost me nearly four years of time off in the nine years of my employment with the company I must now retire from, it was only Dr. Carnow who has been able to confirm that. I assure you that it is only my faith in Dr. Carnow, his confidence in his tests and ultimate diagnosis, not my suspicions, that are responsible for my belief in his opinion.

The diagnosis has given me both fright and relief. I know, and the doctor has confirmed, that I am not a healthy man. From my conversations with Dr. Carnow, I know that without the same good fortune that delivered me from the jungle fourteen years ago, I may be called away very soon. I am thirty-six years old, gentlemen, and that terrifies me. But at the very least, the darkness of uncertainty has passed and I can rest with the fact that I know what to expect.

I did not travel miles from . . . Illinois to the Capitol to accuse anyone or any organization of any wrongdoing, indifference, or malpractice of medicine. Nonetheless, certain questions exist in my mind and the minds of thousands of other Vietnam veterans. What can one doctor in Chicago do that the largest health-care-delivery system in the world cannot? What can one man examine, understand, and diagnose, that the largest health-care-delivery system in the world cannot? Can men who may not have years to wait for the completion of research be asked to stand by while there is a doctor who can answer their questions today? I submit, gentlemen, that we have a right to know, just as we did in Vietnam, why we may have to die.

I have come here today to lend what support I can to Congressman Daschle's legislation for two reasons. First, it will allow the Veterans Administration to give immediate benefits to the men who are suffering, who cannot work, and who can no longer feel the pride of making a contribution that they felt while they were in Vietnam. Secondly, in the long run, approval of this legislation by the Congress will be a definite signal to the nation and the rest of the world that a problem does exist from exposure to Agent Orange and that the greatest deliberative body that the world has ever known wants answers to the problem. Beyond compensation, it will be a call for intensified research in both the public and private sectors into the damage this chemical has caused, the means to halt the damage, and the way to a cure.

A great American hero, Lou Gehrig, of the New York Yankees, once told a capacity crowd in a baseball stadium that, in spite of the fact that he knew he was dying, he considered himself the luckiest man alive. Although I do not consider myself a hero, in light of the fact that Mr. Gehrig is no longer with us, I feel that I am now the luckiest man alive. I have been blessed with a beautiful, loving wife who, in turn, has blessed me with three beautiful, healthy children. I have also been given the rarest of opportunities in serving the greatest nation on the planet in a way few men are allowed to. I pray only that my family be allowed to grow and prosper in the same manner I was, and am left speechless when I consider the bounty that has befallen me.

Another man who was a hero, although perhaps only to me and the rest of his family, was my grandfather. When I returned from Vietnam, he gave me a newspaper clipping that I still carry with me today. The clipping is a rendition of the last two stanzas of Lt. John McCrae's poem "In Flanders Field." I would like to share some of the poem with the committee, because he told me it explained what serving in a war really meant.

> *To you from failing hands we throw*
> *the torch; be it yours to hold high.*
> *If ye break faith with us who die*
> *We shall not sleep, though poppies grow*
> *In Flanders Field.*

I am an American, gentlemen, and therefore too proud and too bullheaded to beg you. But I humbly request that you do not break faith with those of us who answered the call that came from this very building. Think of the legacy you will leave for the next army you may have to raise to stand under our flag should you turn your backs on us. I can only ask you to do what is right.

Thank you for allowing me the honor of being here today.

9

Students were becoming more political as 1968 began and they were expressing themselves more vocally. "There's going to be a fantastic concern in the coming year with the political situation," said one student leader on the West Coast. "Not in the sense of 'We can play the adult game,' but in a sense that the university could have a significant voice in the next election."

As the students began demanding more power to control their lives, they also were drawing a line. At Stanford University during Parents' Day, the student newspaper editorialized, "We would say welcome parents, but on the contemporary university campus, one does not fraternize with the enemy."

At UCLA another student journalist noted, "There is an inherent social activism on the campus, and with civil rights falling away, it's being channeled toward Vietnam." Not only on the liberal campuses, but at conservative schools, the growing student disenchantment with the war was surfacing.

Students at conservative Fordham University heckled Navy recruiters with shouts of, "Hell, no! We won't go!"

Nevertheless, a majority of Americans still supported the American war effort in Southeast Asia. In fact, by January of 1968 a Harris poll revealed that 62 percent of those polled rejected the idea of deescalation of the war. However, actual support of the war was dwindling. In July, polls showed that 72 percent supported the war, but by the end of the year, the support had dropped to 58 percent. Most of those who did not actually support the war, though, didn't oppose it either. This dip in the popularity for the war resulted in increased editorial attacks in the nation's leading publications. Such noted publications as the *Los Angeles Times*, *Detroit Free Press*, *Washington Post*, *New York Times*, *St. Louis Post-Dispatch*, and *Life* magazine were beginning to side with the doves.

Even the *Houston Chronicle*, a Hawkish backer of the administration's policies in Vietnam, was beginning to have doubts: "President Johnson is catching it from all sides. . . . We still support the President on Vietnam, but we're more disturbed at the course of the war."

For several months there were indications that the North Vietnamese and Vietcong were preparing for a major attack around Vietnam and that the tempo of the war was going to pick up. This coming offensive was reported in the nation's news magazines and one U.S. official was quoted in November of 1967: "We have no illusions that the next year is going to be easy; it may, in fact, be the most critical of the U.S. effort in Vietnam."

In January of 1968, the North Vietnamese and Vietcong launched a massive country-wide assault and seized twenty-eight provincial capitals. While the Communists were unable to hold any of these major cities, they left the towns in flames. Pleiku, a highland town of sixty-six thousand, was 50 percent destroyed and eleven thousand were left homeless; Ban Me Thout was 25 percent destroyed and twenty thousand were without homes; Ben Tre, population thirty-five thousand, was 45 percent destroyed, nearly a thousand civilians were killed and ten thousand were left without a roof over their heads; and in Saigon many sections were completely destroyed and over one hundred twenty thousand were left homeless.

The viciousness of the fighting was brought home to the Americans as they watched the nightly television news. In Saigon, the national police chief for Vietnam, Gen. Nguyen Ngoc Loan, was trying to extract information from a Vietcong suspect. However, the suspect was stubborn and would say nothing. Loan pulled out his .38 pistol, aimed it at the prisoner's head, and killed him with a single shot to the temple. It was the shot seen 'round the world and it earned Associated Press photographer Eddie Adams a Pulitzer Prize. Loan turned to Adams as blood gushed from the prisoner's head after he fell to the ground and said, "They killed many of my men—and many of yours."

But it was the ancient capital of Hue that suffered the most. On the first day of the fighting, a Vietnamese schoolteacher opened the door of her family home and found her two brothers in the uniform of the North Vietnamese Army. They burst into the house and asked their grandfather where their uncle was. When the old man said he didn't know, one of the grandsons murdered him. When another relative protested, he, too, was killed. The young teacher fainted, and when she regained consciousness all ten members of the household had been executed.

The North Vietnamese units that captured Hue were accompanied by political commissars. They had clipboards and photographs of government officials to be arrested and executed. They went from house to house in search of their prey, and when the twenty-four-day battle for the city ended, twenty-eight hundred residents of Hue had been executed. The victims included priests, civil servants, teachers, and any men who appeared to be of military age. After regaining control of the city, U.S. Marines found two executed Americans who had had their testicles cut off.

GARY WETZEL

Rank: Private First Class
Unit: 173rd Assault
Helicopter, U.S. Army
Birthplace: South
Milwaukee, Wisconsin

Place: Near Ap Dong An
Date: January 8, 1968

Birthdate: September 29,
1947

"I arrived in Vietnam in October 1966. I came back home in the latter part of August and returned to Vietnam around Thanksgiving 1967. The first couple of months I was in Vietnam I was attached to an ordnance outfit just outside of Vung Tau. We'd load the convoys up with weapons and ammo. It was really easy duty, but I loved flying, so I waited until I was in the Army for a year and a day and signed up for helicopters.

"I was in III Corps just outside of the Iron Triangle at Lai Cay. We'd shoot up to Loc Ninh and Tay Ninh, and over into Cambodia. We'd have one dog tag on our boots, nothing else that said Army. We'd fly in there and do what we had to do, but we weren't supposed to be there.

"If I could get any hours, I'd fly. At one time I had aspirations of being a pilot, but when I lost my arm, that kind of blew that career.

"We were flying Eagle Flights that day which was a group of helicopters with G.I.s on them and we'd fly around like an eagle. We'd look for anything that didn't look right on the ground, swoop down, and let the troops off. They'd go on S and D for a while and we'd pick them up, go back up, and circle around. On this particular day we were the spare helicopter and we were flying with the maintenance helicopter.

"One of the choppers was coming in and the guy behind him got a little too close and blew out his wash. He dropped, but nothing too bad. We picked up the troops and flew down by a place called the French Fort. We landed our choppers—we had ten Slicks and some gunships—and we had some time to kill so we opened up some C-Rats. I split a turkey loaf with my A.C. [aircraft commander] and heated it up with some C-4 [explosives].

"An Australian outfit got shot up pretty good about a mile from us. We got our helicopters cranked up and we took off. We figured it was going to be some shit, a hot LZ. I was talking to some of the troops and said, 'It's not going to be a picnic where we are flying in.'

"The gunships made a gun run first. There was an air strike across the river, wrong area, and we got hit with an R.P.G. It blew out the front of the chopper on Timmy's side. We dropped and came to a skidding halt, and there were all of these gooks shooting at us.

"I had a Thompson on my shoulder and I lifted the door off. I hung on to Timmy [the A.C.] and got him out, and a grenade went off about four feet behind me. It didn't blow my arm off; it just blew everything out. I fell back into the mud—I was all fucked up—and this VC was going to throw another grenade. I had my Thompson and he got the grenade about up to his ear and I got him in the head. He fell back; I blew his people up.

"I looked over to see how bad I was hit. I knew the arm was gone; I knew they couldn't save it. Then I kind of skidded around to the front of the chopper. Timmy's hands were okay, but his legs were chopped meat. I put tourniquets on both his legs.

"The gooks came up and started killing the wounded. I laid on top of my gun and played dead like everybody else. Then one of our guys started shooting at them. They moved around to the side of the helicopter and I figured, 'Fuck it. I'm going so I might as well take a few of them with me.' I skidded around on my belly and they were trying to get my M-60 out of the chopper.

"So I said, 'Hey!' and they looked at me. I blew them away, eight of them.

"I went back by Timmy and he was looking like, Hey, man, this is it. He said, 'Tell Jane I love her.' She was his wife.

"I said, 'Fuck you, tell her yourself. We're going to get out of this.'

"It was about dusk and the tide was coming in and we had to get his head out of the water. Bart and I dragged him across a rice paddy to this dike. That's where they were coming right at me and, I don't know. We got his head up. Bart had numerous wounds in the head and he was all screwed up.

"I have Timmy in my arm and he says, 'Tell Jane I love her.'

" 'We'll get out of this mess.'

"He said, 'No, ah . . .' and he died.

"You don't have time for crying at that moment. I took my arm and tucked it inside of my fatigues so it wouldn't flop around and grabbed my Thompson. 'I'm going to get a few more of the bastards before I go.'

"I got into what I call my John Wayne run and was halfway between the dike and the helicopter when I got hit in the leg. I was on one knee going brrrrp, brrrrp, brrrrp with my Thompson and I passed out. How I got to the helicopter, I don't know.

"The next thing I know I'm in the chopper pulling my sixty up. I had a belt of ammo and I could fire it one-handed. My guns never jammed. I hoped they wouldn't now. I had maybe eight hundred to a thousand rounds. The gooks started to group up and were going to launch a human-wave assault. I just started blowin' the hell out of them. All I had to do was go bang and they were dropping six feet away from me.

"They went back to the tree line, regrouped, and came out again. Bullets were a-flyin', zing, zing, zing. I saw a bunker off to my right about a hundred meters. I watched this black guy charging the bunker and he got cut in half by a fifty. His legs went flying. He was killed outright.

"All of a sudden it dawned on me—'Do I still have my nuts?!' I put the sixty down and grabbed: 'Whew! Still there!' Stupid thoughts.

"I grabbed my sixty and was shooting at the bunker and the bunker was shooting at me. I got off about twenty or thirty rounds and must have gotten lucky and hit a satchel charge. It went up and about thirty of the bastards went flying in the air all over the place. Then they were coming at me again, and I leveled my sixty.

"I started shooting like this, level, and ended up shooting at a twenty-degree angle, bodies were stacking that high. They tried one more time, but with all that was going on—losing their commanders, bodies all over the place—they became disarrayed and went back into the tree line.

"I ran out of ammo, but I still had my forty-five and I got a few of 'em with it. I got one with a knife and I heard these guys yelling, 'Medic!' One medic was shot in the back over by the rice dike and couldn't move, so I was dragging wounded over to him. It was like sliding on ice.

"I tucked the forty-five in my pants and dragged them over. They'd say, 'Thanks a lot, buddy!'

"This went on for about an hour or so, I don't know, and I thought I got ten or fifteen guys over to the medic. I found out later in the hospital that it was over thirty that I dragged in. You don't stop and count at the time you're doing it, because you're busy.

"I figured I had enough spunk in me and I didn't want to die in a lousy rice paddy. So I got one more guy out and just laid there.

"They dropped American troops about a mile away and they worked their way over to us. A lieutenant threw me onto a poncho. I was all screwed up. They brought me to higher ground and shipped me out on one of the first choppers."

Reflections

We came back home and we were the best, damn it, we were the best. You tell that to a lot of World War II vets and it tightens their jaws, but then you say, "But, gentlemen, the reason we are the best is because of our fathers and our forefathers. We all fought for the same flag, so don't associate the warrior with the war. We were in the same fight."

We didn't lose the war. The politicians lost it for us. When we were there, they never kicked our ass. When we left, the North Vietnamese came down because there was no resistance. But they couldn't get past us.

Over in Vietnam in a combat situation it didn't matter —we were brothers. That's a bond that nobody can take away from us. We don't say "fellow veterans," we say, "brothers." That's what it is all about.

Fighting over there and coming back, and sure you are mixed up. One day you're out making a gun run and the next you're back in civilized society. Being immature politically and not being aware of the conditions back here, I was happy the first couple of days with my family and all of that.

Probably the third day, I found myself watching the six o'clock news on television and watching the war. I'd take my dinner in and see what was going on. I couldn't wait to get back. I love my family very much, but there was such a strong bond for my brothers over there, because I knew they were getting their butts shot up. I wanted to be with them. Not for the fighting or the killing, but to be with them in case I could help.

When I got hit over there, I talked to a colonel who said it wasn't so bad losing a limb. He'd lost his leg below the knee, and I accepted that I had lost it. He was in a combat zone and a limb was gone.

So I talked to the surgeon general at the Fitzsimons Hospital outside of Denver. I came hobblin' up with my cane and asked, "How soon before I'm fixed up. I want to go back to my outfit."

He said, "You've seen enough. Two tours is enough."

I said, "No. I've got to get back to my people. I'll be a clerk or a cook, but I've got to get back." I knew if I got back to my outfit, they'd let me fly. They hadn't messed up my trigger fingers.

He said, "No, Gary, you can't. It's better this way."

I said, "Okay, if I'm no goddamn good, get me out of this chicken army." In the latter part of June I got discharged. That was kind of bad because of the Fourth of July. I really had the heebie-jeebies.

Some of my friends thought it was cute to set off firecrackers behind me and my buddy. We were at a beach once and somebody blew a firecracker off behind us and—*whooosh*—we were in the sand. It broke these guys up.

I got up kind of embarrassed like and said, "Hey, if you guys have to set them off, let us know. We don't want to look like a bunch of idiots. You've got to understand where we just came from."

This place I used to hang out in high school was called Betty's Chocolate Shop. It was like Al's on "Happy Days." Back in them days my nickname was Red, and I was kind of like Fonzie. Whatever happened, I'd make it happen.

Coming back after the first tour, I saw how childish these guys were who didn't go. We didn't have anything in common or to talk about except cars—who's got the fastest car, who's got the hottest engine. Goofing off at beer parties and beach parties wasn't fun anymore.

I became more or less of a loner. I wasn't old enough to buy beer, but a couple of places around town knew who I was and let me have a six-pack now and then. I'd get into my car and cruise around sipping beer and listening to "oldies but goodies." I wasn't with a group of people any longer.

Once you've been in 'Nam and close to somebody who dies, you deal with people, but you don't let them get close to you. You build a wall around you with a small door. If you want somebody in, you open the door a little bit. If you don't, you slam it and keep them the hell out.

To this day, I still find I'm that way. "If you let somebody get close to you, you're going to get burned." So you kind of shy away from it. I have seen a lot of guys experience that.

I didn't graduate from high school. At school the dean of boys was poking me in the chest one day, and I said, "Don't do that."

He said, "What are you going to do about it?"

I said, "Just don't," and he kept on and—*boom*—I dropped him.

So I got expelled. My mother and father both served in World War II, and I wasn't doing anything, so why not enlist. At that stage of my life—being a punk and fighting —my first choice was the Marines. I tried to join with my buddy on the Buddy Program. I needed three recommendations; one from the school, but I had punched the dean out, so I went down the street and joined the Army.

I took my basic at Fort Knox and I got my GED. In fact, I got my diploma before the guys graduated in June. A lot of guys in the Army who didn't have a diploma would say, "I'll get it someday, I'll get it someday," but they never did. At least, I went for it and got it.

Two and a half years later, I was invited to speak at a Veterans' Day Banquet. The day before I had been informed that I was being awarded the Congressional Medal of Honor. These two Marine recruiters were still in Milwaukee, and I told them, "See, boys, you passed up quality."

They saluted me and said, "Yes, sir. Yes, sir."

I went to junior college for a while in welding engineering. I was working the third shift and going to school full time during the day with a lot of other vets—Navy guys, Army, and Marines. I'd go to school in the morning, get home at 4 P.M., and try to go to work that night.

At that time I was giving two or three speeches a week and missing on an average of one day of work a week. I'd go to a banquet and get a little shit-faced and call into work and say, "I'm not going to be able to make it in to work."

They'd ask, "What's wrong, Gar?"

"I'm drunk." I couldn't see calling in and saying my kid's got a toothache, or the wife's sick. I had to be honest with me.

They put up with it for about a year and then they asked me to leave. The union didn't want me to leave, but I had to move on to bigger and better things. I left there and went back to construction because I liked being outside. I still do. I can't see punching a clock and getting a gold watch in twenty years. That's not my cup of tea. This is nicer because I can help the vets and be freer.

I'm doing a lot of work with Vietnam veterans now and, well, when I'm with the brothers, I know my back is covered. In Washington two years ago for the Memorial dedication, there were over three hundred thousand Vietnam veterans. *Whoa!*

We were with our own people and our backs were covered, and nobody could take that away from us. The Veterans Administration calls everybody a Vietnam Era vet. Your Era vets are from that era and, fine, they did their thing, but my 'Nam brothers take priority, take precedence, and that's what I deal with.

There is the Vietnam Veterans of America. I'm glad there is an organization for Vietnam vets, but I'm not particularly fond of their leader. In the spring of 1983, he went to Hanoi and placed a wreath on Ho Chi Minh's grave. Within the last couple of months he said that Jane Fonda was one of the heroes of the Vietnam War.

No. That's why I don't associate with the Vietnam Veterans of America. I'll do things for some of the brothers, but not any particular organization.

We are the only veterans so far who have their own memorial attributed to us. The only thing we borrowed was a little piece of real estate from the government. We put on our own parade for us.

You can ride around Washington in a cab and see all of the memorials—the Jefferson Memorial, the Lincoln Memorial, the Marine Memorial. But you can't see our memorial from the road. If you want to see it, you have to get off your fat ass.

I had my doubts when it was built—black marble, below ground level, and all of that. My best friend died in my arm, and I will never, ever have a best friend again. I'll always have good friends.

When I went to the Vietnam Memorial I was afraid to walk on the grass. I walked down to the V, looked at the names, and saw my reflection. "Whoa, how come they're on there and I'm not?" It hits everybody in their own way.

I found my buddy's name, touched it, and, poof, I was on my knees. I paid my tribute to him. He'll always be with me. I'll never forget him.

When we were in Washington for Carter's inauguration, the night before we signed a petition denouncing the free ticket for the guys who went to Canada. I went along with Ford's idea of letting them come back on a conditional amnesty; let them work to get back in, let them pay their dues. Not come back on a free ticket and spit in my face. What does Carter do? "Welcome back. We love you."

I have compassion for human beings, but there are times I have to draw a line. I saw too many friends get hurt, too many friends get killed for what this flag stands for. They went in because America needed them and it was their duty.

One guy came up to me a while back and said that he was sorry, but he had gone to prison instead of going to Vietnam. I told him that he didn't have anything to be sorry about, because he had paid his dues.

When some of them came back from the war, they were

213

Vietnam Veterans Against the War. They were over there and they saw some of the real horrors of war. They expressed their views politically, not condemning the country, but rather the politics.

I don't wear the Medal of Honor for me. I wear it for all of us. I got the DSC when I was in the hospital. I was all screwed up in this bed and some of the guys I saved came over to my bunk with pictures of their wives and said, "Thanks a lot. This is what I've got to go back to."

But once you get the medal, people think you live in this nice little house, with a white picket fence, a couple of kids, a nine-to-five job and go to church on Sunday. It's not that way. People who have received it come from all walks of life and were not all churchgoers, and some drink more than one day a week. We don't blend in the way people want us to. We are individuals.

I looked at it as survival. There were guys in combat who enjoyed the killing. If you get into a combat situation it is a high, but once it is over and you get time to think about it, you can't top it. Nothing in your life can top that high.

Getting married: that was neat. Having my two kids born: that was neat. But nothing could top that high of being in combat and getting out alive. Not the killing.

Like when you are rolling in and you are too high to shoot, but you see the tracers coming at you. "Whoa!" I'd shut my eyes until I pulled the trigger. Or when you are resupplying or picking up the wounded. We saved a lot of lives over there, more than other wars because Vietnam was a helicopter war. That's how people got around.

The only problem was that when you were getting shot at, there was no place to hide.

I slugged a lieutenant once. We were over at Duc Loc, and he would open a can of C-Rats halfway and throw it into the muddy water. About fifteen of the kids would dive for it. They were stumbling around and getting beat up jumping for it.

I said, "Lieutenant, don't do that. These kids have a hard life. Have a little consideration."

I went back to my chopper and he did it again. I looked over and said, "Lieutenant, don't do that, please."

He did it again, and I said, "Come on, lieutenant, please don't do that." He did it again and I told him, "I asked you three times to not do that."

I dropped him and went back to my helicopter, got some C-Rats, and told the kids, "You all get one meal."

The kids were saying, "Number one, G.I., number one, G.I."

The lieutenant was knocked out and when he woke up, he said, "I'll have your ass."

Well, my colonel heard all of this and he said, "You can do that, but I wouldn't recommend it."

He turned out to be a pretty good pilot, but he was just green. He had to get his feet wet like the rest of us.

I'd go to the villages and help the mama-sans and the kids. I kind of miss that, seeing those smiles and the love in their eyes. A lot of them just used the G.I.s, but the majority wasn't like that. You've got your good and your bad just like back here. When I was over there if I could put a smile on somebody's face, it was okay.

You've got to realize where they are coming from. They believe in their Buddha, we believe in our God. In Vietnam when they would launch human-wave attacks and overrun certain outposts, they'd cut off heads, arms, legs. They figured if you were whole when you died, you were going to Number One Land, if you were in pieces, you were going to Number Ten Thou. That's why they eliminated heads and limbs.

It's just that being so young and being exposed to something that traumatic. I still remember the first dead gook I saw over there. When we picked him up in the chopper, all that was left of his head was a little piece of hair and some teeth. The rest was gone.

When we brought him in, his own people wouldn't take him. "Number ten, won't touch."

We hauled in one dead G.I. that day. He was a big guy and had had his head blasted. At least someone had put a towel around his head and what was left of his face.

And when you come back here, people wonder why you've changed, why you're hard. But it's not being hard; it's dealing with things in that light.

A few weeks ago, we had to put my dog who was thirteen and a half years old to sleep. My wife and daughter went along and they wanted me to go into the room and watch Duke get the shot.

I said, "I can't be doing that. Just put him in there." They were going to turn him into ashes and, fine, I'd pick him up the next day, but I don't need to see them put my dog to sleep.

Or if everybody else is cryin' and you aren't, then you ain't got no feelings. If we all cried, we'd never get the job done.

I don't have to show a tear to prove that I care. They wonder why I have to be so goddamn hard at times. It's not being hard; it's just the way it is.

When they play taps, I get misty eyed, but it took years to get to that stage.

When I got hit, one of the guys I used to hang around with brought the telegram at midnight. He said, "Don't worry, Mrs. Wetzel, he ain't dead yet."

I had told them, "Don't send anything home. Wait 'till I get over it." But they did it anyway, and it pissed me off.

When my mom came down to see me, wow, that was a trip.

My wife, Bonnie, was a senior in high school and her graduation present was to fly down to the hospital to see me. I wasn't ready for anybody—132 pounds soaking wet, arm gone, cheeks sucked in.

It was on a Sunday, the day before Valentine's Day. I was getting my bandages changed and a medic came in and said, "Hey, a chick with dark hair wants to see you."

Being a little cocky, I said, "Bring her in."

They finished changing my bandages and put my jammies back on, but I didn't have a top and my ribs were sticking out. I took a couple of steps with my cane and I looked up: There she was.

I fell back into my room and my buddies came running over and said, "What's wrong, what's wrong?"

I said, "Is there a chick out there with dark hair?"

They said, "Yeah."

I said, "Aw hell, get me a top, do something, help me."

I figured sooner or later I'd have to face her, so I hobbled up to her with my cane and gave her a little kiss on the cheek. I said, to her, "Just help me to my bed."

I was hobbling and she was going to guide me by my left arm, but she backed off. She didn't think I saw it, but I saw it.

I got back to my bunk. It was in the corner 'cause I wanted to be shut off from the world. We chatted for about twenty minutes and she looked at me like a pitiful piece of crap. I was fairly athletic when I went in and now I'm garbage. She said, "Betty's here"—her sister.

I said, "Swell, let's go down and see sis, but you'll have to push me in the wheelchair because I can't hoof it that far."

We got them checked in to the billeting and I told them that I'd meet them Monday in the commissary for coffee and a sandwich. That night I didn't sleep at all because I knew they were there.

The next morning I'm walking—I ain't bothering nobody—and I look up and who's there—my mother. I started to fall back and my buddy stuck the wheelchair out and I fell right into it. She came up and started hugging me and kissing me, "Oh, my son, my son!"

I said, "Aw, come on, Ma, it ain't that bad." Macho, got to be tough in front of the guys. But it was a real kick in the teeth.

When I got there, maybe five or six days before, Timmy's parents called me. He was the only son—father was a doctor and mother a nurse. Grandma was there, too, and I said, "Is Jane there?"

She said yes and I said, "Jane, I've got to do this."—I'm bawling, the tears are running down—"I was there when Timmy went on and I'm supposed to give you a message."

"What is it?"

I'm bawling—okay, Gary, get it out, "I'm supposed to tell you he loved you."

Then we were all crying.

FREDERICK EDGAR FERGUSON

Rank: Chief Warrant Officer   **Place:** Hue
Unit: Company C, 227th   **Date:** January 31, 1968
Aviation Battalion, First
Cavalry Division
(Airmobile) U.S. Army
Birthplace: Pilot Point,   **Birthdate:** August 18, 1939
Texas

"It was a mess.

"We had been briefed for months, 'There is something up, there is something up. Be ready for it.' We got to the point of saying, 'Oh yeah, There Is Something Up—Briefing Number Three.' We were hearing the same old thing over and over, but sure enough, something was up.

"I was working with the First CAV Division in I Corps

at LZ Baldy just a little north of Chu Lai. Most of the division was in II Corps and we moved into southern I Corps into the Que Son Valley. We worked out of Baldy but parked our airplanes at Chu Lai. It was only a fifteen-minute flight.

"We got the word that the whole division was going to move north to just south of the DMZ. We were moving to a place called LZ Evans, about five minutes at ninety knots just south of Dong Ha.

"We were living at a CB [construction battalion] we called Sandbag. We were parking on a baseball field about five minutes from the Hue-Phu Bai airstrip between the Citadel in Hue and the strip near the hills.

"But we were staying with the CBs and it is interesting because they wouldn't let us warrant officers eat in the officers' mess. They didn't consider us as officers.

"They did let us into their officers' club, but they wanted us to leave our guns at home, but we didn't go anywhere without our guns. They played to the tune of a different drummer than what the CAV did. Let's face it; we were used to being in the bush all of the time. We acted that way anyhow.

"We operated our missions out of there—Ash and Trash, Resupply, Combat Assaults. All of the things a combat pilot in the helicopter business does. I guess we'd been there a couple of weeks—it's been over fifteen years and the time frame is beginning to slip away from me. I'm not sure of the time, but I went on R & R to Australia and came back. I remember we did Christmas at Chu Lai so it couldn't have been more than a couple weeks.

"We had been getting a little more indirect fire than what we had been accustomed to and, of course, the CBs blamed it on us. The fact that the helicopters were parked on their ball field was drawing fire.

"We had learned through the process of being shot at that when the stuff starts falling, you don't get up and run. You wait a second and say, 'Okay, let's see what we've got here.' As long as you stay flat on the ground, the chances are you aren't going to get hit unless one lands right on top of you.

"You have a cone of fire that goes up, so if you're up and running around, you have a better chance of getting hit even if you are running to a bunker. But you don't get up and split. That's stuff you learn after being shot at a while.

"One night it was really getting heavy—mortars, rockets landing on us. We were a little afraid they were going to blow up the helicopters. What we decided to do was to get the heck out of there. Little did we know the firing was going on everywhere and there wasn't anyplace to go.

"Everybody slipped down to the ball field and cranked them up—no lights so we wouldn't create a target—and took off. We didn't want to lose our helicopters because that's the way the CAV does business. If we run out of helicopters, then the grunts out there don't have anybody to bring them food or ammunition and they are in deep *kimshi*.

"So somebody said, 'Let's go up north and land at Evans.' We headed up that way but Evans was under attack and fogged in.

" 'Let's go look over at the Citadel in Hue. They have an airstrip there. Let's take a look at that.' Well, that son-of-a-gun was under attack.

" 'Well, let's go back down to Hue-Phu Bai [air strip].' We only have two hours of fuel and were up there puttering around and beginning to get low on fuel. We're getting a bit concerned about where the hell we are going to land.

"We raised Hue-Phu Bai on the radio and the operator said he didn't think it was a good idea to land there because they were under attack. In fact, his tower was on fire and he was leaving. So we heard the last from this guy for a while.

"We discussed it up there in the airplanes—there were about twelve of us. We're saying, 'Hey, my twenty-minute light is coming on and I'm down to three hundred pounds of fuel.' We've got to go somewhere pretty quick. We are going to land somewhere either under power or when the engines stop from fuel starvation, but we are going to land sooner or later.

"We landed inside the barbed wire in a rice-paddy area just as the tower west of the main runway fell over. We scattered the helicopters out, turned them off, and got away from them. We just waited because they were just paperweights until we could get some more fuel. We didn't figure the Marines at Hue-Phu Bai were going to come out at that particular time to refuel us.

"As morning came it was obvious a lot of stuff was going on, but the enemy didn't launch a ground attack at Hue-Phu Bai. Had they done that, they probably could have had the damn place and us. They didn't. They didn't launch one at the CB camp either.

"As daylight came the rocketing stopped, and we refueled and went back to Sandbag to get our mission for the day. At that point, we didn't have any conception about what had happened. We knew it was pretty widespread and a lot of stuff was going on, because we were detached from everybody else.

"My mission was to take a group of engineers south to where the enemy had cut the highway, leave them, and come back. On the way back, we began picking up radio traffic about one of our airplanes that had gone down. It was from my company, one of our planes and they were down inside of Hue. Five planes had gone in to pick them up but were driven off by the intense fire.

"I couldn't understand why they were receiving such intense fire inside of Hue, a place we believed was secure. As we were coming up, another crashed. That's when we got the word that Hue had fallen and was in the hands of the enemy. After other planes had been driven off by the intense fire, we got the word from Division to stay away from Hue. 'The antiaircraft fire is too hot. Don't go near the darn place.'

"We knew that some of our people were still alive in there some place because they were talking on the radio after taking refuge in the South Vietnamese compound. Evidently, the NVA had decided not to put forth the effort to get them. They were being mortared but that was about it.

"I said, 'Hey, I think we ought to try and get those guys out 'cause if you and I were in there, we'd want them to come after us. What do you think?'

"My copilot, Buck Anderson from South Carolina, said he was willing. My crew chief and gunner also said they'd go. So I said, 'Tell you what let's do—you guys get the airplane ready, strip her down. We don't want to take anything we don't need. Ammunition only. Everything else comes out.'

"Meanwhile, I was able to find three gunship crews that were flyable, had bullets, and were willing to cover us on the way in and, hopefully, on the way out. We sat down and hashed it out between us and then we started out.

"I called the guys in the compound on the radio and told them I was on my way in. However, they were being mortared and radioed back, 'Don't come in now. We are under a mortar attack. We'll call you when it quits.'

"So, we knew they were getting mortared, but we didn't know how many tubes were firing at them. Depending on the trajectory that they were dropping them in, we figured we would have between thirty and forty-five seconds at most after it, once it left the tube.

"We were talking in the airplane and I said, 'Once they figure out what we are up to, they are going to start dropping rounds down their tubes. They've already got it sighted so we are only going to have fifteen or twenty seconds on the ground loading time before the first rounds start to hit.

" 'So we are really going to have to hustle. Pull them [the five downed soldiers] in, drag them in, but, whatever you do, don't get out of the airplane. Once it starts hitting, I've got to go. If one of those things hit us, we're dead meat, too.'

"The radio guy in the compound called and said he

hadn't had any rounds for a few minutes, so we started in. I told the gunships I was going to low-level down the Perfume River, turn right into the compound, and pick these folks up. They said, 'That's cool.'

"If I had to go in, I wasn't going to put it into a building. I could hit the water and maybe survive the crash, but not nosing right into a building. That was the primary reason we went down the Perfume River.

"When we started down, we began taking very heavy fire—automatic weapons fire, 12.7s, big-caliber machine guns; they were just eating us up. But with three gunships covering me, they had four ships to shoot at instead of just one. Also, the gunships were shooting back which helped. Of course, our door gunners were doing their thing. I think that—the four of us together and our shooting back—is the only reason we were able to get in and get out, although we did take a lot of hits.

"God, Buddha, or Whatever was with us. The enemy didn't hit anything critical. The airplane shuddered and shook a lot, but she kept going. The gunners were having a field day. The enemy was walking down the street. There were bad guys everywhere. The gunships were hosing them down with mini-guns and firing rockets into them.

"I remember looking out of the corner of my eye as we went past the Citadel and seeing the VC flag—the blue-and-red with the yellow star in the middle—flying on the flagpole inside the Citadel. My gunner on that side—a guy named Ford who we called Edsel—said, 'Let's stop and get the flag on the way out.'

"I laughed and said, 'Yeah, sure, you are bad, but come on. Get serious.'

"I was flying the airplane and concentrating on making the approach and Buck was directing our gunners and talking to the other gunships about targets. Of course, there was no shortage of targets. 'Point it and shoot it. You are going to hit something.' They were in buildings, on boats, just all over the place.

"We called them on the radio and said we were coming

in. 'We are two minutes out.' They were ready to load because they also knew that the mortars would be coming in as soon as we touched down. There had been nine people on board the helicopter when it crashed. Five were still alive, but they had all been wounded.

"I just kept my tunnel vision on the place we were going.

"There was a lot of dust in there and a big flagpole in the middle with a building off to the right. There wasn't that much room [about two feet] between the rotor blade and the flagpole and the rotor blade and the house.

"How I got that airplane between that flagpole and that building with all that dust without crashing is beyond me. I'm not exactly sure how I pulled that one off. But you don't look a gift horse in the mouth. It shouldn't have worked. I'm a pretty good helicopter pilot, but there are limits.

"I remember one guy in the compound, a lieutenant colonel. All he had on was his Jockey shorts and bandages. He was just covered with battle bandages, almost like he was wearing a white suit. Really hit with shrapnel.

"He was the one flying the airplane when it went down. He made a pretty good auto-rotation landing. As he was coming in the helicopter was gone, but nobody on board was injured, but when they hit the ground, they were nailed with a B-40 rocket and machine-gun fire.

"We landed and started loading the guys into the helicopter, dragging them in. A mortar round went off behind the airplane, and Buck said, 'Jesus Christ!'—it was almost like a prayer—'Let's get out of here!'

"I yelled, 'Is everybody on?'

"They said, 'Everybody's on.'

"While we were in the compound, there was a wall that kept us from taking any direct small-arms fire, only mortar fire. But I had to pick this baby straight up between the pole and the building.

"My plan was to take out of Hue as fast as I could in the same direction I had landed, just keep going on out. I picked her up in a hover just above the wall and another mortar round went off—they were really coming in now. It picked my tail up and swung me around 180 degrees.

"Now I'm sitting up there above the wall pointed in the wrong direction taking small-arms fire. I don't know what kind of helicopter business you've been in, but it takes a few seconds to turn around. I'm sitting there with my nose down in a take-off posture headed in the wrong direction, and the gunships are expecting me to go out in the other direction. That's what we had briefed on.

"But because of the mess I was in, I didn't want to wait and go the other way, so I just put the nose down, applied all the power I could, and headed out the way I had come in.

"I called the other gunships on the radio—praying it was still working; it was—and explained that I was headed in the opposite direction, and that I'd be mighty obliged if they could come back and cover me. It really didn't matter because I was going that way regardless, but they did.

"At this particular point they were out of rockets, out of machine-gun ammunition, and about the only thing they were doing was to help take off some of the fire. The pilots were shooting out their windows with their thirty-eights— that's all they had left. While we were on the ground inside the compound loading, we—the pilots, Buck, and I—gave the crew chief and gunner our thirty-eights because they were out of machine-gun ammunition too.

"I said, 'Here, shoot this. I can't shoot it 'cause I'm flying the aircraft. Do something with it. Make noise if nothing else. It probably won't do any good, but it can't hurt.' So, they were leaning out their doors going pow, pow, pow with our thirty-eights. It was better than nothing.

"Because there were four aircraft coming out together, it divided the enemy's attention somewhat. I think that is why we got out alive.

"All four aircraft were damaged beyond feasible repair and had to be evacuated back to the States. In fact, I think two of the gunships were destroyed in place. The three had all crashed on the way back to Hue-Phu Bai.

"The helicopters were a mess. Mine was the only one to make it in to Hue-Phu Bai. Had it not been that I had five wounded people on board, I'd have probably put mine down sooner than I did.

"The transmission was gone, zero oil pressure. It was stinking, you could smell it. It was hotter than hell in the back. The airplane was shaking so bad you couldn't read the instrument panel, but it was still flying. So I pushed it into the Hue-Phu Bai air strip and when I cleared the fence, I just slid it onto the sand out front. If that barbed-wire fence had been another strand higher, I don't think I'd have made it over.

"It was a hairy mission, but we were all alive. There was a lot of, 'Oh boy! You guys did great.' A lot of slapping each other on the back. You know how it is when you have a real high like that. Everybody is real happy and excited.

"It took us a day to come down, but we were back in the war the next day."

Reflections

It was a thing we did, and now we go on with our lives. It is the same with any war. It is over and I want it to be over.

It seems that every time they publish something about Vietnam veterans it is the bad stuff. That incident in California where that guy went into [a fast-food restaurant] and killed all of those people. The first thing that came to me was, "Please, don't let him be a Vietnam veteran."

You don't hear about the Jim Taylors or the Leo Thorsnesses or the good things that came out of the war—if you can say that anything good comes out of a war: the acts of valor and unselfishness.

When I'm talking to reporters, I sometimes accuse them of biased reporting. They jump up and say, "Biased reporting? What do you mean?" I'll mention some names—"Did you ever hear of Pat Brady or Mike Novosel," and four or five other Medal of Honor recipients out of Vietnam.

The reporters say, "No, never heard of them."

Then I'll ask, "Did you ever hear of William Calley?"

They say, "Oh, yeah, yeah."

I say, "I rest my case."

I remember on the plane going over to Vietnam. There was a lot of enthusiasm—*"Da da ta da ta da, charge!"* Coming back was a whole different airplane. It was quiet, subdued, almost somber.

We flew out of Cam Ran Bay and as the plane was flying out, I was thinking as I watched the shoreline, "We're out of thirty-seven-millimeter range, we're out of fifty-seven-millimeter range, we're out of SAM range."

Then it was, "Out of range. Going home."

We landed at McCoy Air Force Base in Seattle. We got off the plane and had to go through customs. No biggie. I had packed everything away except for my AWOL bag. In it I had my personal things and my Silver Star, Bronze Star, and Air Medal.

The medal cases were opened and the cases' cloth lining peeled back. Then it was all shoved over to the other side of the table. The medals were not put back or anything. My stuff was just lying there in pieces. I guess they were looking for dope or something.

When I was there, nobody smoked dope that I was aware of. We were all very matter-of-fact about what we were doing. We were there to win this thing, giving it our best shot. There just wasn't any of that kind of thing.

The maintenance guys and everybody else—we were the First CAV, and we were damned sure going to give it our all.

The thing about Tet was that the press turned the thing into a major defeat. The enemy had given us everything they had, and we knocked the living crap out of them. Now how in the hell the press turned that into a goddamn defeat is what I want to know.

Take Bastogne in World War II for instance. The 101st Airborne is surrounded, "Nuts!" Rah-Rah. Patton came charging in with the Third Army and knocked the hell out of the Krauts. We turned it into a great victory.

It was the same thing with the Tet Offensive. They came in, got a little foothold, and we knocked the el toro poo poo out of those people. We killed so many bad guys, it cost them a lot of folks. It was a major victory, but was turned into a defeat.

I don't understand that.

10

• In Saigon at 3 A.M. on February 1, 1968, twenty-three guerrillas from the Vietcong C-10 Sapper Battalion attacked and entered the American Embassy. Shortly before noon all of the VC had either been killed or captured and the Marine embassy guards raised the Stars and Stripes, five hours later than normal.

• In the streets of Saigon, the VC ran from house to house shouting, "We have come to liberate Saigon." They beheaded the commander of a South Vietnamese training school in his home, blew up his wife and six children with hand grenades, and executed any civilians caught with South Vietnamese flags in their possession.

• In Hue after the twenty-four days of bitter house-to-house fighting, two divisions of American and South Vietnamese Marines and soldiers retook the city. A U.S. commander in Hue said, "Seoul [during the Korean War] was tough, but this—well, it's something else." The American losses were put at 142 Marines killed in action, the South Vietnamese listed 384 combat deaths, and the North Vietnamese and Vietcong lost over 8,000 men KIAs in their effort to liberate the city.

In Saigon after the fighting had ended, General Westmoreland told his troops, "You have destroyed more of the enemy in seven days than the U.S. has lost in seven years." The total number of enemy killed during the country-wide assault was put at thirty-one thousand, or fourteen thousand more than the number of Americans killed since 1961.

An official in Washington said at the time, "This is the Vietcong's Bay of Pigs. The Vietnamese people did not arise and overthrow their government as Hanoi predicted."

But somehow, the Americans and South Vietnamese were robbed of the victory. *Time* called it a "humiliating surprise." North Vietnam's defense minister Vo Nguyen Giap was labeled "brilliant" while General Westmoreland was being depicted as embattled and beleaguered.

Columnist Clayton Fritchey, a former aide to Gen. George Marshall wrote, "It is time to change generals as Lincoln did when he replaced McClellan with Grant to break the Civil War stalemate. It is time to send a commander to Vietnam who is capable of plotting a winning strategy or, if there is no such thing, who is capable of telling the President so."

Time reported,

In less strident tones, others recalled that when Westmoreland returned to Washington last fall he had painted a sanguine picture of the war and stated that it was even conceivable that the U.S. could begin a staged withdrawal from South Vietnam "within two or three years." Now, in the light of the shattering events of the past two weeks, his critics concluded that Westmoreland had either consciously misled the public or, equally unforgivable, had completely misjudged the outlook on the battlefield. For the first time since he took command in South Vietnam three and a half years ago, Westmoreland is being compared by some to Gen. Henri Navarre, the aggressive French commander whose miscalculation of enemy capabilities was responsible for his country's final defeat in Indochina fourteen years ago.

This comparison to the French defeat at Dien Bien Phu was incredible for the American service personnel who had been involved in the bitter fighting. They had fought so bravely and suffered so much, only to come home and be told that they had been defeated or be ignored altogether. It added a new dimension to psychological warfare.

At this time the *New York Times* reported that there was a contingency plan to send over two hundred thousand more troops into Vietnam. The military explained that the plan was only to be initiated if an emergency arose that endangered the American personnel already in Vietnam. Nevertheless, the plan was attacked as a further example of American escalation. As a result, it was quietly shelved by the Pentagon. There would be no more plans to increase the troop levels in Vietnam, contingency or otherwise.

After the Tet Offensive the Americans were no longer fighting their way into Vietnam; they were fighting their way out. The American public discovered, though, that it was much easier going in than it would be coming out. It took less than three years from the landing of the Marines at Da Nang to get into Vietnam; it would take twice as long to get out.

There would be more suffering, more dying, and more brave men, but the perception of the war and the warriors would change after Tet. They would no longer be fighting for freedom or democracy or other noble causes. Now, and for the next seven years, the policy makers would tell the country that America was fighting for "peace with honor."

But the soldiers, sailors, Coast Guardsmen, and Marines knew differently. They were fighting for the same thing that all warriors fight for. As Ernie Pyle said during World War II: "They were fighting for, well, at least for each other."

☆ ☆

After the war had ended, many people tried to forget the turmoil of the sixties. Gen. William Westmoreland said, "Out of this war are going to come some of the finest people this country has ever known." But some Americans choose to forget the deeds of these men and women.

Not all, though.

Years after the war had ended, Jim Taylor was driving on a California highway in his pickup, which bore newly issued Medal of Honor license plates, when he was pulled over by the flashing red lights of a patrol car. As the patrolman got out of his vehicle, Jim nervously thought, I wonder what I did wrong.

"I watched on television," the patrolman said after Jim had rolled down his window, "when the governor presented those license plates to you men. It made me feel good to see you younger fellows standing up there alongside the other veterans. I don't care what anybody else says, I'm proud of what you guys did in Vietnam. I just thought you ought to know."

Later Jim told another Vietnam veteran, "That made me feel good, real good."

History of the Medal of Honor

F. E. Ferguson

Steeped in controversy at its inception, the Medal of Honor has evolved into our nation's most respected award for valor. From the beginning the United States has recognized its fighting men's deeds of distinction with various medals. In the two hundred years since our nation's birth, a complex system of medals has developed into a "Pyramid of Honor."

The practice of awarding medals for deeds of distinction began in ancient times. One of the first, and longest lasting, forms of award was the laurel wreath, bestowed by the Greeks on citizens who were outstanding. In the late Roman era rulers adopted the laurel wreath, and when their profiles appeared on coins, it was with the wreath upon their heads. "Medals developed as more or less special kinds of coins, and it is not startling that the laurel wreath is part of the Medal of Honor today."[1] When the Roman Empire fell apart and feudalism replaced it, the

> feudal system was accompanied by a growth of "rewards" in the form of titles and prerogatives. . . . Feudalism died a natural death. . . . But the ancient system of "decorations for the aristocracy only" continued.[2]

Later, Napoleon Bonaparte "originated a decoration that could be worn by anyone, regardless of rank or social background . . . the decoration of the Legion d'Honneur."[3] He used it skillfully to bolster his empire. The Legion d'Honneur was the spearhead of the system he so shrewdly used to instill loyalty in the nation he led.

Before Napoleon died he had almost all of the Christian world united in competition against him. And the other states of Europe were forced to the realization that in order to fight him—or a revival of his ideas after his death—they would have to be as efficient as he was in everything . . . they adopted systems of using medals for bravery which could be won by anyone worthy of them.[4]

Thus there arose the "Russian Cross of St. George, the Iron Cross of Germany, and the English decoration of the Victoria Cross."[5]

The first of the American forerunners to the Medal of Honor was given to George Washington, "by a resolution passed by the Continental Congress and approved on March 25, 1776."[6] Congress awarded the second in 1777, to "General Horatio Gates for the defeat of the British . . . at Saratoga."[7] The third went to Henry Lee in 1779, "in recognition of his attack upon the British at Paulus Hook, . . . during which he captured 160 of the enemy without sustaining any loss to his own forces."[8]

The next three special awards issued by the United States were the "André" medals, given in 1780 to the three enlisted men who captured the British intelligence major, John André, as he was en route from West Point to New York, wearing civilian clothes, after having conspired with Benedict Arnold.[9]

In 1782, George Washington created a decoration for "singularly meritorious action," known as the Purple Heart. He awarded it to three men "in 1783. The records show no others."[10]

From 1783 to 1847 when the demands of the Mexican War brought the soldier to public attention again, the United States government awarded no decorations. It was at this time that Congress authorized the "Certificate of Merit" for soldiers. The award did not provide for a medal, but only for a certificate—a document. "Congress provided that the holders of the certificate who were still in the service should have extra pay of two dollars a month; but money alone could not honor the serviceman for his deed."[11]

There was also the "brevet" system of promotion, which provided that a serviceman "mentioned for gallantry in dispatches could be granted a 'brevet rank' higher than that of his actual rank, and be entitled to wear the insignia which went with the brevet."[12] But this system suffered greatly from political abuse and much of its honor grew meaningless.

In the winter of 1861, following the beginning of the Civil War, there was much thought in Washington about honoring the deeds of American soldiers who were distinguishing themselves in battle. Congress seemed unaware that George Washington had already established the Purple Heart to honor the gallant deeds of all brave American fighting men. Thus in December 1861, Congress passed a bill which created the Navy Medal of Honor for enlisted men of the Navy and Marine Corps. The bill authorized the preparation of two hundred medals.

> ... with suitable emblematic devices, which shall be bestowed upon such petty officers, seamen, landsmen, and marines as shall most distinguish themselves by their gallantry in action and other seamanlike qualities during the present war.[13]

The Navy Medal of Honor became the first decoration formally authorized by the American government to be worn as a badge of honor.

Two months later, in February 1862, Congress began

action to create an Army medal. It provided for awards to enlisted men of the Army and Volunteer Forces who distinguished themselves by their gallantry in action and other soldierlike qualities. Congress approved this action in July 1862 and amended it to include officers in March 1863. Now the Medal of Honor became an American reality.

The first Medals of Honor awarded were Army medals issued . . . to six soldiers on March 25, 1863. . . . The recipients were six survivors of the Andrews Raid, a group of twenty-one volunteers led by a mysterious spy calling himself James J. Andrews, who in April of 1862 penetrated nearly two hundred miles south into Confederate territory and captured a railroad train at Big Shanty, Georgia. In the wild railroad chase which followed, they attempted to destroy bridges and tracks between Atlanta and Chattanooga. When their fuel ran out, they had to forsake their train and take to the woods. All were captured by Confederate cavalry. Seven, including James J. Andrews, were executed. The remaining fourteen stayed in a Confederate prison until October 1862, when eight escaped. The six remaining in prison were paroled on March 17, 1863, and made their way to Washington. These six were the ones who got the first Army Medals. Nineteen of the raiders ultimately received Medals. James J. Andrews, the civilian leader, never won the award.[14]

Just nine days later, "on April 3, 1863, the first Navy Medals of Honor were awarded to a number of sailors taking part in the attacks on Forts Jackson, Fisher and St. Philip on April 24, 1862."[15]

Following the award of the first medals, Americans became very much aware of them. Many were given not for acts of extreme gallantry or even to fighting men; all one had to do was ask, and a medal was almost assured. Award, after award, after award of the Medal of Honor made it seem a token or war souvenir. Abuses of the medal were common; for example, President Lincoln authorized the award of the medal to members of an entire regiment as a reward for reenlisting. These medals were later reconsidered and stricken from the record.

Concern developed, and in 1890, a group of former Medal of Honor winners interested in perpetuating the ideals of the medal, organized the Medal of Honor Legion. Their principal objective was to obtain legislation from Congress that would give the Medal of Honor the same position which similar medals of other countries occupy.

In 1904, Congress passed legislation calling for official documents describing the deed involved to accompany claims for the Medal of Honor. This act of Congress also changed the design of the medal, as certain veterans' organizations had imitated the original design approved in May 1862. The medallion, a five-pointed star, was done in

> . . . bas-relief, on the star, the Union held a shield in her right hand against an attacker, who crouched on the left, holding forked-tongued serpents which struck at the shield. In the left hand of the Union was held the fasces, the ancient Roman symbol of unified authority, an axe bound in staves of wood. . . . The thirty-four stars which encircle these figures represent the number of states at the time the Medal was designed. The reverse of the Medal bore a blank for the name of the winner and the date and place of his deed. . . . The only difference between the Army Medal and that of the Navy was that the Army Medal, instead of being attached to its ribbon by an anchor, was attached by means of the American Eagle symbol, standing on crossed cannon and cannon balls. . . . The Medal was designed by Christian Schussel.[16]

Because the original design had been copied, the Medal of Honor was redesigned by Major General George L. Gillespie in 1904. General Gillespie patented the design and then transferred the patent to the Secretary of War and his successors, so that further imitations of the award could be prohibited by law.[17]

Currently, the Army Medal of Honor is a

> . . . gold-finished star, its five points tipped by trefoils, superimposed on a laurel wreath of green enamel. In each point of the star is a green enamel oak leaf. The medallion in the center bears the head of the goddess Minerva, emblem of righteous war and wisdom, encircled by the words United States of America. On the reverse, above the space for the recipient's name, is the inscription "The Congress to." The medal is suspended from a horizontal bar bearing the word Valor; above it is an American eagle, wings spread, grasping laurel leaves in one claw and arrows in the other.[18]

The present Navy Medal of Honor uses Schussel's design. On the reverse, above the space for the recipient's name, is the inscription "Personal Valor." The medal hangs "from the flukes of an anchor, fouled by a cable; the anchor is attached by a ring at the top to an open clasp of fasces, with a five-pointed star at the center."[19] The medal is extended from a light blue pad studded with thirteen stars, which is attached to a light blue cravat. The pad on the Navy Medal of Honor is square or rectangular while the Army one is octagonal.

In 1905, Congress authorized a medal to be worn by all holders of the Certificate of Merit. However, in 1918 a special act of Congress discontinued the Certificate of Merit Medal and replaced it with a new medal: the Distinguished Service Cross.

At different times Congress established boards of review to investigate not only the individual acts, but the whole policy involved in the award of the Medal of Honor. One such board, established in 1916, provided that "all of the 2,625 Medals of Honor that had been awarded up to that time were reconsidered. By February 15, 1917, 911 names were stricken from the list."[20] Eight hundred sixty-four of the stricken names were those of the members of the Twenty-seventh Marine Volunteer Infantry which had been awarded the medal for reenlisting. Among the others who lost their medals were William F. Cody (Buffalo Bill) and Dr. Mary Walker, the only woman ever to receive the Medal of Honor.[21] (In 1977, Dr. Mary Walker's medal was again reconsidered and her name was restored to the list of those having received the Army Medal of Honor.[22])

Finally, in 1918, Congress decided to clear away any inconsistencies of previous legislation regarding the Medal of Honor and made a set of perfectly clear rules for its award. The law passed in July 1918 stated as follows:

> . . . the provisions of existing law relating to award of Medals of Honor . . . are amended so that the President is authorized to present in the name of Congress, a medal of honor only to each person who, while an officer or enlisted man of the Army, shall hereafter, in action involving actual conflict with an enemy, distinguish himself by gallantry and intrepidity at the risk of his life above and beyond the call of duty.[23]

It also created the Distinguished Service Cross, the Distinguished Service Medal, and the Silver Star Medal. For the first time in American history, it was established by law that there were degrees of service to the country, each worthy of recognition, but only one which could be given supreme recognition. The building of the "Pyramid of Honor" had begun.

In August 1956, Congress enacted legislation to create the Air Force Medal of Honor and provide for its award to members of the Air Force. However, it was not until 1963 that regulations for the awarding of the Navy Medal of Honor were amended to prevent award of the medal for deeds done "in line of Profession," but not necessarily in actual conflict with an enemy. An act of Congress in July 1963 clarified the criteria for awarding of the medal for all of the service branches, stating that award of the medal was "for service 'in military operations involving conflict with an opposing foreign force' or for such service with friendly forces engaged in armed conflict."[24]

Today our "Pyramid of Honor," the system of individual decorations in order of precedence is as follows: the Medal of Honor; Army Distinguished Service Cross, Air Force Cross, Navy Cross (these three equal in value); Defense Distinguished Service Medal; Distinguished Service Medal; Silver Star Medal; Defense Superior Service Medal; Legion of Merit; Distinguished Flying Cross; Soldier's Medal, Navy and Marine Corps Medal, Coast Guard Medal, Airman's Medal (equal in value); Bronze Star Medal; Meritorious Service Medal; Air Medal; Joint Service Commendation Medal; individual service Commendation Medals; and Purple Heart. These decorations are followed by United States Unit Citations, U.S. Service Awards, Foreign Decorations, Foreign Unit Citations and Non-United States or Service Awards of Foreign Countries, in that order of precedence.[25]

Nowadays, we think of the award of the Medal of Honor in terms of a colorful military pageant or a solemn White House ceremony. But for many years the presentation involved little or no pomp and ceremony. Often the local mail carrier presented the medal in the form of a registered parcel.

This rather indifferent attitude regarding presentation of the medal came to a halt in 1905, when President Theodore Roosevelt signed an executive order outlining basic policy still in use. The order provided that the recipient would, when possible, be ordered to Washington, D.C., and the presentation would be made by the president as commander-in-chief, or by a representative designated by the president. If it should be impractical for the recipient to come to Washington, the order provided, the chief of staff would prescribe the time and place of the ceremony in each case.[26] President Roosevelt presented the first medal at the White House on "January 10, 1906, . . . to one of his 'old boys'—Assistant Surgeon James Robb Church, who had served in Teddy's famous First U.S. Volunteer Cavalry."[27]

Legislation and regulations currently allow no margin

of doubt or error when judging whether a man is entitled to the Medal of Honor. The deed must be

> ... proved by incontestable evidence of at least two eye-witnesses; it must be so outstanding that it clearly distinguished his gallantry beyond the call of duty from lesser forms of bravery; it must involve the risk of his life; it must be the type of deed which, if he had not done it, would not subject him to any justified criticism.[28]

A recommendation for the Army or Air Force Medal of Honor must be made within two years of the date of the deed and award of the medal must be made within three years of the date of the deed. A recommendation for the Navy (Marine and Coast Guard) Medal of Honor must be made within three years from the date of the deed upon which it depends and award of the medal must be within five years after the date of the deed.[29]

Along with the great honor receipt of the medal conveys, there are certain small benefits. A medal holder may, when space is available, obtain free military transportation. A veteran who has been awarded the medal for combat is eligible for additional pay of two hundred dollars per month tax free from the Veterans Administration for the rest of his life. In addition, the children of Medal of Honor recipients are eligible to enter any of the U.S. military academies on a nonquota basis.

Since the inception of the Medal of Honor during the Civil War, a total of 3,408 medals have been awarded. The Army, simply because of the greater numbers it normally has engaged in time of war, has been and continues to be the most important custodian of the Medal of Honor. This is shown by the following count of the numbers of medals awarded by the services, from March 1863, to the most recent award in January 1978: Army, 2,355; Navy, 744; Marine Corps, 292; Air Force, 16 (The Air Force was part of the Army from 1907 to 1947, during which time it received 43 Medals of Honor. These are included in the Army total.); and Coast Guard, 1. A great many of those medals have been awarded posthumously and, as of 1978, there are only two hundred seventy-nine living recipients of the Medal of Honor.[30]

In summary, it may be said that no other U.S. medal was born of such imprecise legislation or has suffered so much administrative abuse. Yet it has triumphed over all obstacles to become an object of awe and veneration unmatched in our nation's history, as amplified in the following:

While observing the award of the Medal of Honor to a soldier at Casablanca in 1943, General George S. Patton said, "I'd give my immortal soul for that decoration!" Apparently the devil was not aroused by Patton's Faustian invitation, for although Patton fought well and won many military honors for his display of courage and gallantry during two of America's wars, the Medal of Honor was not one of them.[31]

President Harry Truman had served as a captain of field artillery in World War I and well understood the meaning and value of the Medal of Honor. He is reported to have often said that of all his presidential duties, "awarding the Medal of Honor was the one from which he derived the greatest pleasure."[32]

At one time it was suggested that the medal be awarded to General of the Army Dwight D. Eisenhower in recognition of his leadership during the European campaigns of World War II, but when "Ike" learned of it, he refused to consider the idea. Many years later, Eisenhower told a young war hero upon whom he had just bestowed the medal, "Son, I would rather have the right to wear this than be President of the United States."[33]

Perhaps the best comment available is that of General Joshua Chamberlain, who received the Medal of Honor for his action at Gettysburg in July 1863. He later wrote:

Only the Congressional Medal of Honor had been held sacred—not to be bought or sold, or recklessly conferred. It was held to be the highest honor—recognition of some act of conspicuous personal gallantry beyond what military duty required. Knowing what has happened with the cross of the Legion of Honor in France, and how sacred the Victoria Cross is held in England, we trust that no self-seeking plea nor political pressure shall avail to belittle the estimation of this sole-remaining seal of honor whose very meaning and worth is that it notes conduct in which manhood rises above self. May this award ever be for him who has won it, at the peril of life, in storm of battle, but let us not behold the sublime spectacle of vicarious suffering travestied by the imposition of vicarious honors.[34]

Although General Chamberlain's comments were made years ago, they are just as appropriate today as they were when he made them; his message is timeless.

Notes

1. *Medal of Honor of the United States Army, The* (Washington, D.C., 1948), p. 9.
2. *Ibid.,* pp. 9, 10.
3. *Ibid.,* p. 10.
4. *Ibid.*
5. *Ibid.*
6. *Ibid.*
7. *Ibid.*
8. *Ibid.*
9. *Ibid.,* p. 11.
10. *Ibid.,* p. 5.
11. Irvin H. Lee, *Negro Medal of Honor Men* (New York, 1969), p. 3.
12. *Medal, op. cit.,* p. 5.
13. *Ibid.,* p. 430.
14. Joseph L. Schott, *Above and Beyond* (New York, 1963), p. 26.
15. Lee, *op. cit.,* p. 4.
16. *Medal, op. cit.,* pp. 5, 6.
17. Lee, *op. cit.,* p. 6.
18. *Ibid.,* p. 7.
19. *Ibid.*
20. *Ibid.,* p. 5.
21. *Congressional Medal of Honor Roster, July 4, 1975* (Boston, 1975), p. 41.
22. Senate Committee on Veterans' Affairs, *Medal of Honor Recipients 1863–1978* (Washington, D.C., 1979), p. 267.
23. *Medal, op. cit.,* p. 442.
24. *Congressional, op. cit.,* p. 41.
25. Senate Committee on Veterans' Affairs, *op. cit.,* pp. 15, 16.
26. Bruce Jacobs, *Heroes of the Army* (New York, 1956), p. 82.
27. *Ibid.*
28. *Medal, op. cit.,* p. 3.

29. *Congressional, op. cit.,* p. 38.
30. Senate Committee on Veterans' Affairs, *op. cit.,* p. 1079.
31. Schott, *op. cit.,* p. 13.
32. Jacobs, *op. cit.,* p. 85.
33. *Ibid.,* p. 86.
34. John J. Pullen, *A Shower of Stars* (Philadelphia, 1966) pp. 179, 180.

Bibliography

Congressional Medal of Honor Roster, July 4, 1975. Boston: The Congressional Medal of Honor Society of the United States of America, 1975.

Jacobs, Bruce. *Heroes of the Army.* New York: W. W. Norton and Company, Inc., 1956.

Lee, Irvin H. *Negro Medal of Honor Men.* New York: Dodd, Mead and Company, 1969.

Medal of Honor of the United States Army, The. Washington, D.C.: U.S. Government Printing Office, 1948.

Pullen, John J. *A Shower of Stars.* Philadelphia: J. B. Lippincott Company, 1966.

Schott, Joseph D. *Above and Beyond.* New York: G. P. Putnam's Sons, 1963.

Senate Committee on Veterans' Affairs. *Medal of Honor Recipients 1863–1978.* Washington, D.C.: U.S. Government Printing Office, 1979.